P9-APN-674

MARK WAID · DIEGO BARRETO

IRREDEEMABLE

VOLUME 10

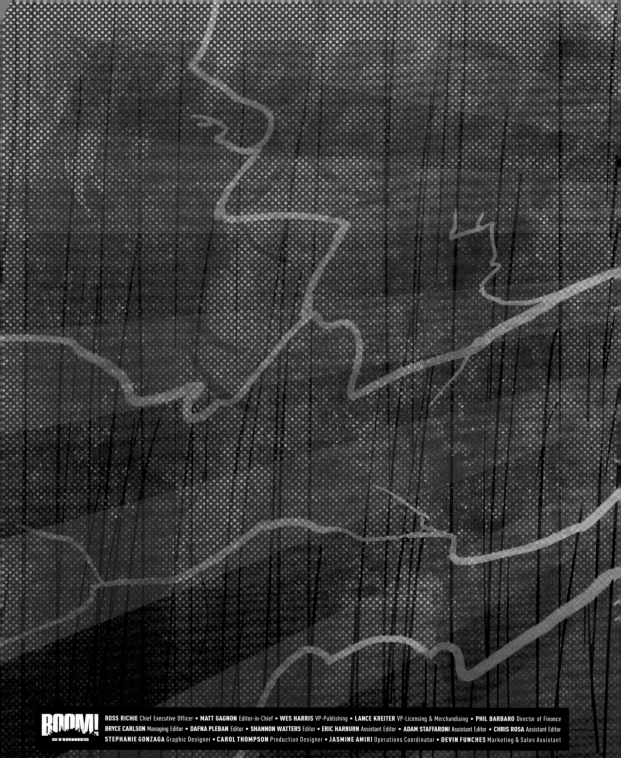

BOOM! STUDIOS

ROSS RICHIE Chief Executive Officer • MATT GAGNON Editor-in-Chief • WES HARRIS VP-Publishing • LANCE KREITER VP-Licensing & Merchandising • PHIL BARBARO Director of Finance
BRYCE CARLSON Managing Editor • DAFNA PLEBAN Editor • SHANNON WATTERS Editor • ERIC HARBURN Assistant Editor • ADAM STAFFARONI Assistant Editor • CHRIS ROSA Assistant Editor
STEPHANIE GONZAGA Graphic Designer • CAROL THOMPSON Production Designer • JASMINE AMIRI Operations Coordinator • DEVIN FUNCHES Marketing & Sales Assistant

IRREDEEMABLE Volume Ten — August 2012. Published by BOOM! Studios, a division of Boom Entertainment, Inc. Irredeemable is Copyright © 2012 Boom Entertainment, Inc. and Mark Waid. Originally published in single magazine form as IRREDEEMABLE 34-37. Copyright © 2012 Boom Entertainment, Inc. and Mark Waid. All rights reserved. BOOM! Studios™ and the BOOM! Studios logo are trademarks of Boom Entertainment, Inc., registered in various countries and categories. All characters, events, and institutions depicted herein are fictional. Any similarity between any of the names, characters, persons, events, and/or institutions in this publication to actual names, characters, and persons, whether living or dead, events, and/or institutions is unintended and purely coincidental. BOOM! Studios does not read or accept unsolicited submissions of ideas, stories, or artwork.

A catalog record of this book is available from OCLC and from the BOOM! Studios website, www.boom-studios.com, on the Librarians Page.

BOOM! Studios, 6310 San Vicente Boulevard, Suite 107, Los Angeles, CA 90048-5457. Printed in China. First Printing.
ISBN: 978-1-60886-275-7

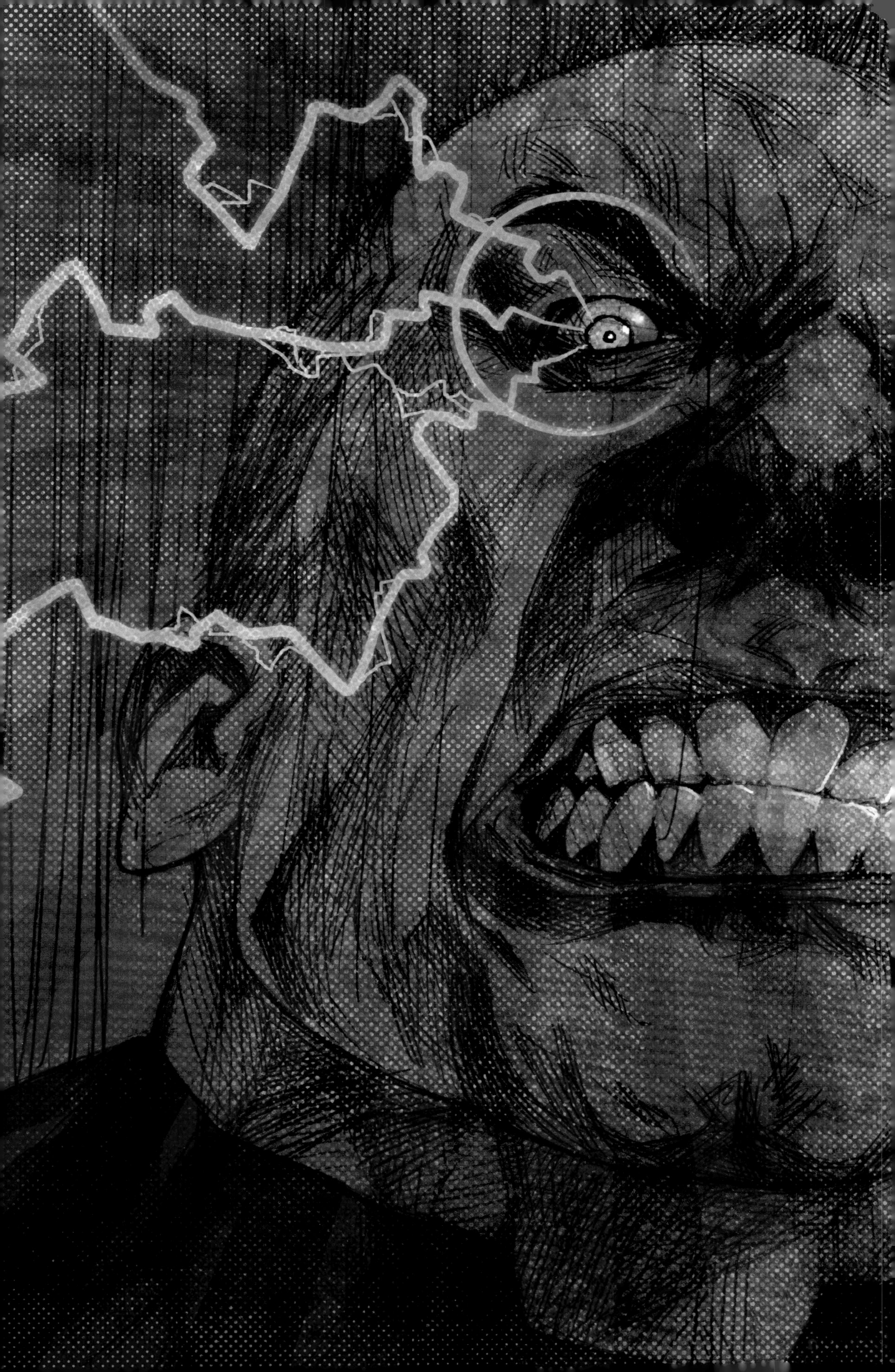

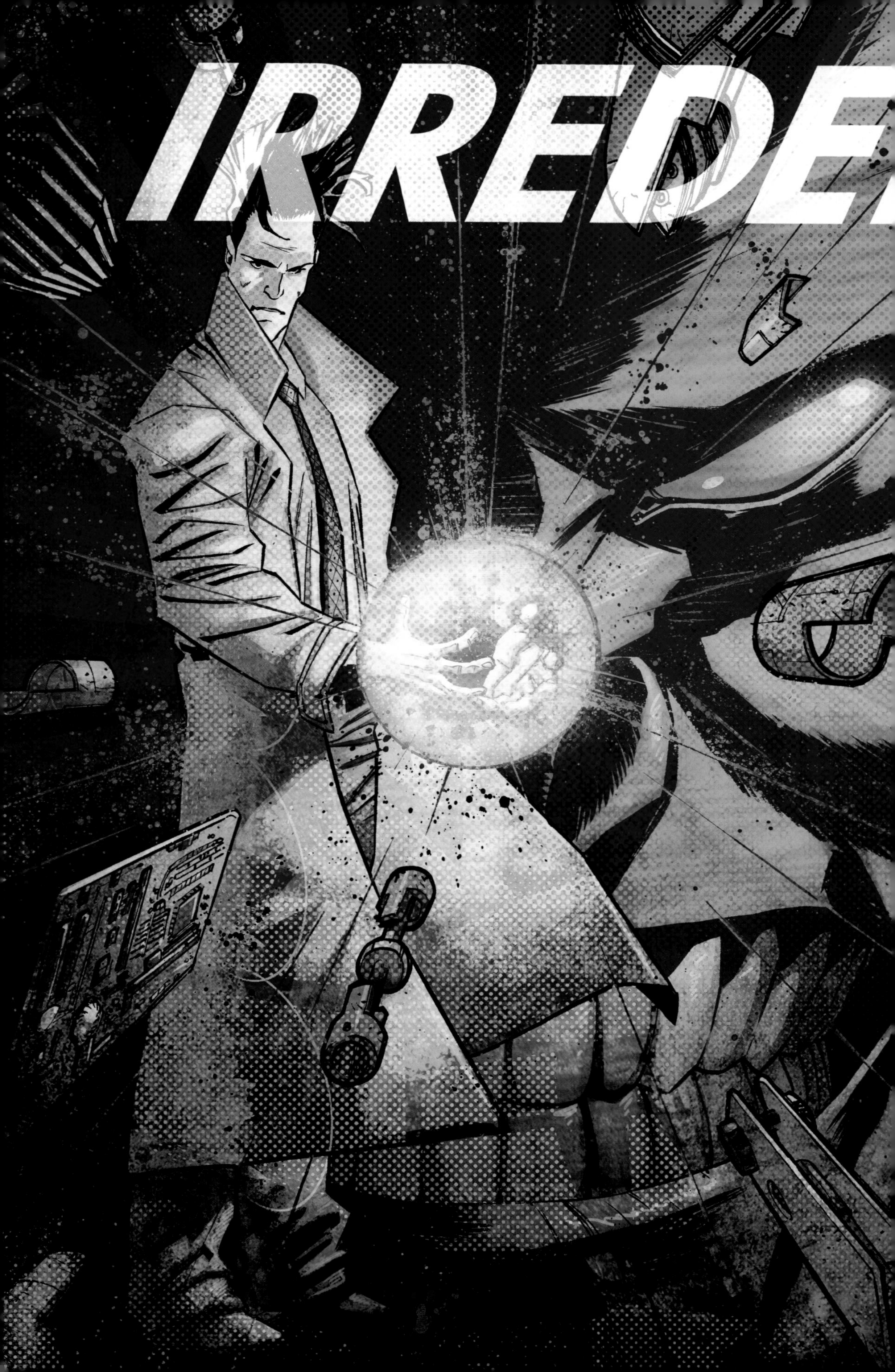
IRREDE

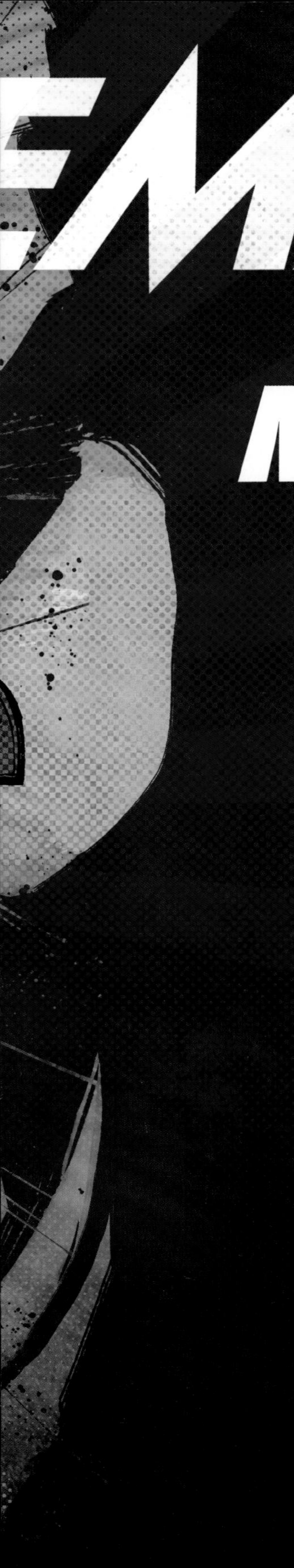

EMABLE

CREATED AND WRITTEN BY

MARK WAID

ARTISTS:

DIEGO BARRETO
& DAMIAN COUCEIRO

COLORIST:

NOLAN WOODARD

LETTERER:
ED DUKESHIRE

EDITORS:
MATT GAGNON &
SHANNON WATTERS

COVER:
TREVOR HAIRSINE
COLORS: ARCHIE VAN BUREN

PLUTONIAN CHARACTER DESIGN:
PAUL AZACETA

TRADE DESIGN:
DANIELLE KELLER

CHAPTER 34

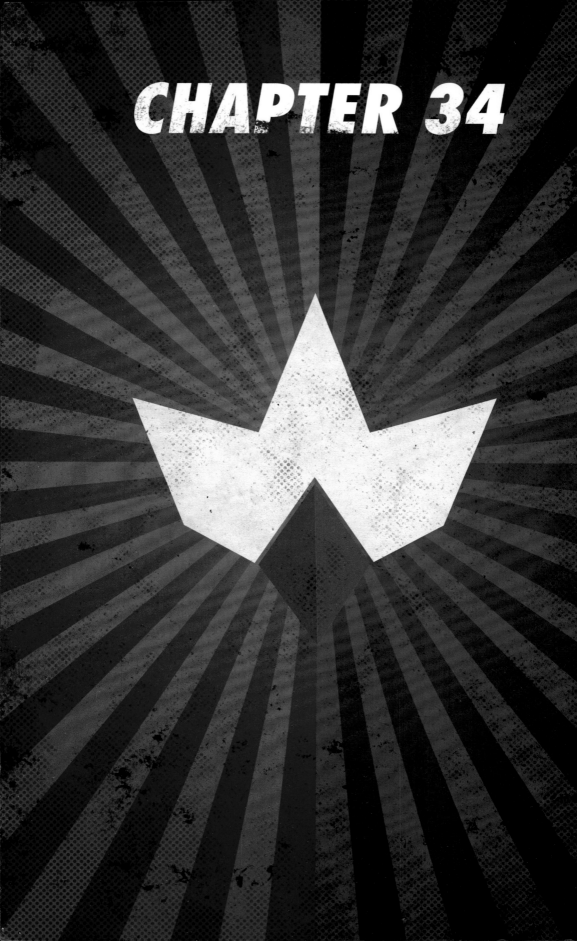

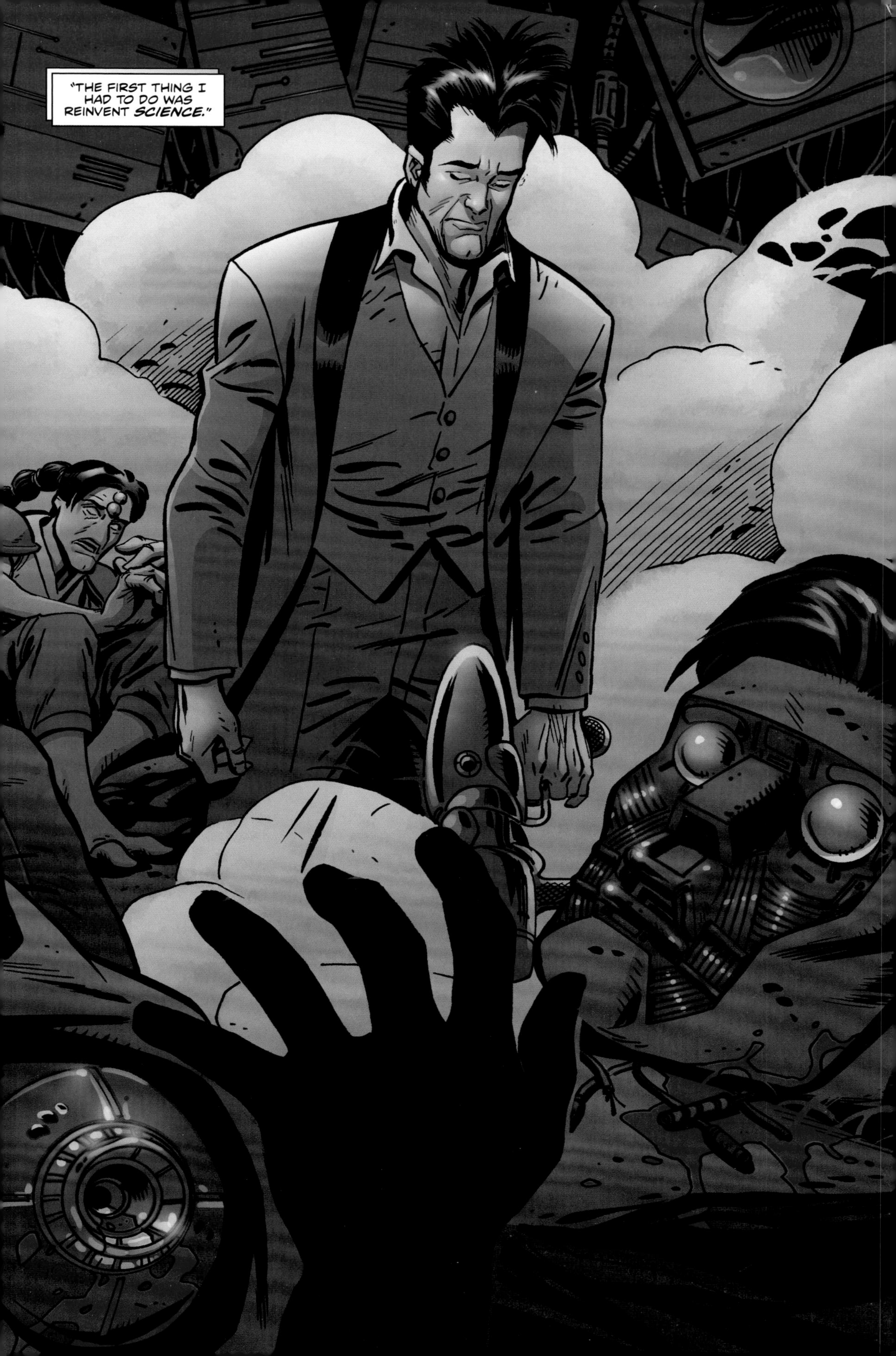
"THE FIRST THING I HAD TO DO WAS REINVENT *SCIENCE*."

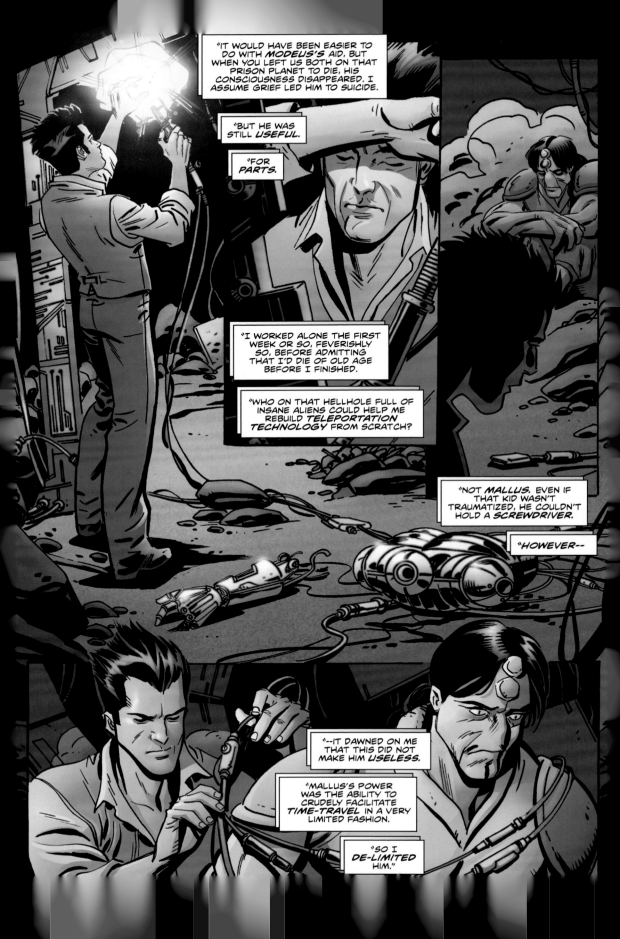

"IT WOULD HAVE BEEN EASIER TO DO WITH *MODEUS'S* AID, BUT WHEN YOU LEFT US BOTH ON THAT PRISON PLANET TO DIE, HIS CONSCIOUSNESS DISAPPEARED. I ASSUME GRIEF LED HIM TO SUICIDE.

"BUT HE WAS STILL *USEFUL*.

"FOR *PARTS*.

"I WORKED ALONE THE FIRST WEEK OR SO, FEVERISHLY SO, BEFORE ADMITTING THAT I'D DIE OF OLD AGE BEFORE I FINISHED.

"WHO ON THAT HELLHOLE FULL OF INSANE ALIENS COULD HELP ME REBUILD *TELEPORTATION TECHNOLOGY* FROM SCRATCH?

"NOT *MALLUS*. EVEN IF THAT KID WASN'T TRAUMATIZED, HE COULDN'T HOLD A *SCREWDRIVER*.

"HOWEVER--

"--IT DAWNED ON ME THAT THIS DID NOT MAKE HIM *USELESS*.

"MALLUS'S POWER WAS THE ABILITY TO CRUDELY FACILITATE *TIME-TRAVEL* IN A VERY LIMITED FASHION.

"SO I DE-LIMITED HIM."

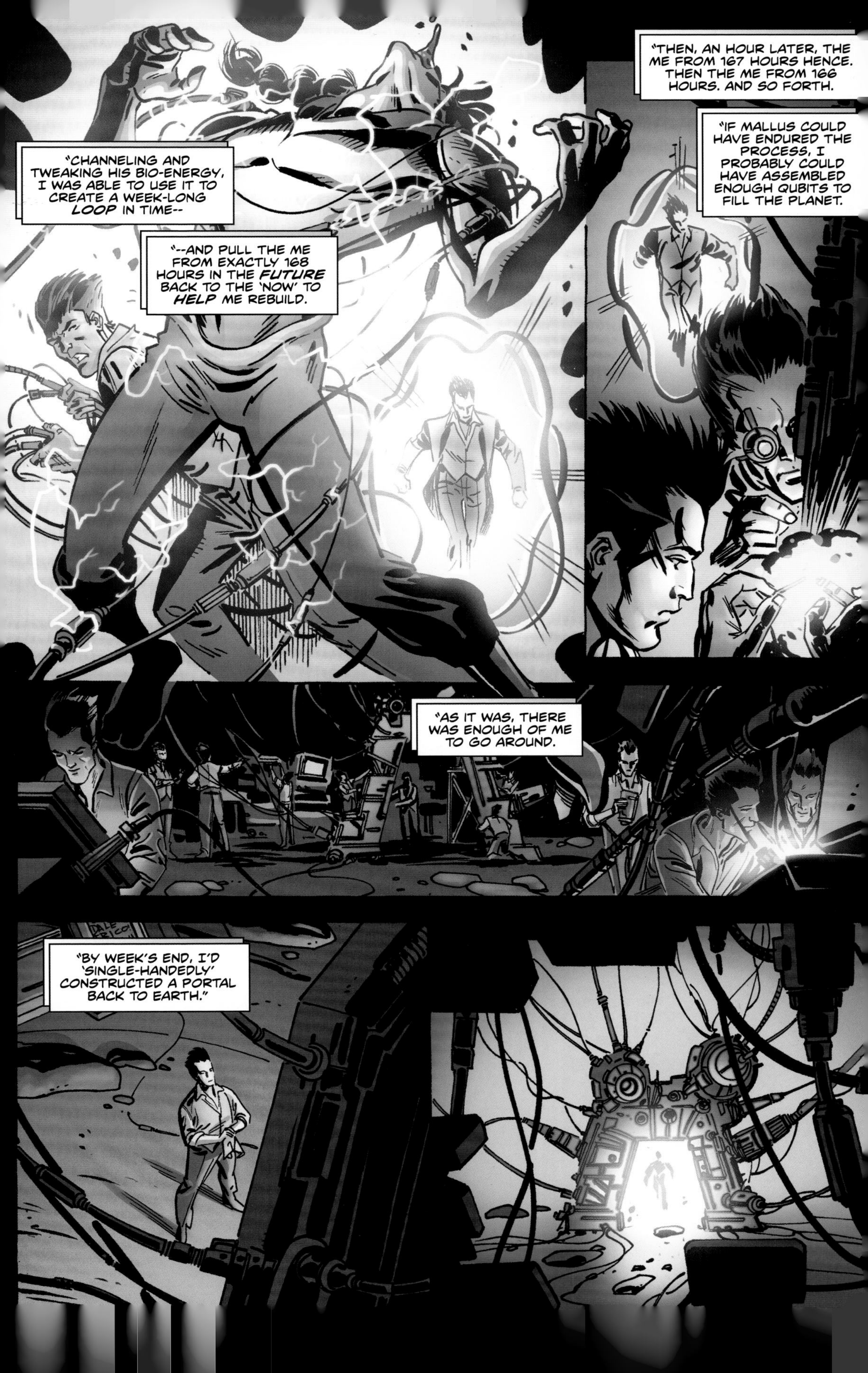
"CHANNELING AND TWEAKING HIS BIO-ENERGY, I WAS ABLE TO USE IT TO CREATE A WEEK-LONG *LOOP* IN TIME--
"--AND PULL THE ME FROM EXACTLY 168 HOURS IN THE *FUTURE* BACK TO THE 'NOW' TO *HELP* ME REBUILD.
"THEN, AN HOUR LATER, THE ME FROM 167 HOURS HENCE. THEN THE ME FROM 166 HOURS. AND SO FORTH.
"IF MALLUS COULD HAVE ENDURED THE PROCESS, I PROBABLY COULD HAVE ASSEMBLED ENOUGH QUBITS TO FILL THE PLANET.
"AS IT WAS, THERE WAS ENOUGH OF ME TO GO AROUND.
"BY WEEK'S END, I'D 'SINGLE-HANDEDLY' CONSTRUCTED A PORTAL BACK TO EARTH."

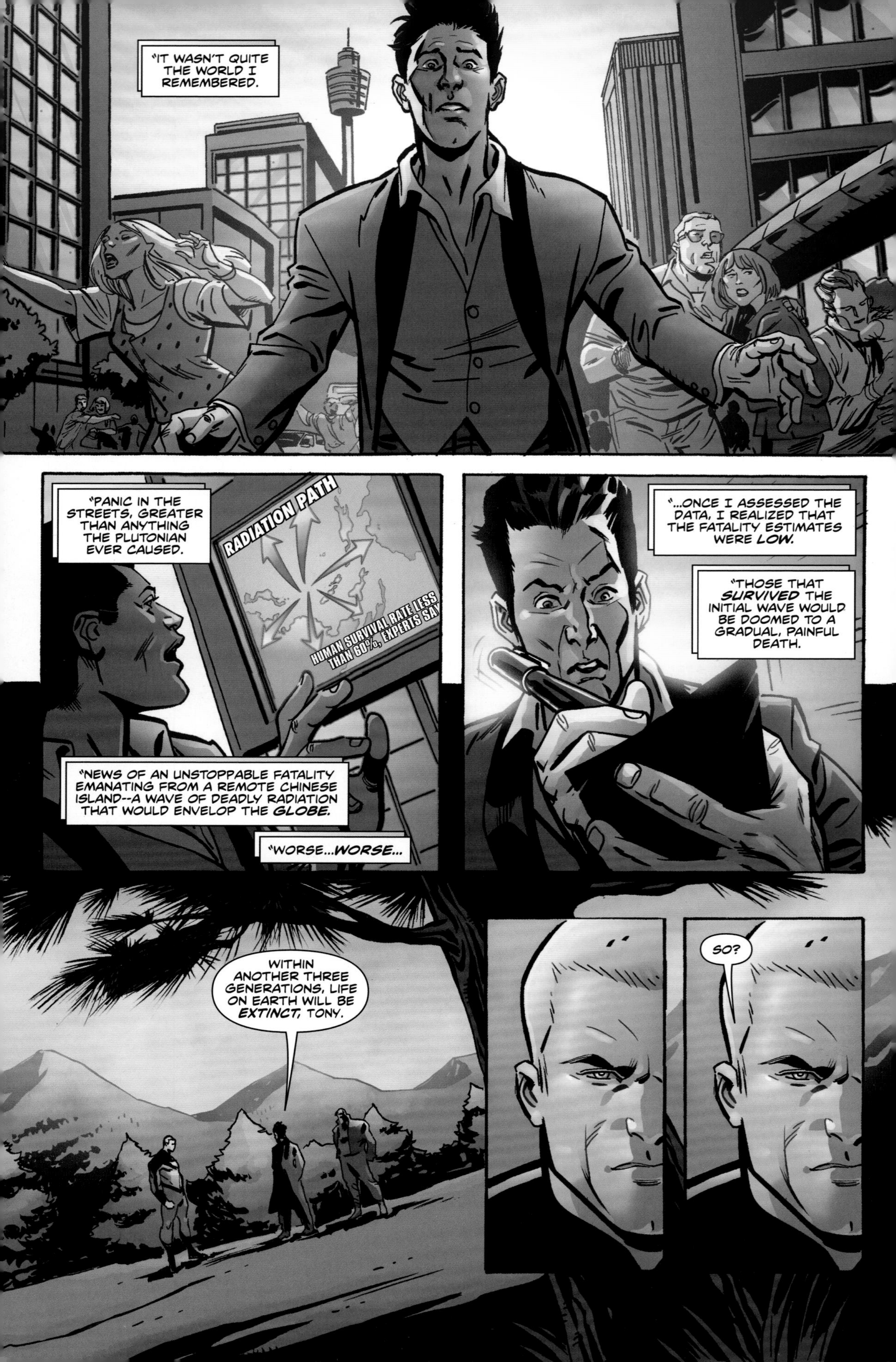
"IT WASN'T QUITE THE WORLD I REMEMBERED.
"PANIC IN THE STREETS, GREATER THAN ANYTHING THE PLUTONIAN EVER CAUSED.
RADIATION PATH
HUMAN SURVIVAL RATE LESS THAN 60%, EXPERTS SAY
"NEWS OF AN UNSTOPPABLE FATALITY EMANATING FROM A REMOTE CHINESE ISLAND--A WAVE OF DEADLY RADIATION THAT WOULD ENVELOP THE GLOBE.
"WORSE...WORSE...
"...ONCE I ASSESSED THE DATA, I REALIZED THAT THE FATALITY ESTIMATES WERE LOW.
"THOSE THAT SURVIVED THE INITIAL WAVE WOULD BE DOOMED TO A GRADUAL, PAINFUL DEATH.
WITHIN ANOTHER THREE GENERATIONS, LIFE ON EARTH WILL BE EXTINCT, TONY.
SO?

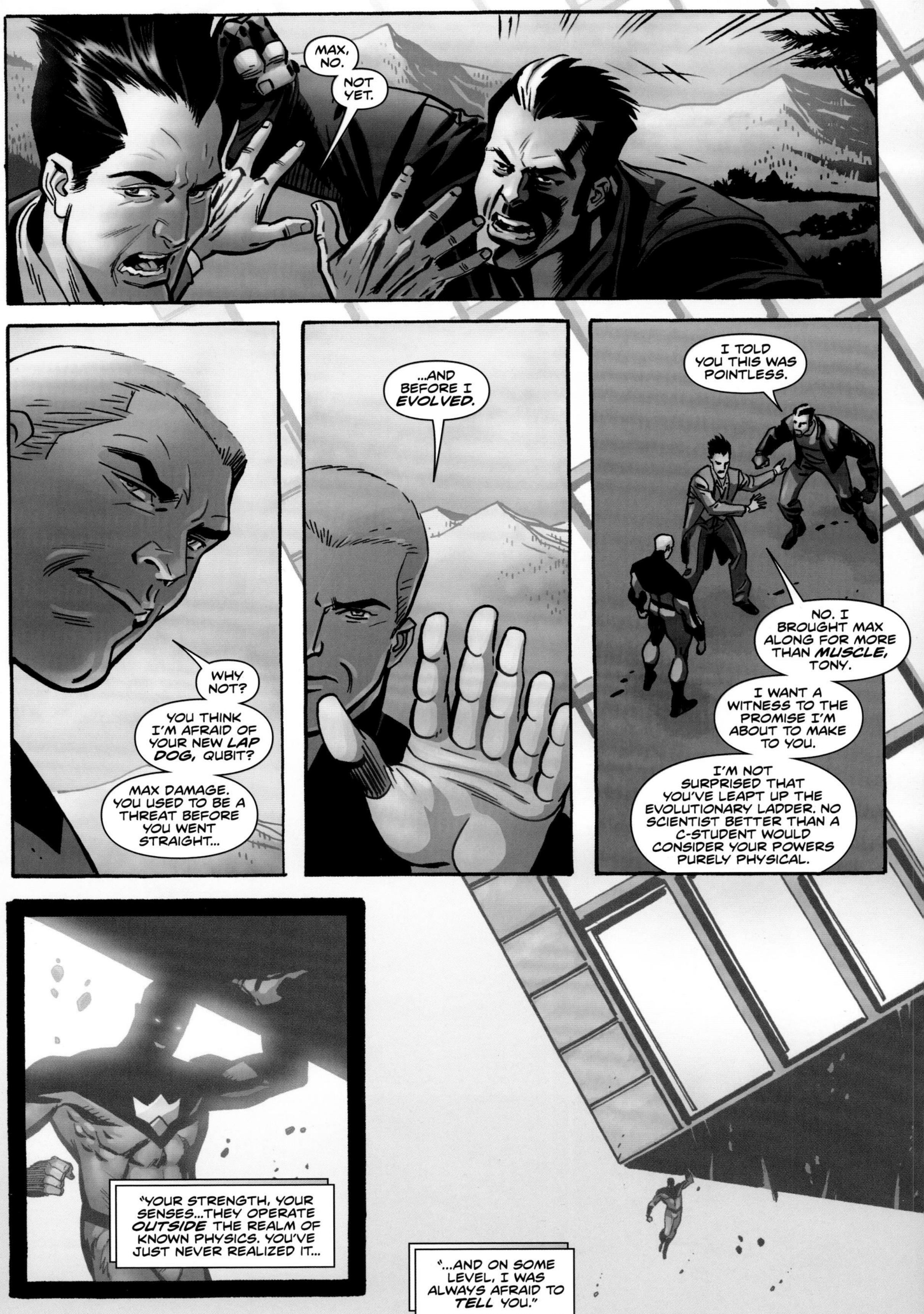

MAX, NO.
NOT YET.
WHY NOT?
YOU THINK I'M AFRAID OF YOUR NEW *LAP DOG,* QUBIT?
MAX DAMAGE. YOU USED TO BE A THREAT BEFORE YOU WENT STRAIGHT...
...AND BEFORE I *EVOLVED.*
I TOLD YOU THIS WAS POINTLESS.
NO. I BROUGHT MAX ALONG FOR MORE THAN *MUSCLE,* TONY.
I WANT A WITNESS TO THE PROMISE I'M ABOUT TO MAKE TO YOU.
I'M NOT SURPRISED THAT YOU'VE LEAPT UP THE EVOLUTIONARY LADDER. NO SCIENTIST BETTER THAN A C-STUDENT WOULD CONSIDER YOUR POWERS PURELY PHYSICAL.
"YOUR STRENGTH, YOUR SENSES...THEY OPERATE *OUTSIDE* THE REALM OF KNOWN PHYSICS. YOU'VE JUST NEVER REALIZED IT...
"...AND ON SOME LEVEL, I WAS ALWAYS AFRAID TO *TELL* YOU."

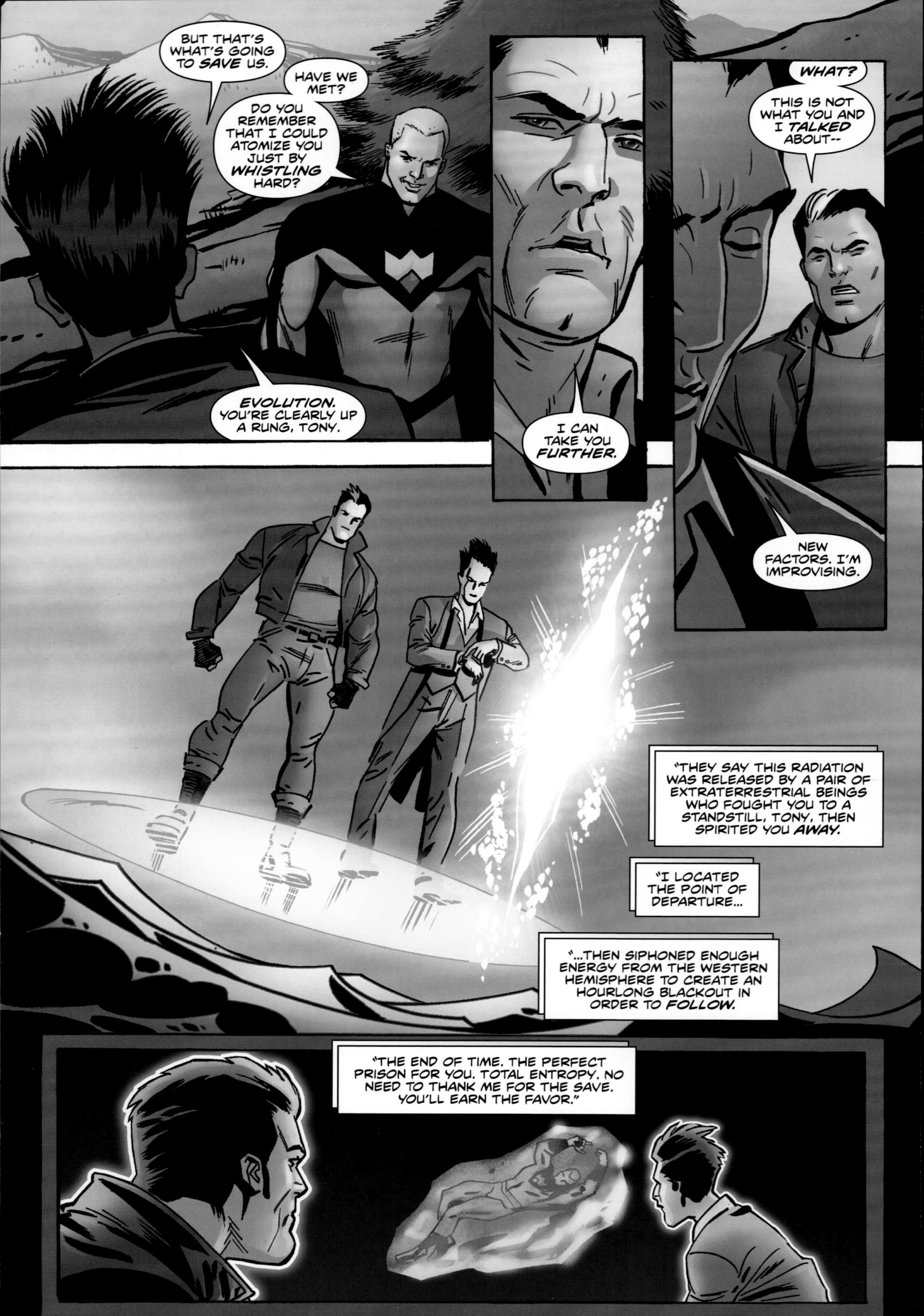

BUT THAT'S WHAT'S GOING TO SAVE US.
HAVE WE MET?
DO YOU REMEMBER THAT I COULD ATOMIZE YOU JUST BY WHISTLING HARD?
EVOLUTION. YOU'RE CLEARLY UP A RUNG, TONY.
I CAN TAKE YOU FURTHER.
WHAT?
THIS IS NOT WHAT YOU AND I TALKED ABOUT--
NEW FACTORS. I'M IMPROVISING.
"THEY SAY THIS RADIATION WAS RELEASED BY A PAIR OF EXTRATERRESTRIAL BEINGS WHO FOUGHT YOU TO A STANDSTILL, TONY, THEN SPIRITED YOU AWAY.
"I LOCATED THE POINT OF DEPARTURE...
"...THEN SIPHONED ENOUGH ENERGY FROM THE WESTERN HEMISPHERE TO CREATE AN HOURLONG BLACKOUT IN ORDER TO FOLLOW.
"THE END OF TIME. THE PERFECT PRISON FOR YOU. TOTAL ENTROPY. NO NEED TO THANK ME FOR THE SAVE. YOU'LL EARN THE FAVOR."

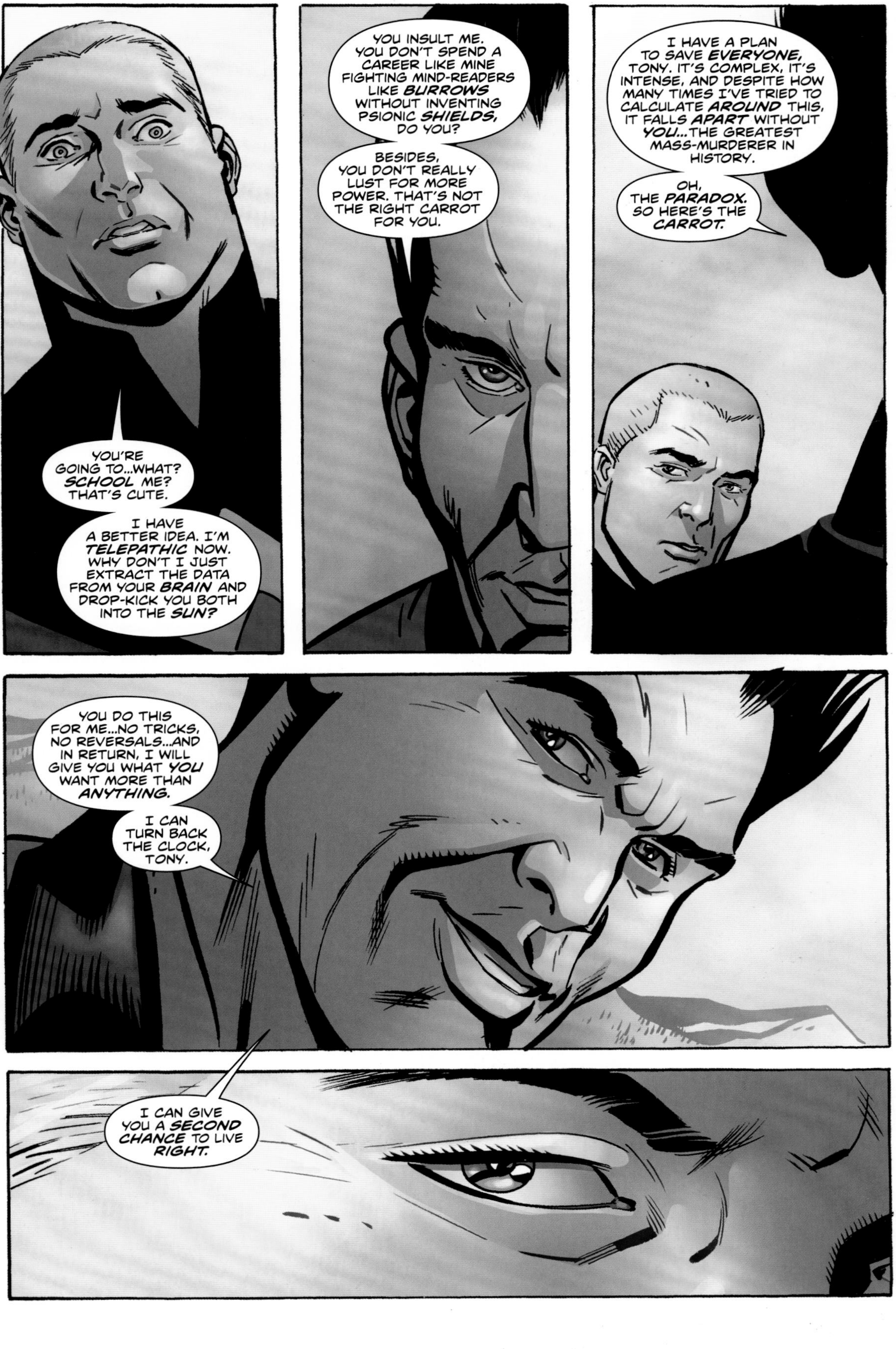
YOU'RE GOING TO...WHAT? SCHOOL ME? THAT'S CUTE.
I HAVE A BETTER IDEA. I'M TELEPATHIC NOW. WHY DON'T I JUST EXTRACT THE DATA FROM YOUR BRAIN AND DROP-KICK YOU BOTH INTO THE SUN?
YOU INSULT ME. YOU DON'T SPEND A CAREER LIKE MINE FIGHTING MIND-READERS LIKE BURROWS WITHOUT INVENTING PSIONIC SHIELDS, DO YOU?
BESIDES, YOU DON'T REALLY LUST FOR MORE POWER. THAT'S NOT THE RIGHT CARROT FOR YOU.
I HAVE A PLAN TO SAVE EVERYONE, TONY. IT'S COMPLEX, IT'S INTENSE, AND DESPITE HOW MANY TIMES I'VE TRIED TO CALCULATE AROUND THIS, IT FALLS APART WITHOUT YOU...THE GREATEST MASS-MURDERER IN HISTORY.
OH, THE PARADOX. SO HERE'S THE CARROT.
YOU DO THIS FOR ME...NO TRICKS, NO REVERSALS...AND IN RETURN, I WILL GIVE YOU WHAT YOU WANT MORE THAN ANYTHING.
I CAN TURN BACK THE CLOCK, TONY.
I CAN GIVE YOU A SECOND CHANCE TO LIVE RIGHT.

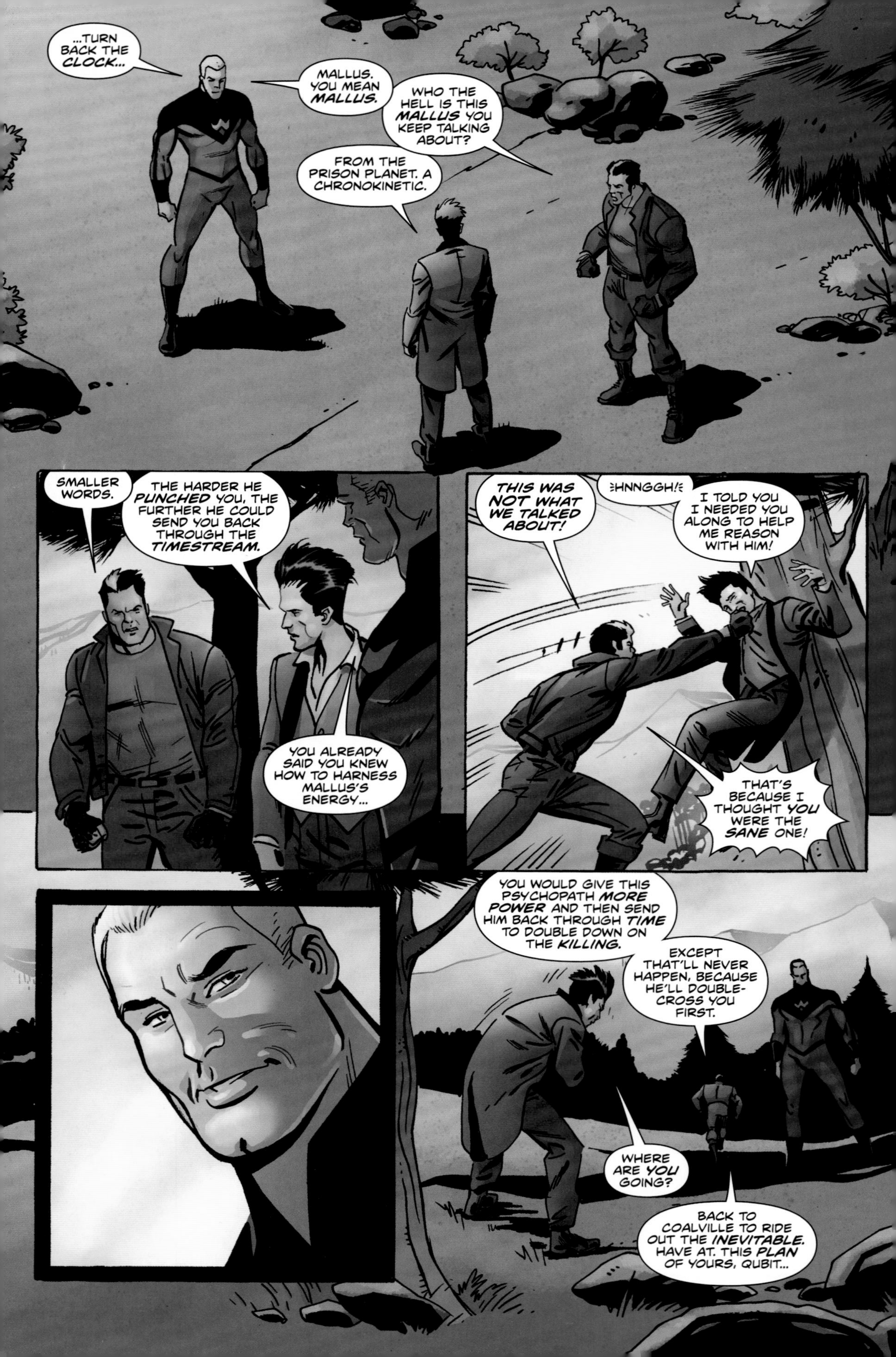
...TURN BACK THE CLOCK...
MALLUS. YOU MEAN MALLUS.
WHO THE HELL IS THIS MALLUS YOU KEEP TALKING ABOUT?
FROM THE PRISON PLANET. A CHRONOKINETIC.
SMALLER WORDS.
THE HARDER HE PUNCHED YOU, THE FURTHER HE COULD SEND YOU BACK THROUGH THE TIMESTREAM.
YOU ALREADY SAID YOU KNEW HOW TO HARNESS MALLUS'S ENERGY...
THIS WAS NOT WHAT WE TALKED ABOUT!
HNNGGH!
I TOLD YOU I NEEDED YOU ALONG TO HELP ME REASON WITH HIM!
THAT'S BECAUSE I THOUGHT YOU WERE THE SANE ONE!
YOU WOULD GIVE THIS PSYCHOPATH MORE POWER AND THEN SEND HIM BACK THROUGH TIME TO DOUBLE DOWN ON THE KILLING.
EXCEPT THAT'LL NEVER HAPPEN, BECAUSE HE'LL DOUBLE-CROSS YOU FIRST.
WHERE ARE YOU GOING?
BACK TO COALVILLE TO RIDE OUT THE INEVITABLE. HAVE AT. THIS PLAN OF YOURS, QUBIT...

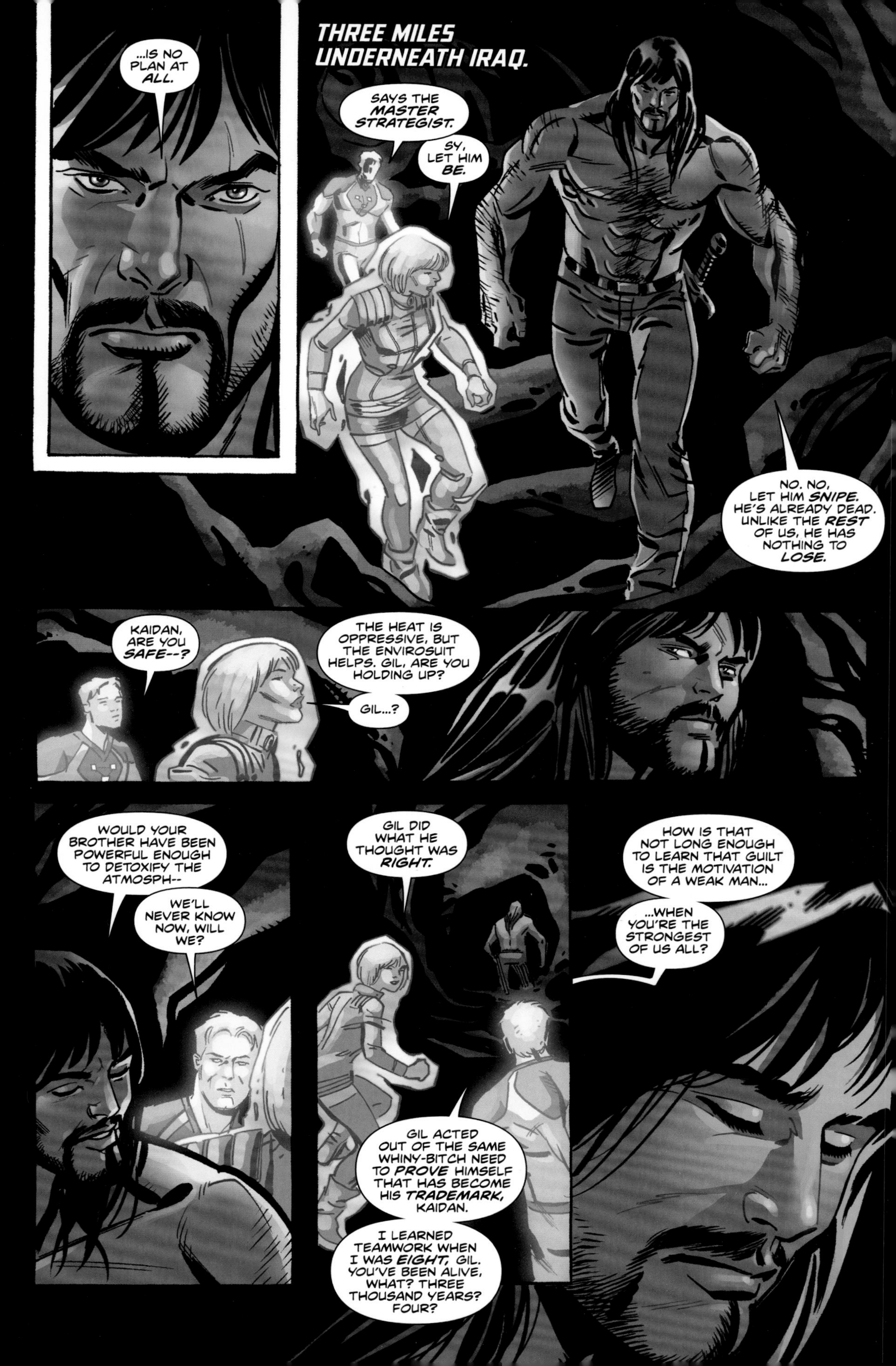
...IS NO PLAN AT ALL.
THREE MILES UNDERNEATH IRAQ.
SAYS THE MASTER STRATEGIST.
SY, LET HIM BE.
NO. NO, LET HIM SNIPE. HE'S ALREADY DEAD. UNLIKE THE REST OF US, HE HAS NOTHING TO LOSE.
KAIDAN, ARE YOU SAFE--?
THE HEAT IS OPPRESSIVE, BUT THE ENVIROSUIT HELPS. GIL, ARE YOU HOLDING UP?
GIL...?
WOULD YOUR BROTHER HAVE BEEN POWERFUL ENOUGH TO DETOXIFY THE ATMOSPH--
WE'LL NEVER KNOW NOW, WILL WE?
GIL DID WHAT HE THOUGHT WAS RIGHT.
GIL ACTED OUT OF THE SAME WHINY-BITCH NEED TO PROVE HIMSELF THAT HAS BECOME HIS TRADEMARK, KAIDAN.
I LEARNED TEAMWORK WHEN I WAS EIGHT, GIL. YOU'VE BEEN ALIVE, WHAT? THREE THOUSAND YEARS? FOUR?
HOW IS THAT NOT LONG ENOUGH TO LEARN THAT GUILT IS THE MOTIVATION OF A WEAK MAN...
...WHEN YOU'RE THE STRONGEST OF US ALL?

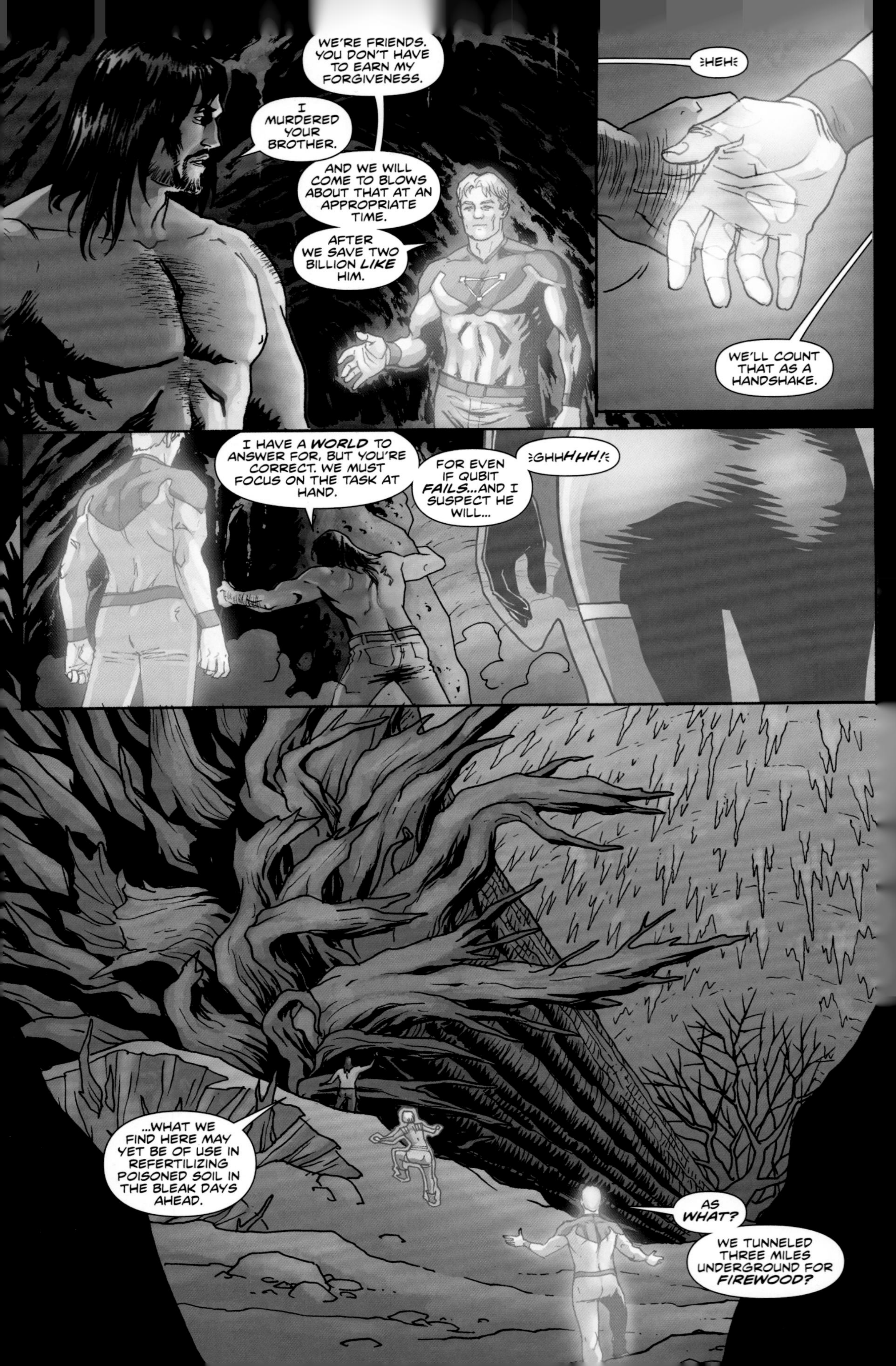
WE'RE FRIENDS. YOU DON'T HAVE TO EARN MY FORGIVENESS.
I MURDERED YOUR BROTHER.
AND WE WILL COME TO BLOWS ABOUT THAT AT AN APPROPRIATE TIME.
AFTER WE SAVE TWO BILLION *LIKE* HIM.
HEH
WE'LL COUNT THAT AS A HANDSHAKE.
I HAVE A *WORLD* TO ANSWER FOR, BUT YOU'RE CORRECT. WE MUST FOCUS ON THE TASK AT HAND.
FOR EVEN IF QUBIT *FAILS*...AND I SUSPECT HE WILL...
GHH*HHH!*
...WHAT WE FIND HERE MAY YET BE OF USE IN REFERTILIZING POISONED SOIL IN THE BLEAK DAYS AHEAD.
AS *WHAT?*
WE TUNNELED THREE MILES UNDERGROUND FOR *FIREWOOD?*

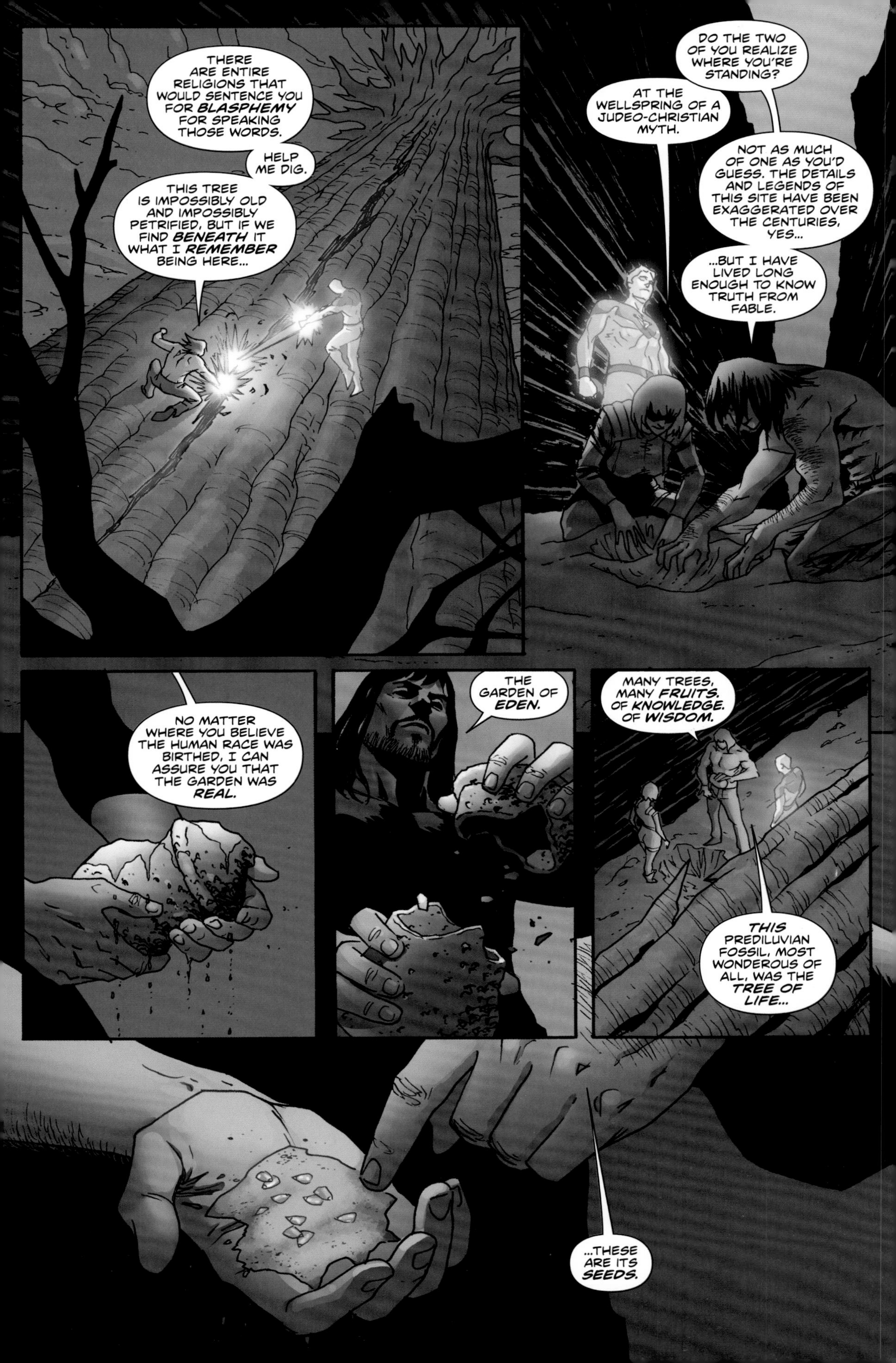
THERE ARE ENTIRE RELIGIONS THAT WOULD SENTENCE YOU FOR BLASPHEMY FOR SPEAKING THOSE WORDS.
HELP ME DIG.
THIS TREE IS IMPOSSIBLY OLD AND IMPOSSIBLY PETRIFIED, BUT IF WE FIND BENEATH IT WHAT I REMEMBER BEING HERE...
DO THE TWO OF YOU REALIZE WHERE YOU'RE STANDING?
AT THE WELLSPRING OF A JUDEO-CHRISTIAN MYTH.
NOT AS MUCH OF ONE AS YOU'D GUESS. THE DETAILS AND LEGENDS OF THIS SITE HAVE BEEN EXAGGERATED OVER THE CENTURIES, YES...
...BUT I HAVE LIVED LONG ENOUGH TO KNOW TRUTH FROM FABLE.
NO MATTER WHERE YOU BELIEVE THE HUMAN RACE WAS BIRTHED, I CAN ASSURE YOU THAT THE GARDEN WAS REAL.
THE GARDEN OF EDEN.
MANY TREES, MANY FRUITS. OF KNOWLEDGE. OF WISDOM.
THIS PREDILUVIAN FOSSIL, MOST WONDEROUS OF ALL, WAS THE TREE OF LIFE...
...THESE ARE ITS SEEDS.

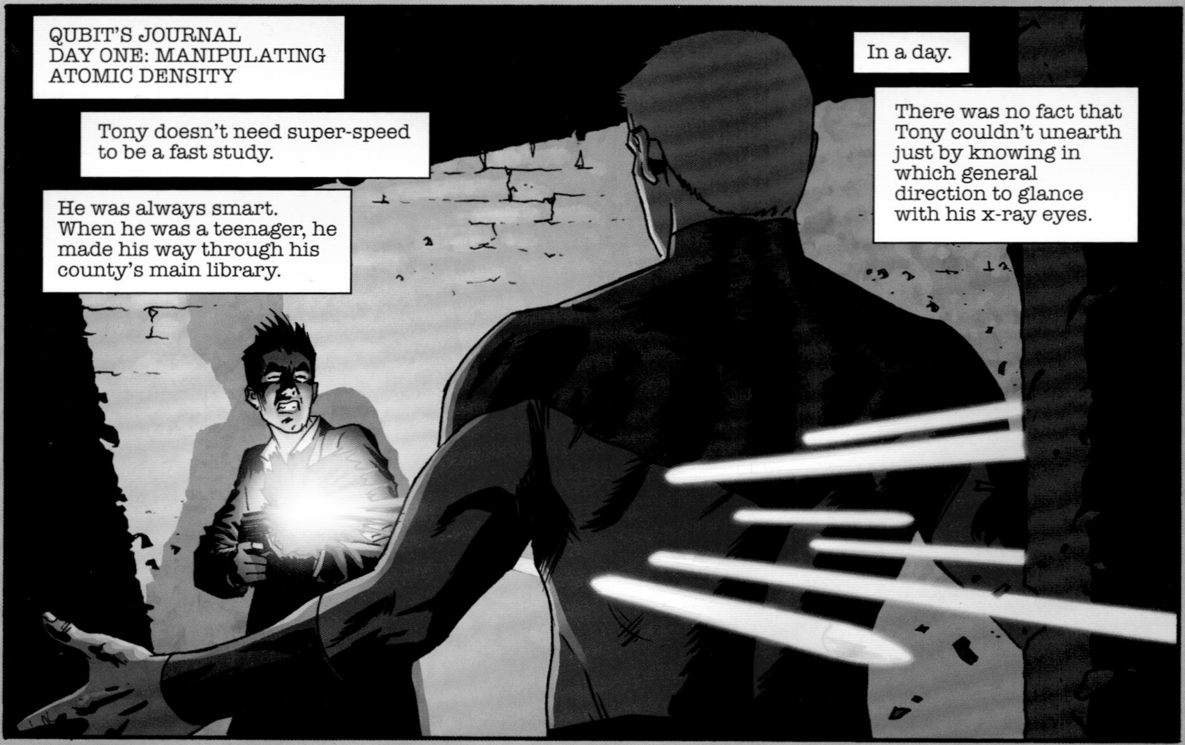

QUBIT'S JOURNAL
DAY ONE: MANIPULATING ATOMIC DENSITY
Tony doesn't need super-speed to be a fast study.
He was always smart. When he was a teenager, he made his way through his county's main library.
In a day.
There was no fact that Tony couldn't unearth just by knowing in which general direction to glance with his x-ray eyes.

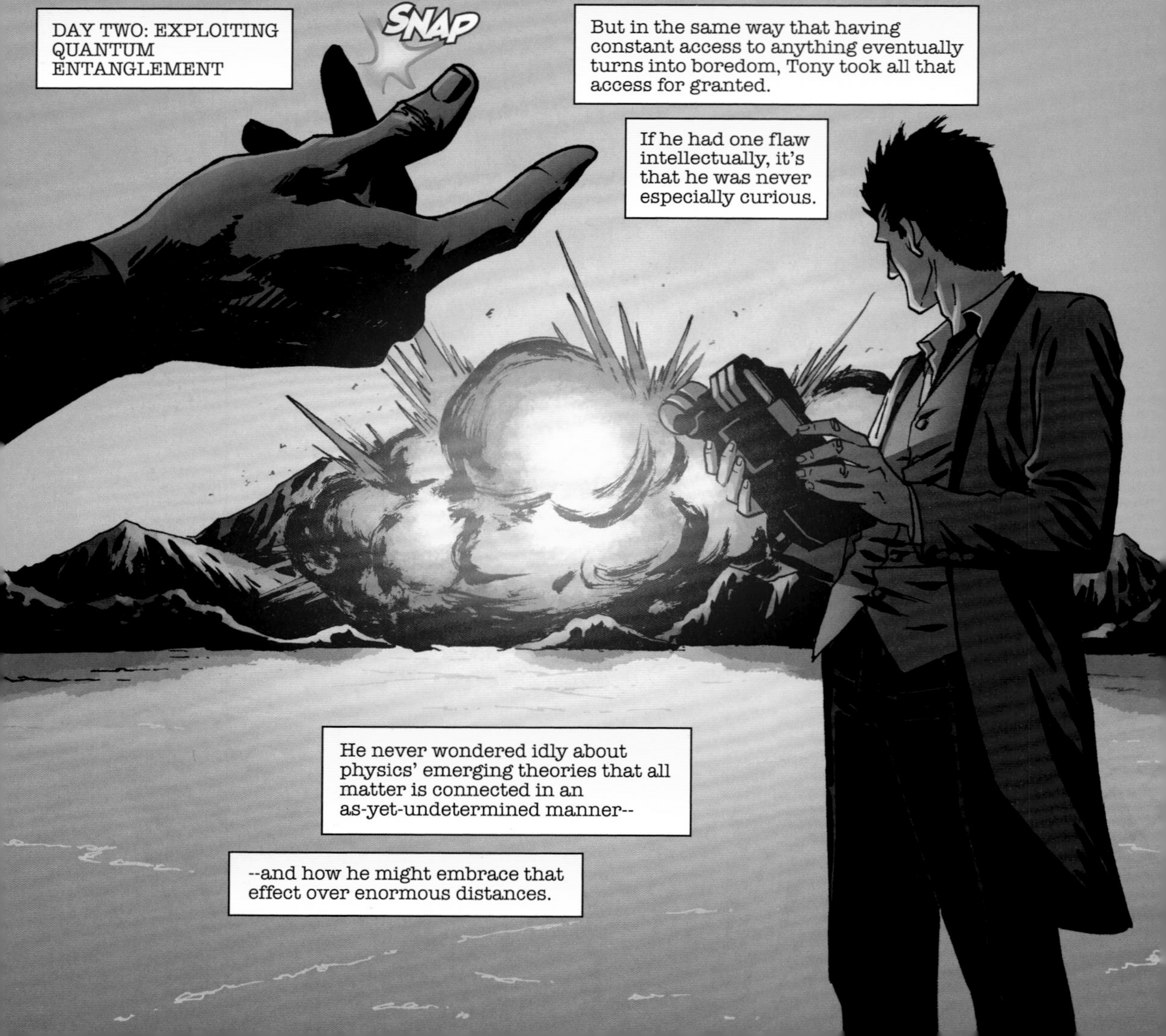

DAY TWO: EXPLOITING QUANTUM ENTANGLEMENT
SNAP
But in the same way that having constant access to anything eventually turns into boredom, Tony took all that access for granted.
If he had one flaw intellectually, it's that he was never especially curious.
He never wondered idly about physics' emerging theories that all matter is connected in an as-yet-undetermined manner--
--and how he might embrace that effect over enormous distances.

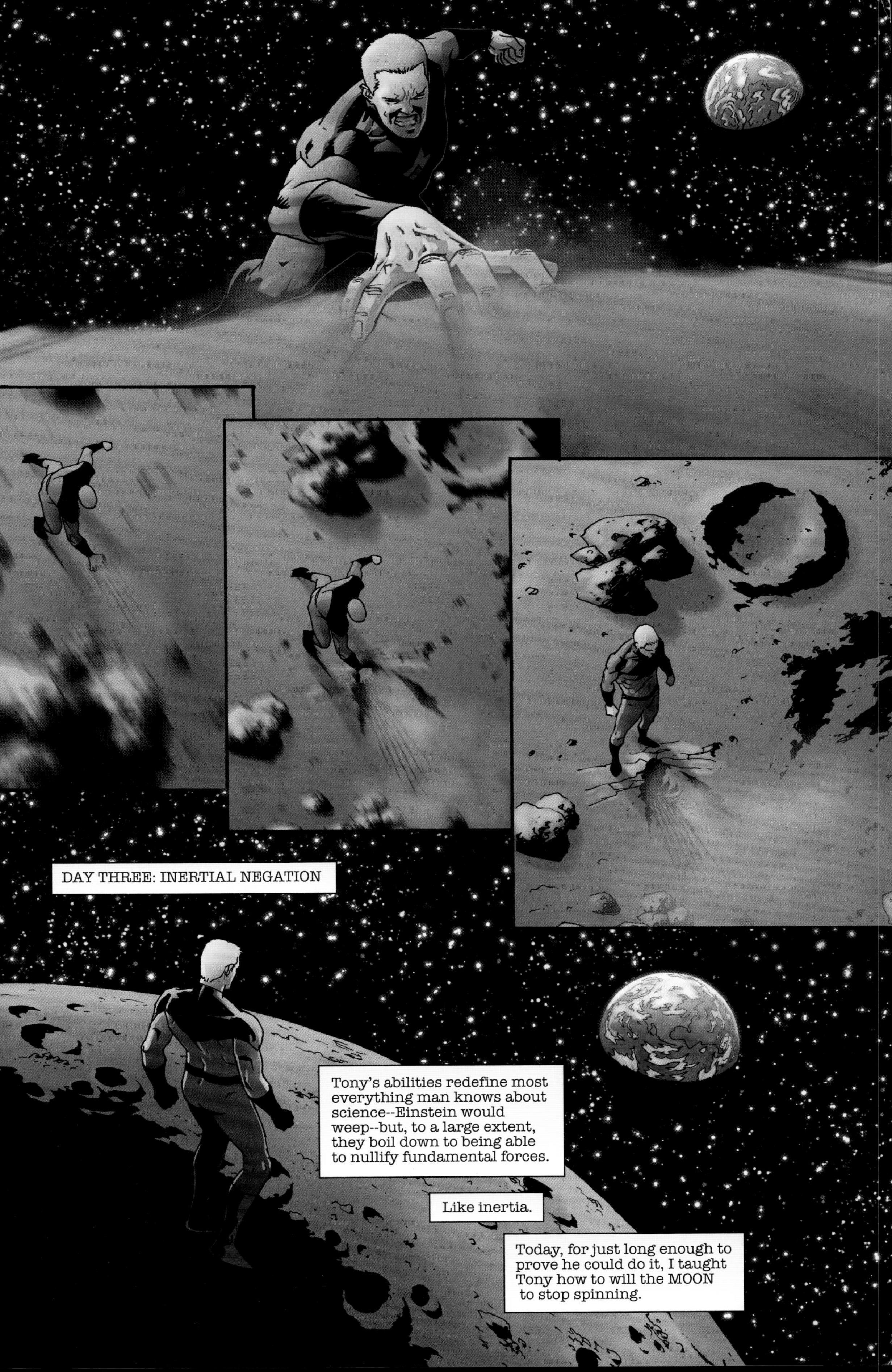
DAY THREE: INERTIAL NEGATION
Tony's abilities redefine most everything man knows about science--Einstein would weep--but, to a large extent, they boil down to being able to nullify fundamental forces.
Like inertia.
Today, for just long enough to prove he could do it, I taught Tony how to will the MOON to stop spinning.

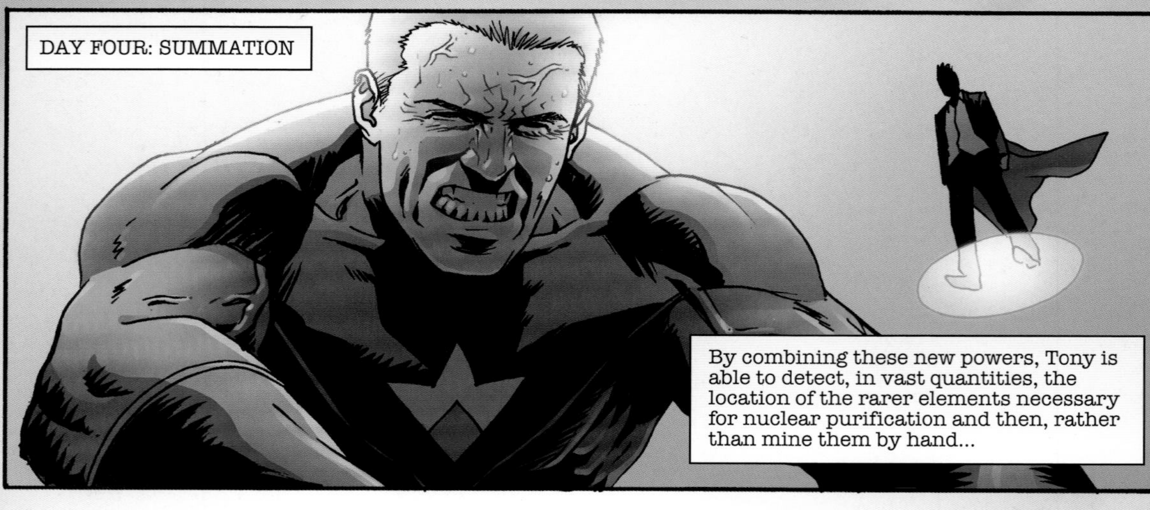
DAY FOUR: SUMMATION
By combining these new powers, Tony is able to detect, in vast quantities, the location of the rarer elements necessary for nuclear purification and then, rather than mine them by hand...

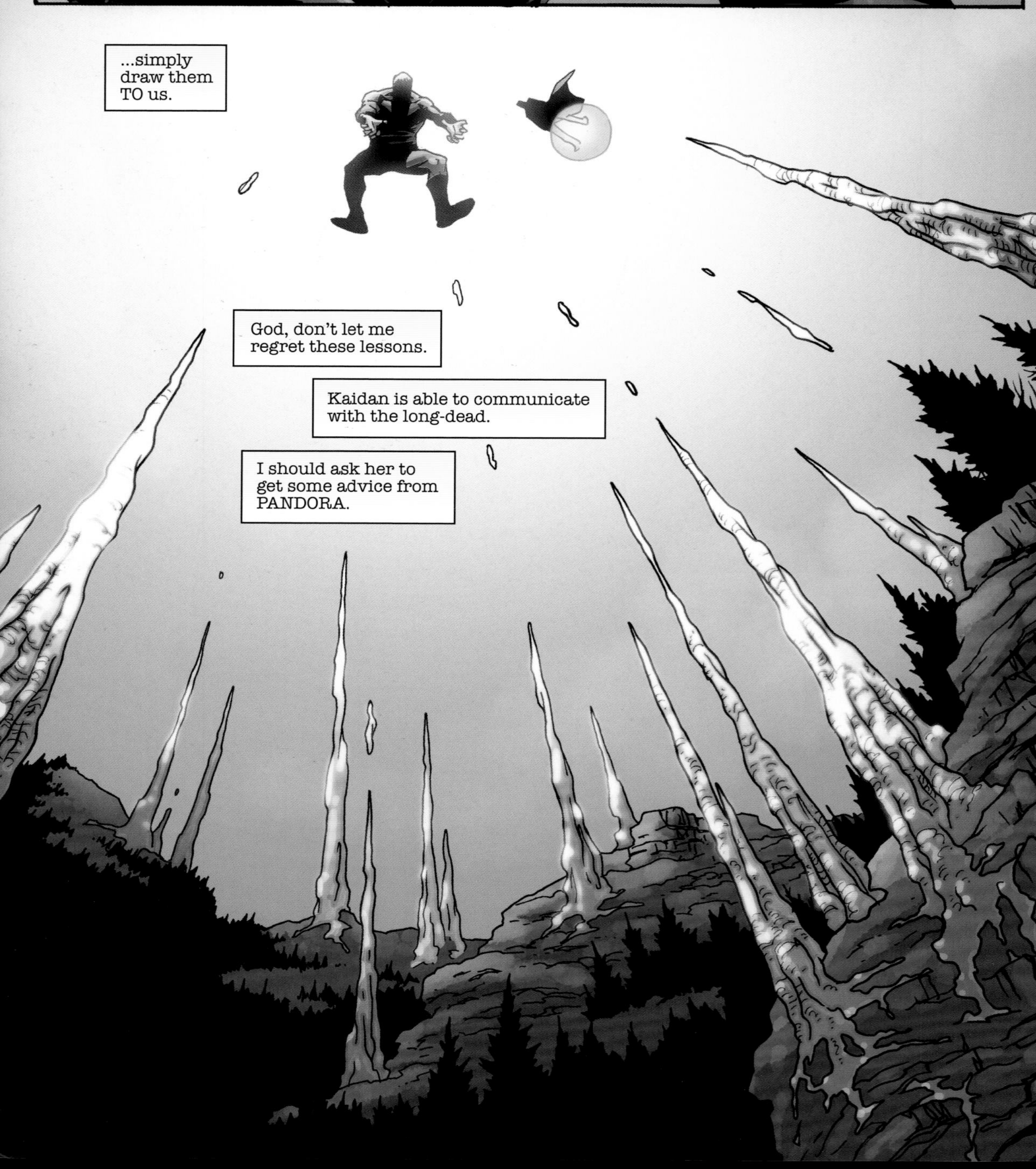
...simply draw them TO us.
God, don't let me regret these lessons.
Kaidan is able to communicate with the long-dead.
I should ask her to get some advice from PANDORA.

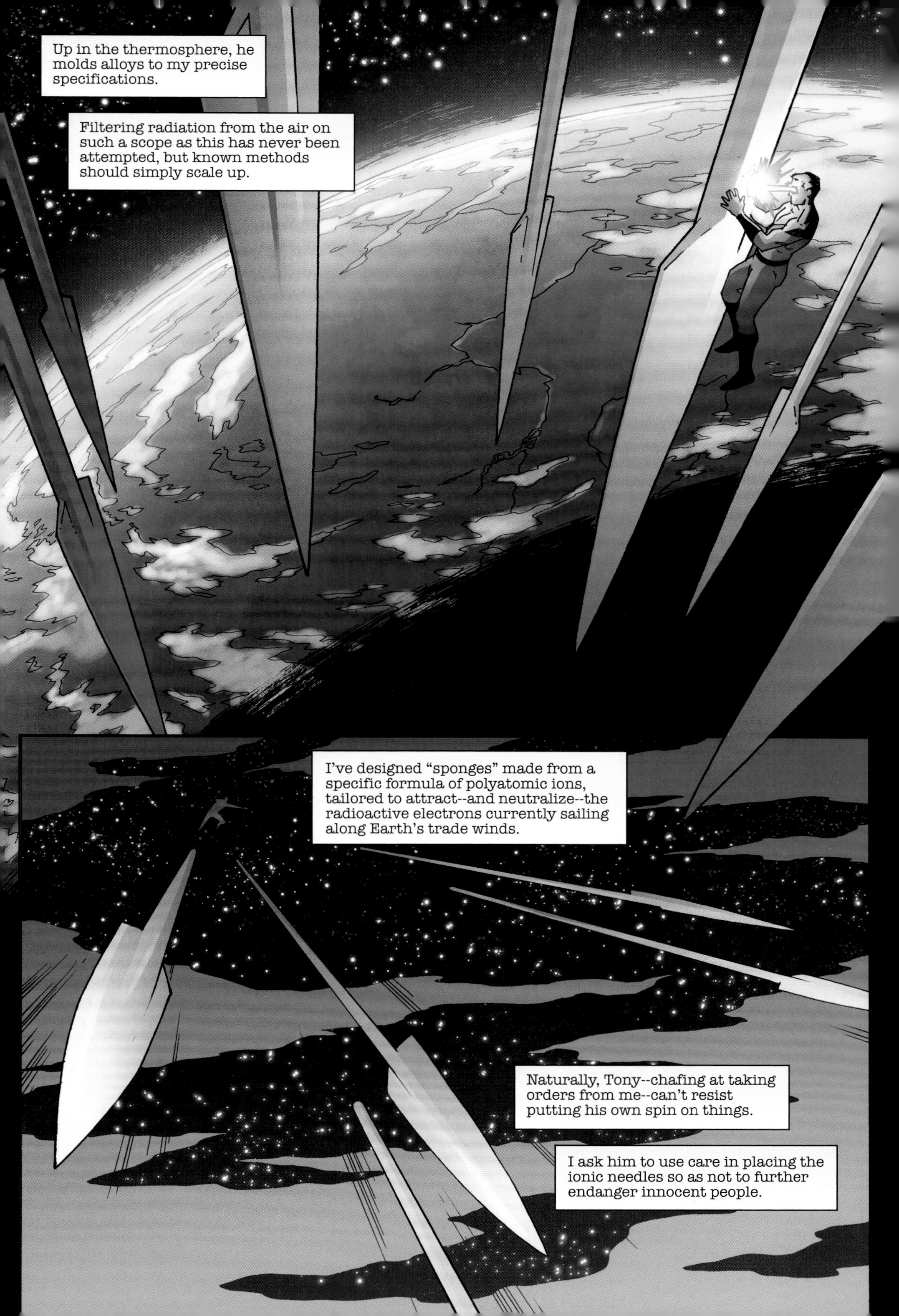
Up in the thermosphere, he molds alloys to my precise specifications.
Filtering radiation from the air on such a scope as this has never been attempted, but known methods should simply scale up.
I've designed "sponges" made from a specific formula of polyatomic ions, tailored to attract--and neutralize--the radioactive electrons currently sailing along Earth's trade winds.
Naturally, Tony--chafing at taking orders from me--can't resist putting his own spin on things.
I ask him to use care in placing the ionic needles so as not to further endanger innocent people.

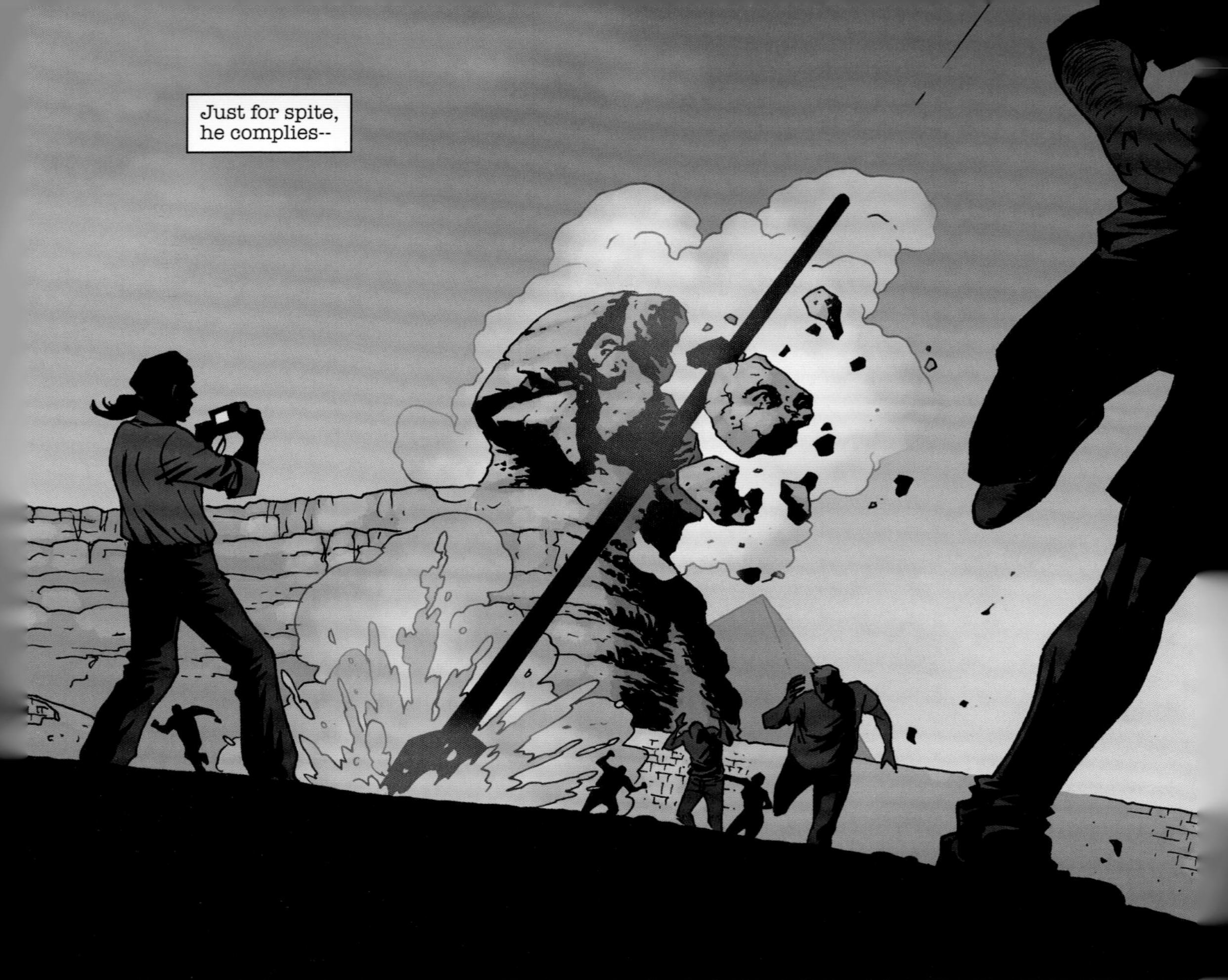
Just for spite, he complies--

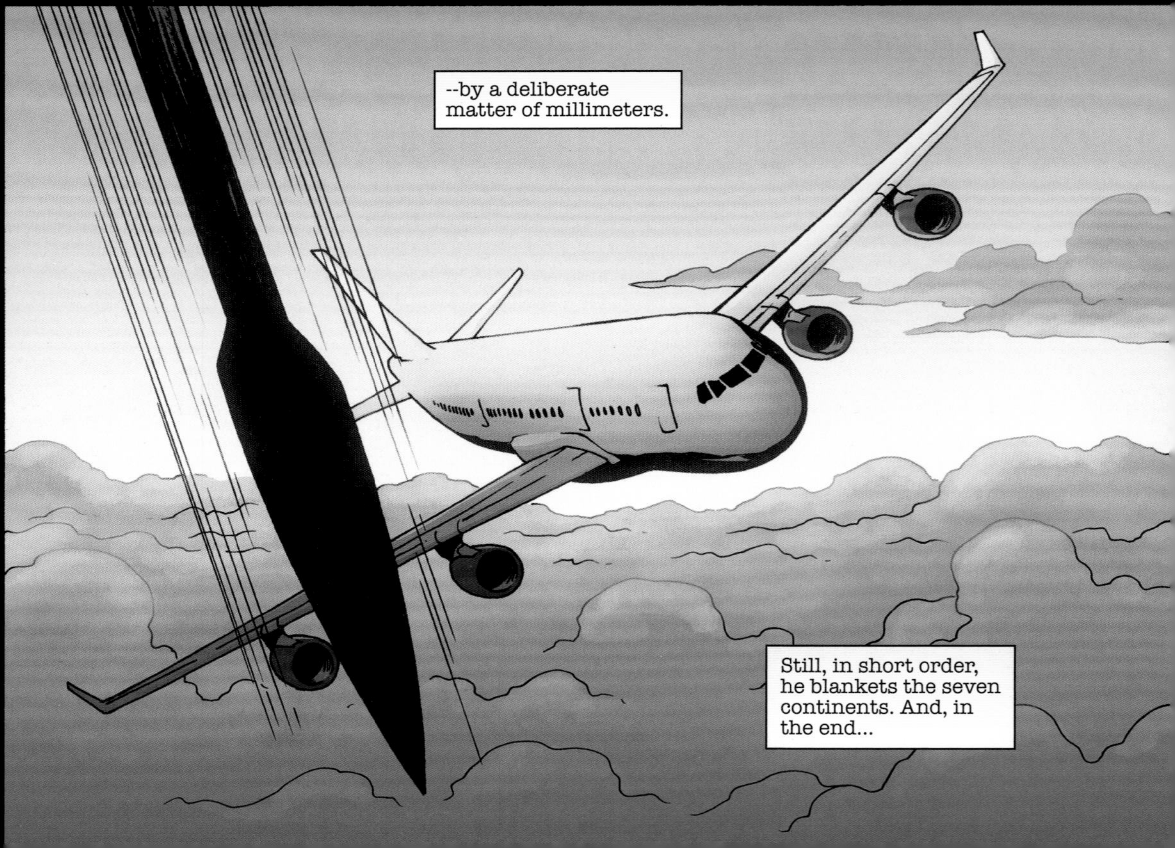
--by a deliberate matter of millimeters.
Still, in short order, he blankets the seven continents. And, in the end...

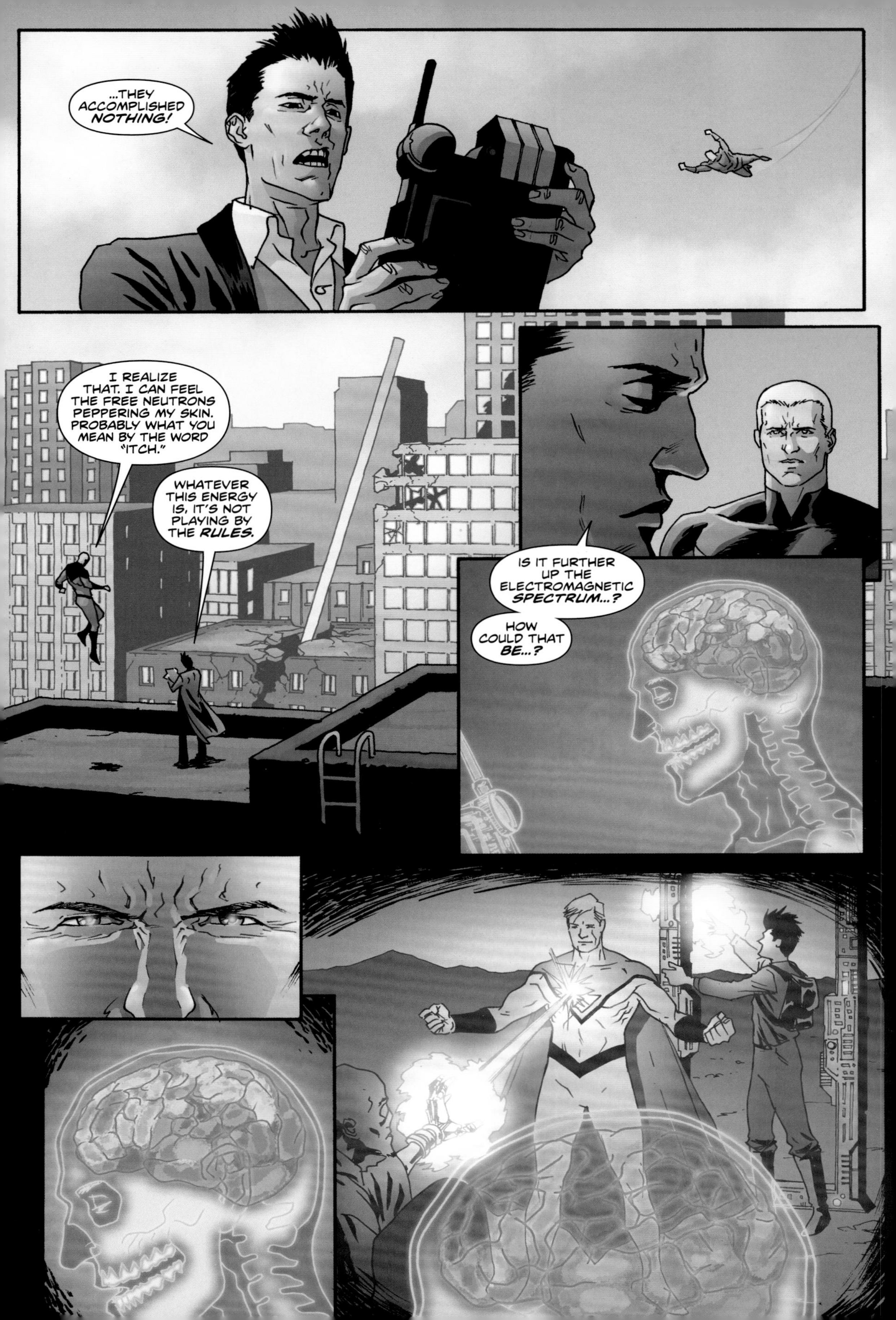
...THEY ACCOMPLISHED NOTHING!
I REALIZE THAT. I CAN FEEL THE FREE NEUTRONS PEPPERING MY SKIN. PROBABLY WHAT YOU MEAN BY THE WORD "ITCH."
WHATEVER THIS ENERGY IS, IT'S NOT PLAYING BY THE RULES.
IS IT FURTHER UP THE ELECTROMAGNETIC SPECTRUM...?
HOW COULD THAT BE...?

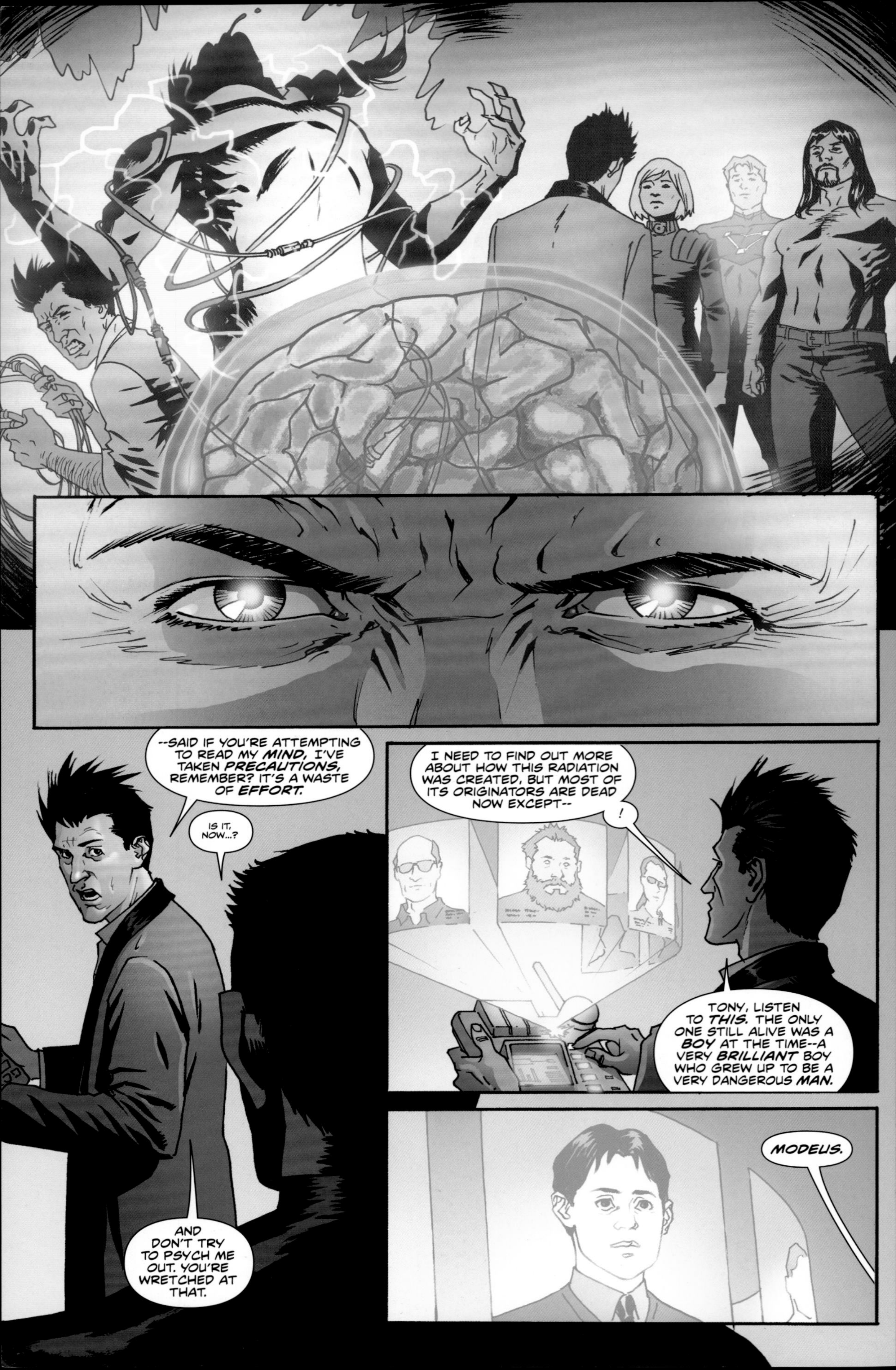
--SAID IF YOU'RE ATTEMPTING TO READ MY *MIND*, I'VE TAKEN *PRECAUTIONS*, REMEMBER? IT'S A WASTE OF *EFFORT*.
IS IT, NOW...?
AND DON'T TRY TO PSYCH ME OUT. YOU'RE WRETCHED AT THAT.
I NEED TO FIND OUT MORE ABOUT HOW THIS RADIATION WAS CREATED, BUT MOST OF ITS ORIGINATORS ARE DEAD NOW EXCEPT--
!
TONY, LISTEN TO *THIS*. THE ONLY ONE STILL ALIVE WAS A *BOY* AT THE TIME--A VERY *BRILLIANT* BOY WHO GREW UP TO BE A VERY DANGEROUS *MAN*.
MODEUS.

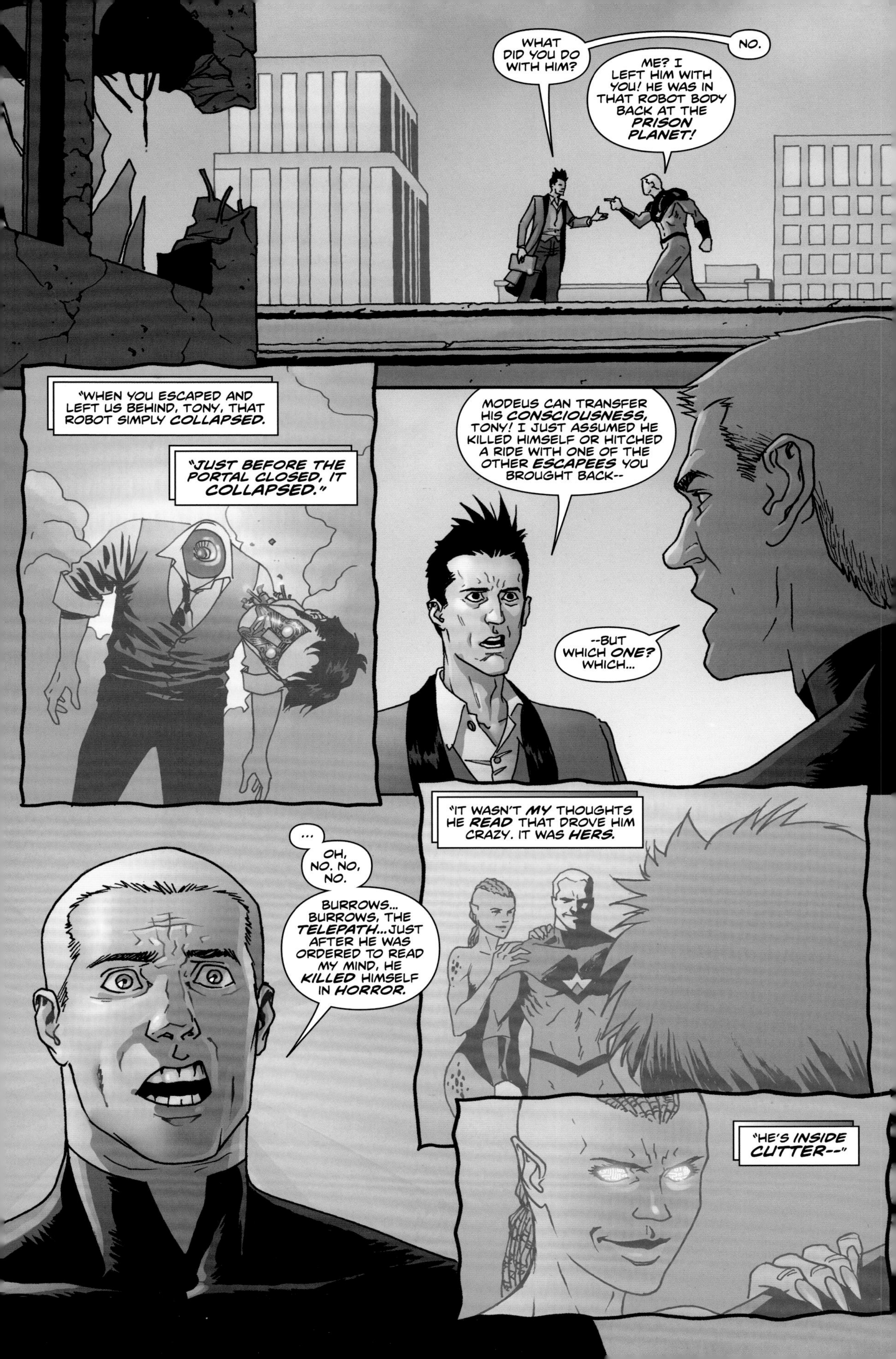
WHAT DID YOU DO WITH HIM?
NO.
ME? I LEFT HIM WITH YOU! HE WAS IN THAT ROBOT BODY BACK AT THE PRISON PLANET!
"WHEN YOU ESCAPED AND LEFT US BEHIND, TONY, THAT ROBOT SIMPLY COLLAPSED.
"JUST BEFORE THE PORTAL CLOSED, IT COLLAPSED."
MODEUS CAN TRANSFER HIS CONSCIOUSNESS, TONY! I JUST ASSUMED HE KILLED HIMSELF OR HITCHED A RIDE WITH ONE OF THE OTHER ESCAPEES YOU BROUGHT BACK--
--BUT WHICH ONE? WHICH...
...
OH, NO. NO, NO.
BURROWS... BURROWS, THE TELEPATH...JUST AFTER HE WAS ORDERED TO READ MY MIND, HE KILLED HIMSELF IN HORROR.
"IT WASN'T MY THOUGHTS HE READ THAT DROVE HIM CRAZY. IT WAS HERS.
"HE'S INSIDE CUTTER--"

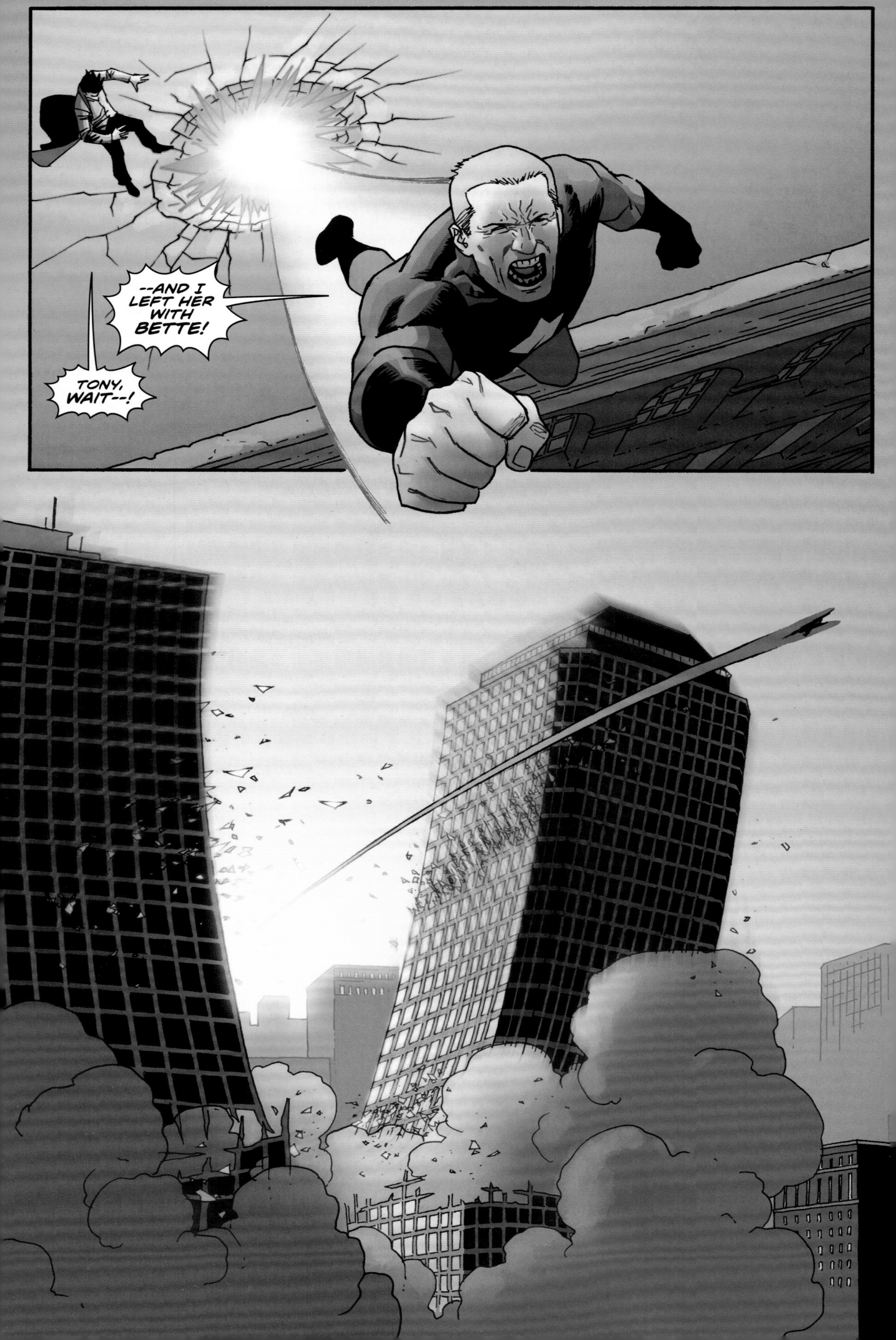
--AND I LEFT HER WITH BETTE!
TONY, WAIT--!

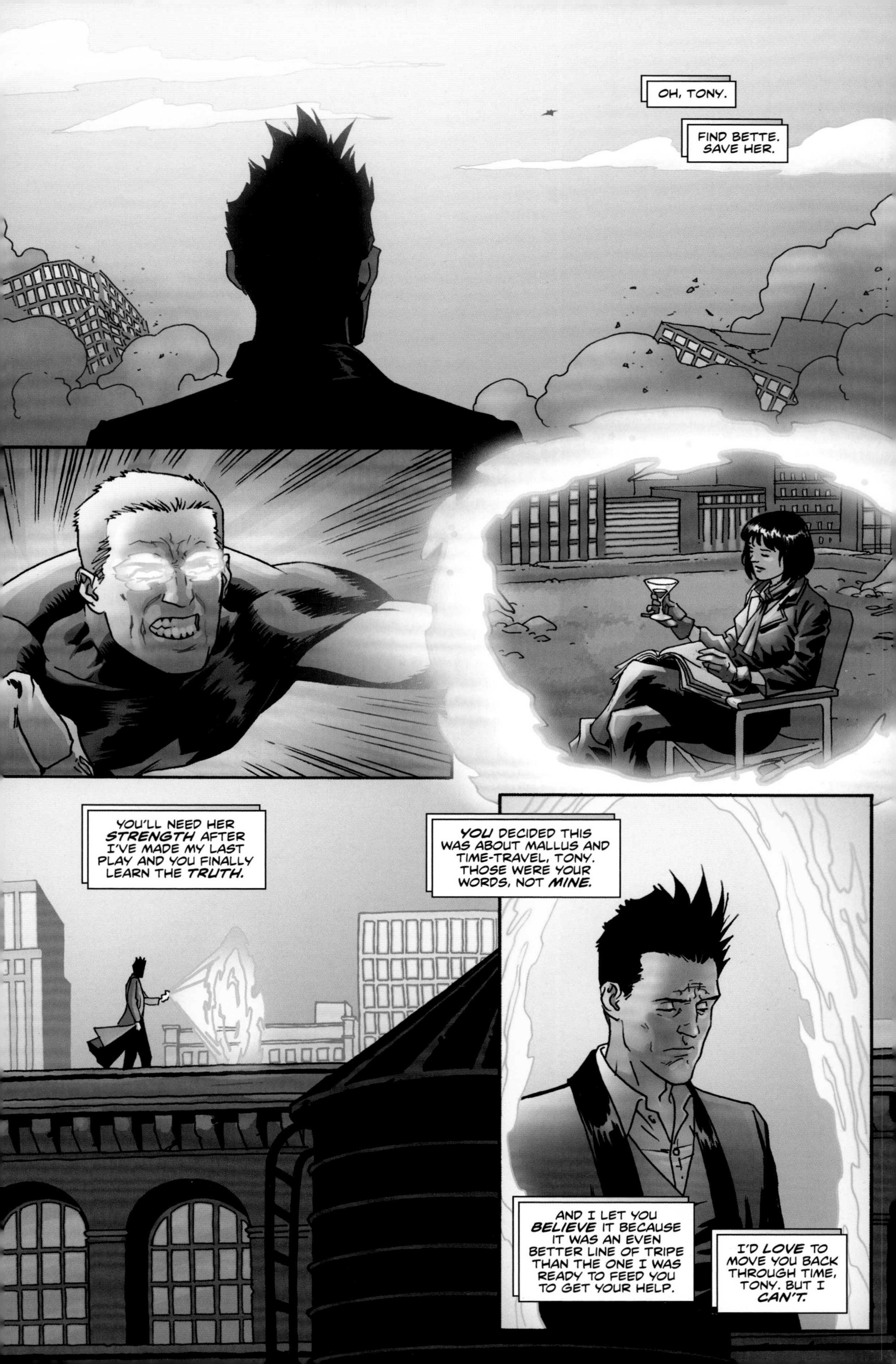
OH, TONY.
FIND BETTE. SAVE HER.
YOU'LL NEED HER STRENGTH AFTER I'VE MADE MY LAST PLAY AND YOU FINALLY LEARN THE TRUTH.
YOU DECIDED THIS WAS ABOUT MALLUS AND TIME-TRAVEL, TONY. THOSE WERE YOUR WORDS, NOT MINE.
AND I LET YOU BELIEVE IT BECAUSE IT WAS AN EVEN BETTER LINE OF TRIPE THAN THE ONE I WAS READY TO FEED YOU TO GET YOUR HELP.
I'D LOVE TO MOVE YOU BACK THROUGH TIME, TONY. BUT I CAN'T.

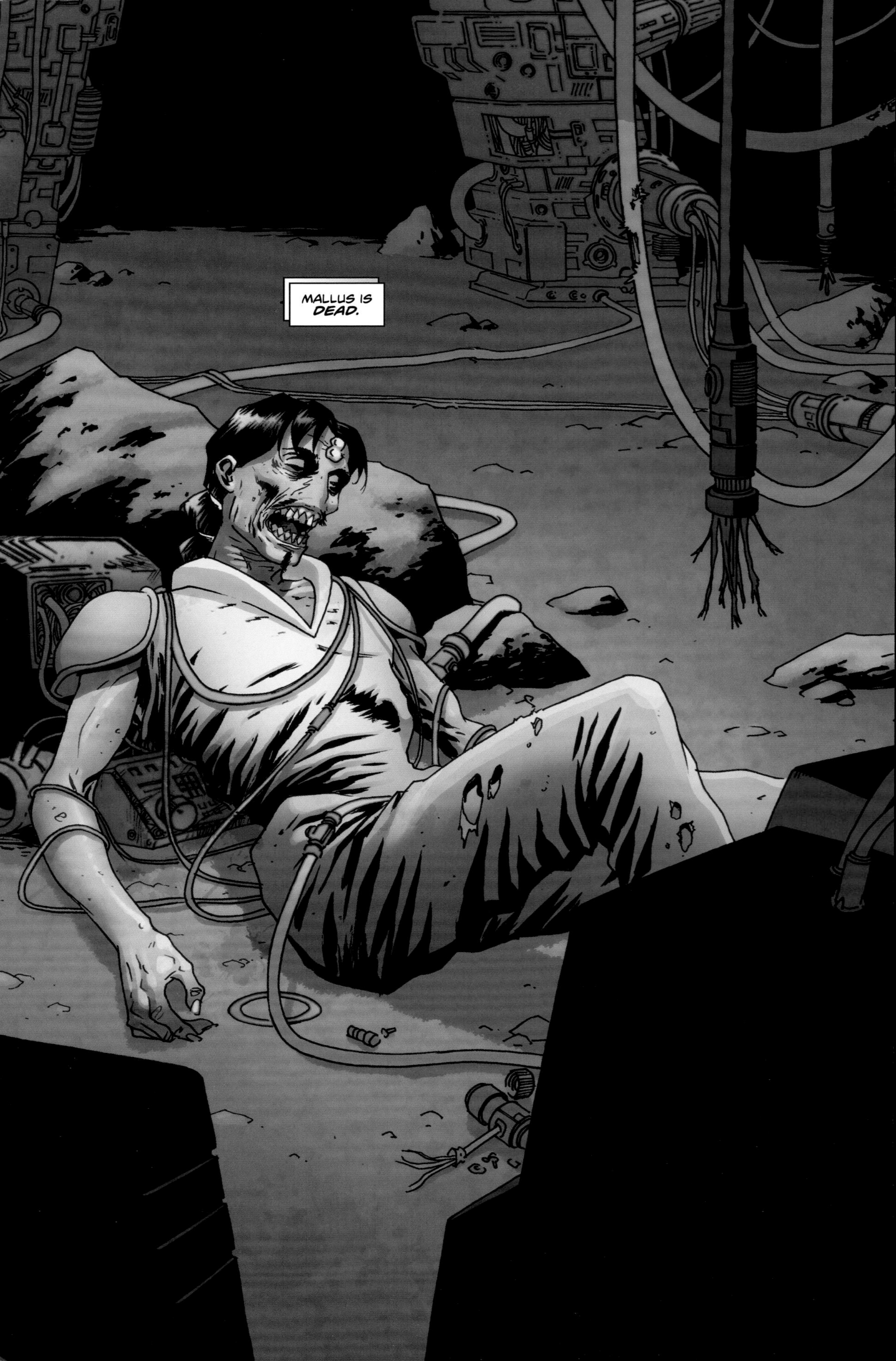
MALLUS IS DEAD.

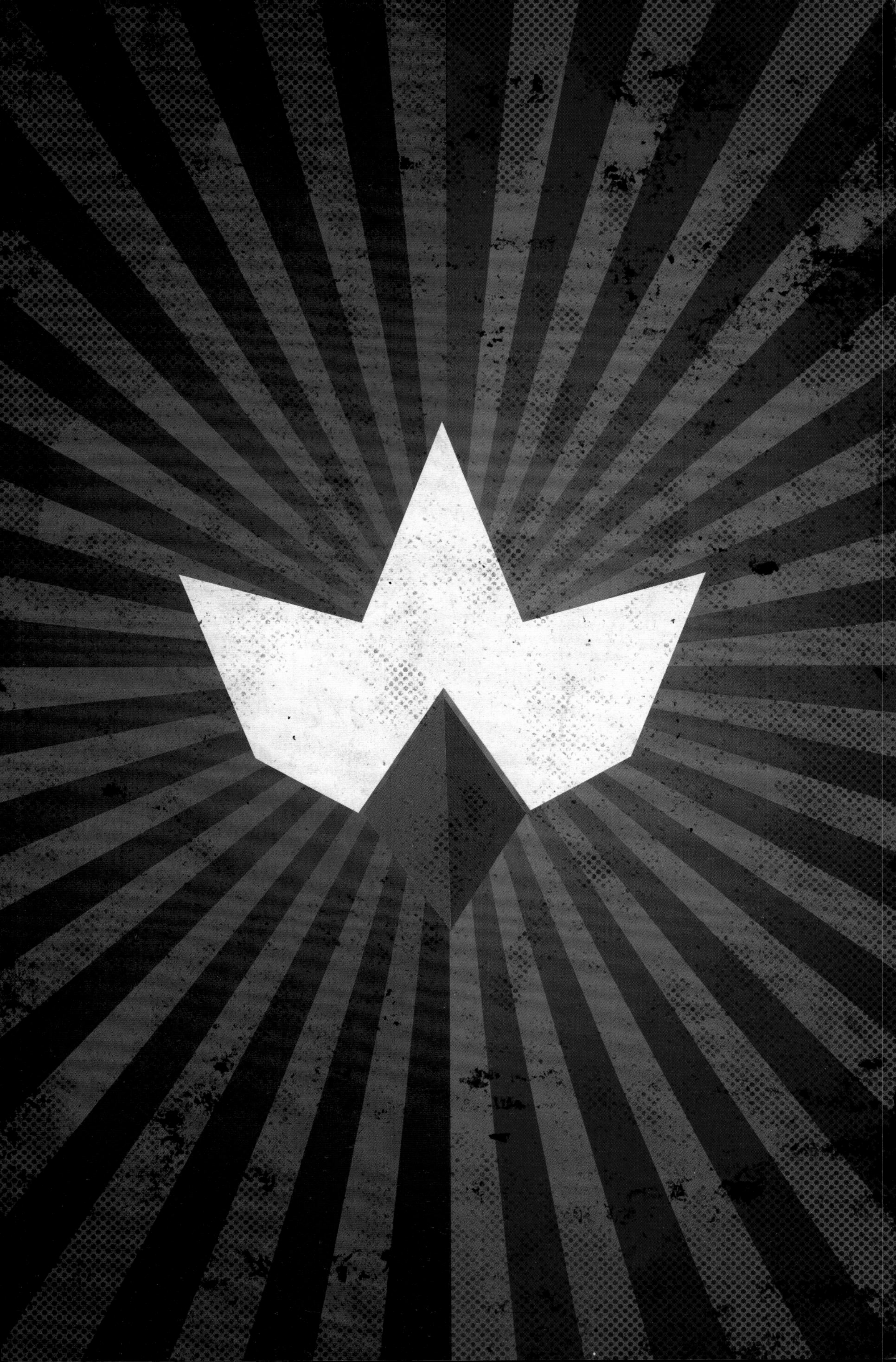

CHAPTER 35

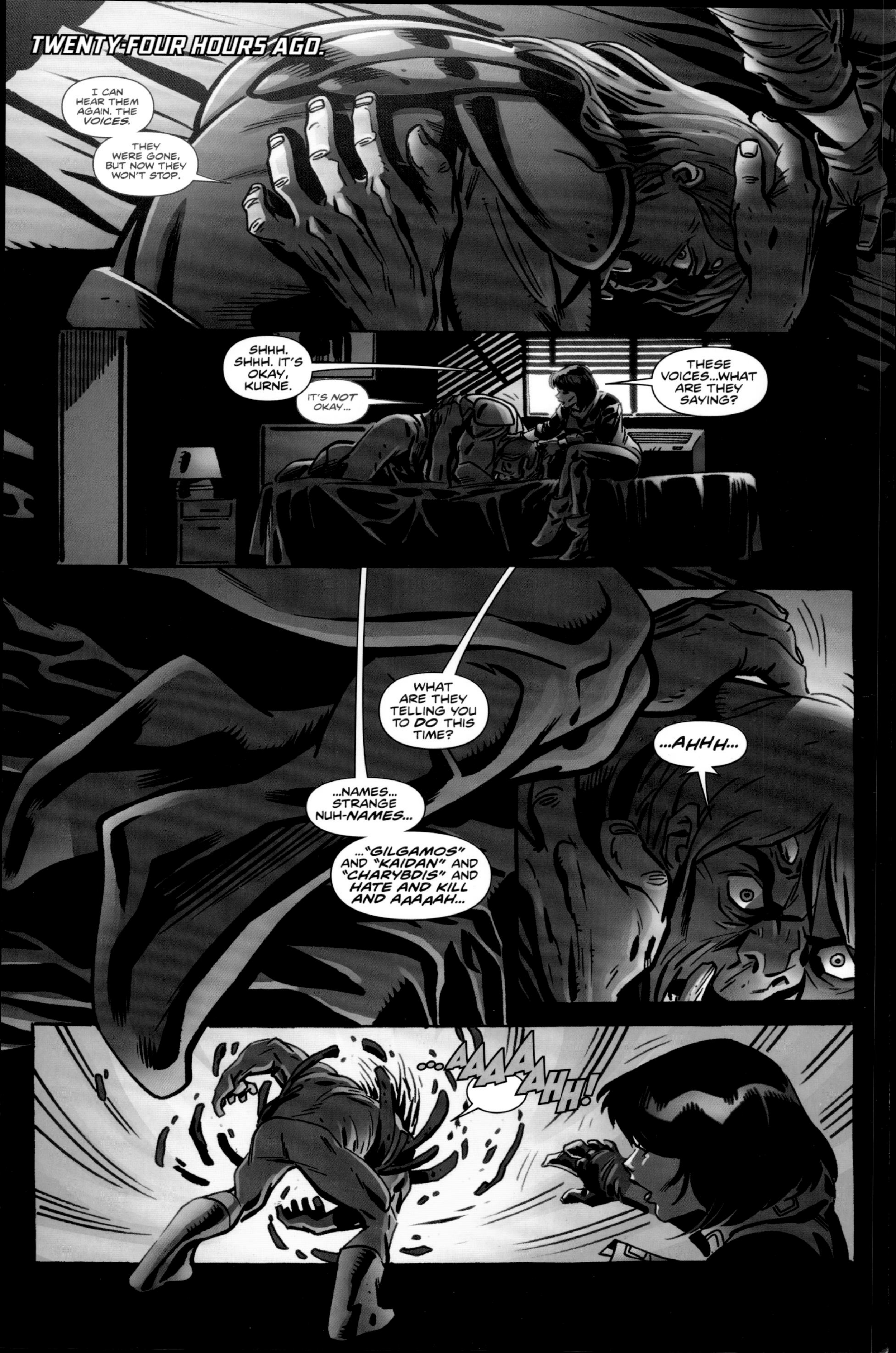
TWENTY-FOUR HOURS AGO.
I CAN HEAR THEM AGAIN. THE VOICES.
THEY WERE GONE, BUT NOW THEY WON'T STOP.
SHHH. SHHH. IT'S OKAY, KURNE.
IT'S NOT OKAY...
THESE VOICES...WHAT ARE THEY SAYING?
WHAT ARE THEY TELLING YOU TO DO THIS TIME?
...AHHH...
...NAMES... STRANGE NUH-NAMES...
..."GILGAMOS" AND "KAIDAN" AND "CHARYBDIS" AND HATE AND KILL AND AAAAAH...
...AAAAAHH!

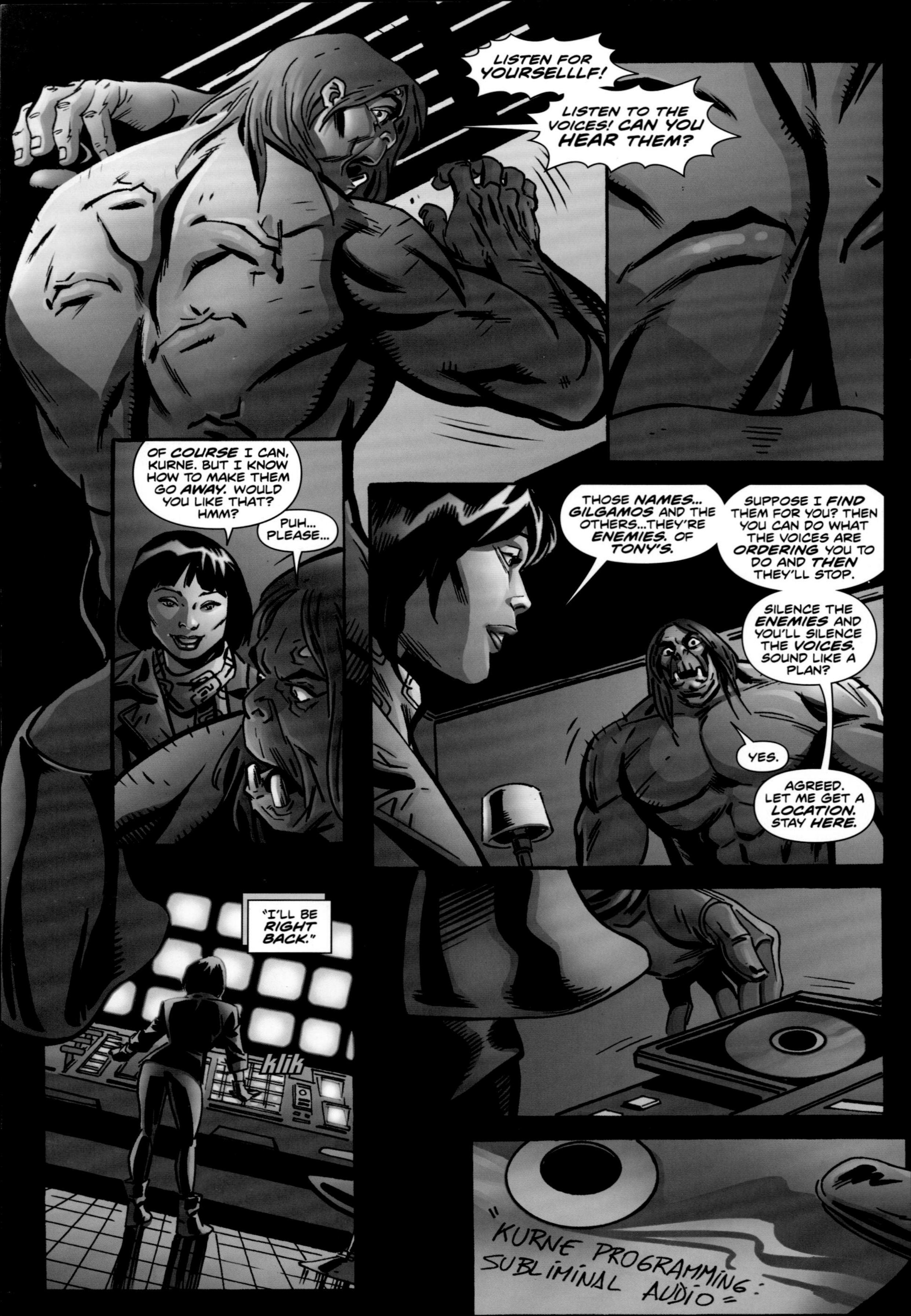
LISTEN FOR YOURSELLLF!
LISTEN TO THE VOICES! CAN YOU HEAR THEM?
OF COURSE I CAN, KURNE. BUT I KNOW HOW TO MAKE THEM GO AWAY. WOULD YOU LIKE THAT? HMM?
PUH... PLEASE...
THOSE NAMES... GILGAMOS AND THE OTHERS...THEY'RE ENEMIES. OF TONY'S.
SUPPOSE I FIND THEM FOR YOU? THEN YOU CAN DO WHAT THE VOICES ARE ORDERING YOU TO DO AND THEN THEY'LL STOP.
SILENCE THE ENEMIES AND YOU'LL SILENCE THE VOICES. SOUND LIKE A PLAN?
YES.
AGREED. LET ME GET A LOCATION. STAY HERE.
"I'LL BE RIGHT BACK."
klik
"KURNE PROGRAMMING: SUBLIMINAL AUDIO"

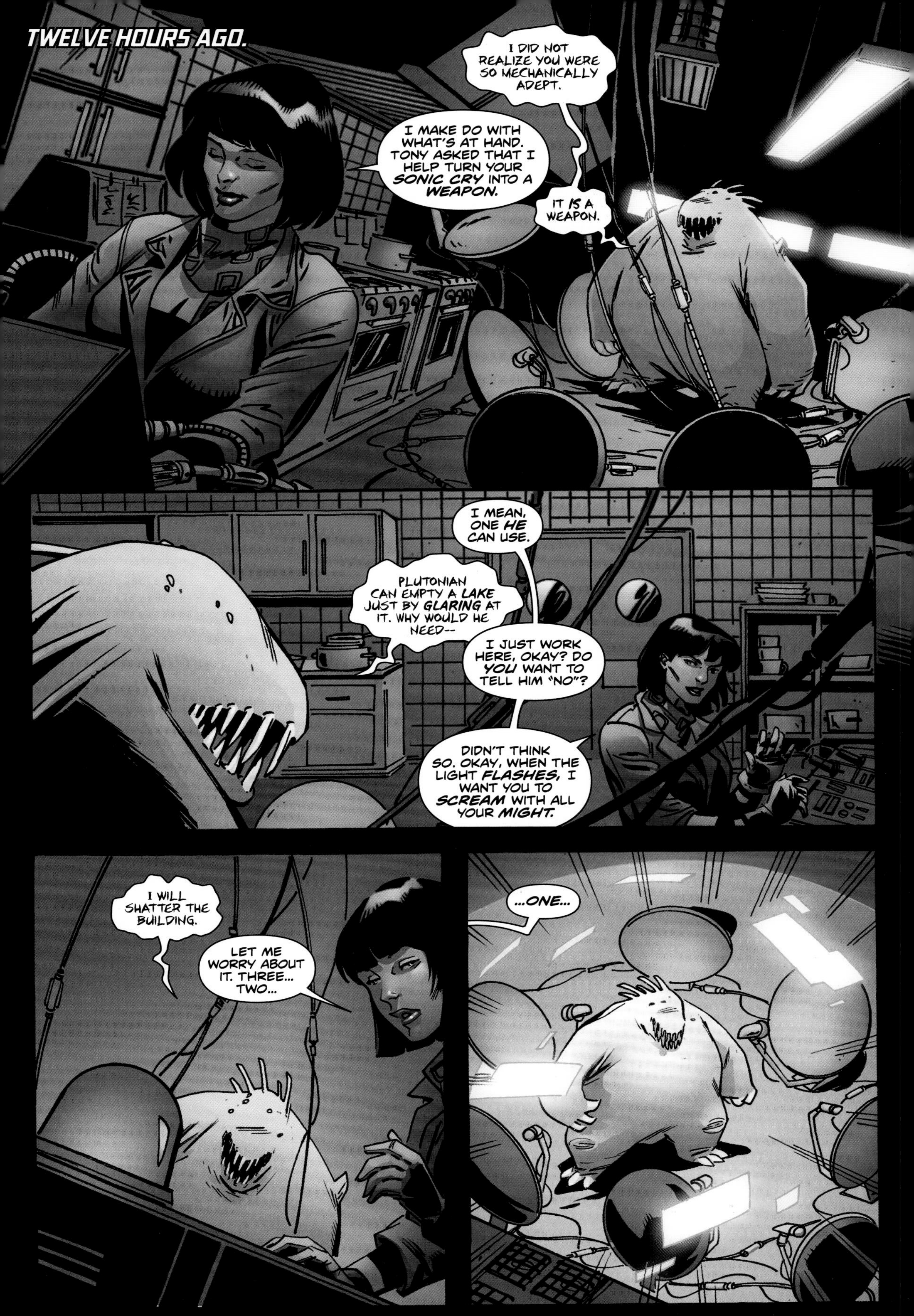
TWELVE HOURS AGO.
I DID NOT REALIZE YOU WERE SO MECHANICALLY ADEPT.
I MAKE DO WITH WHAT'S AT HAND. TONY ASKED THAT I HELP TURN YOUR SONIC CRY INTO A WEAPON.
IT IS A WEAPON.
I MEAN, ONE HE CAN USE.
PLUTONIAN CAN EMPTY A LAKE JUST BY GLARING AT IT. WHY WOULD HE NEED--
I JUST WORK HERE, OKAY? DO YOU WANT TO TELL HIM "NO"?
DIDN'T THINK SO. OKAY, WHEN THE LIGHT FLASHES, I WANT YOU TO SCREAM WITH ALL YOUR MIGHT.
I WILL SHATTER THE BUILDING.
LET ME WORRY ABOUT IT. THREE... TWO...
...ONE...

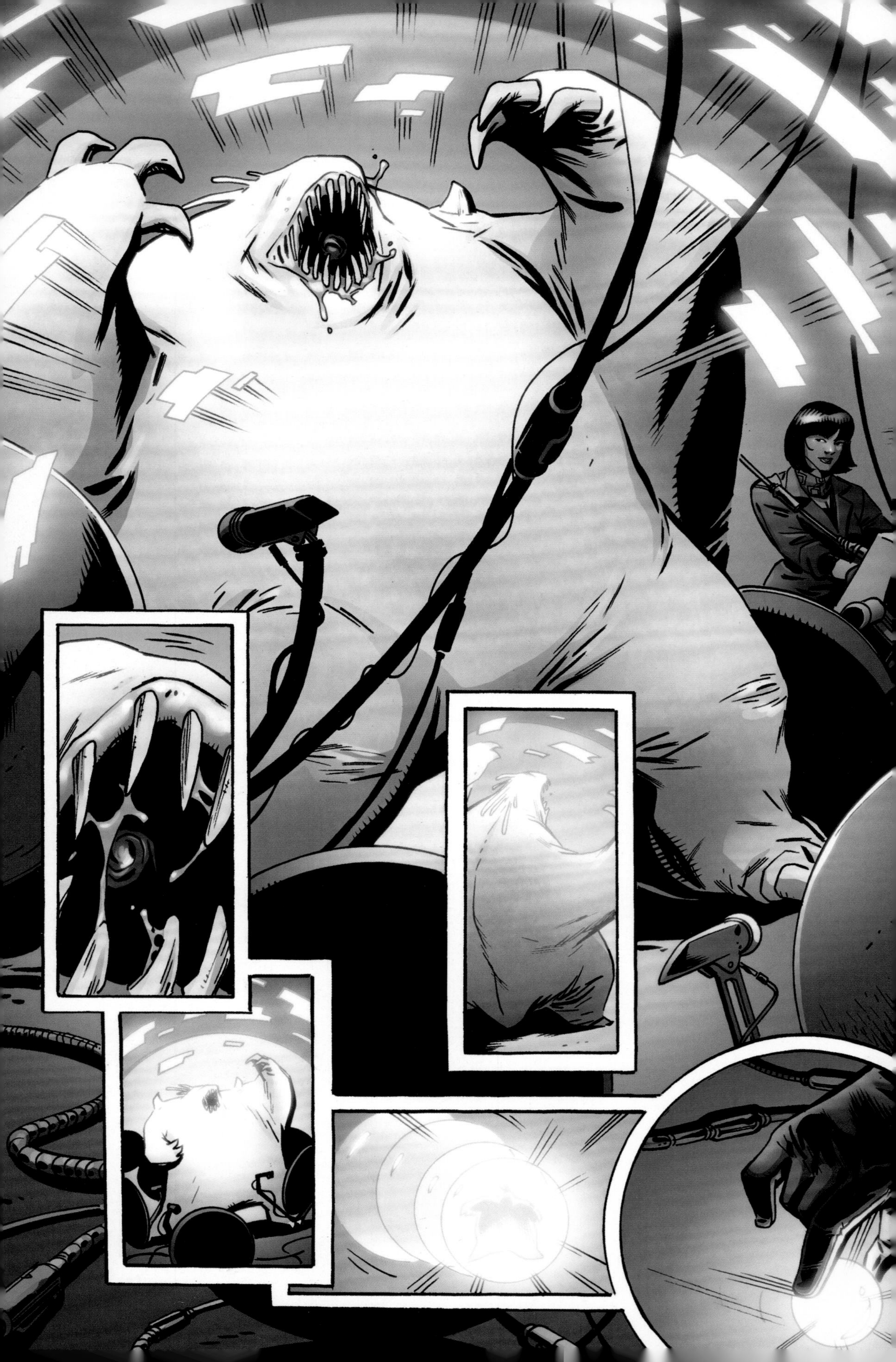

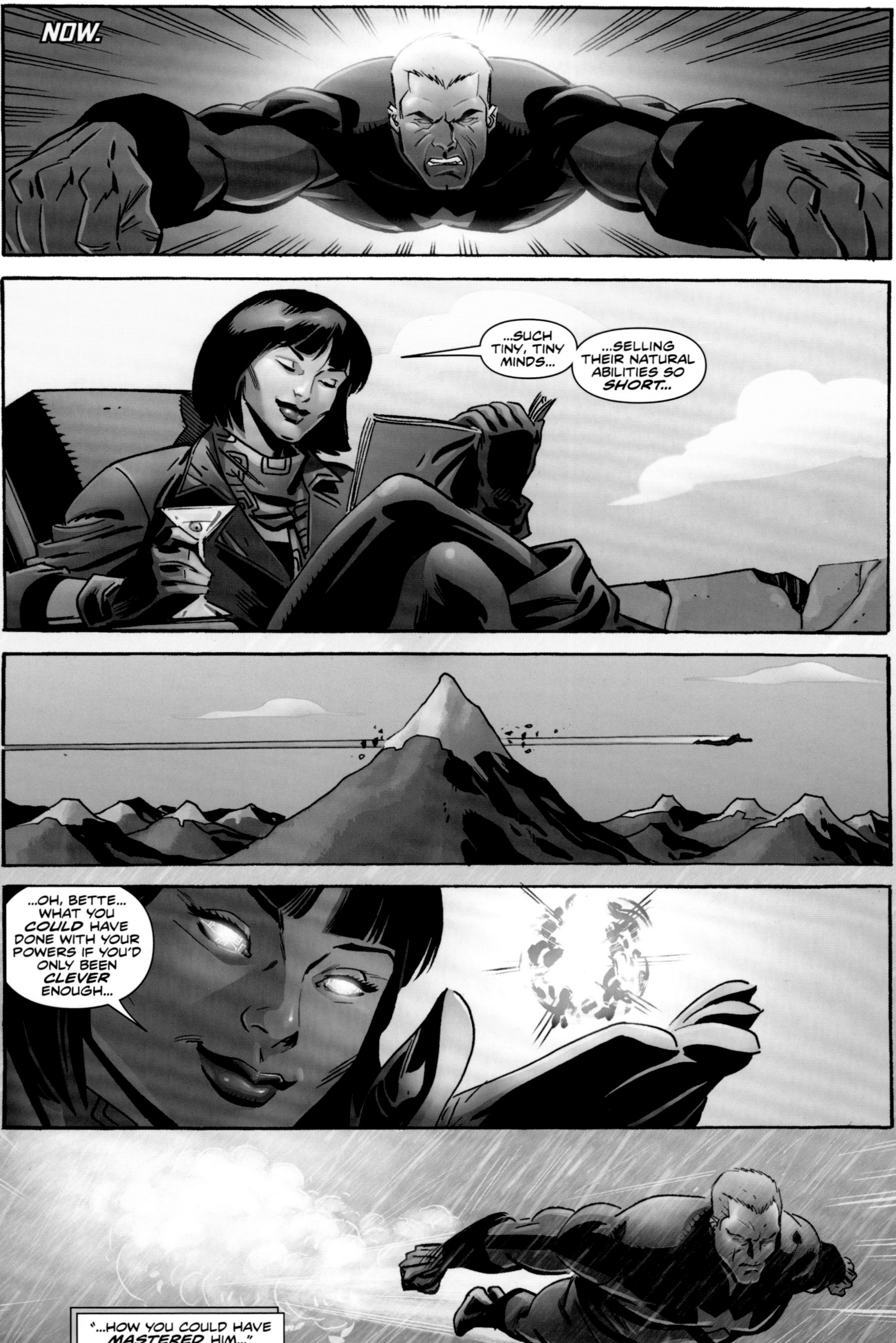
NOW.
...SUCH TINY, TINY MINDS...
...SELLING THEIR NATURAL ABILITIES SO SHORT...
...OH, BETTE... WHAT YOU COULD HAVE DONE WITH YOUR POWERS IF YOU'D ONLY BEEN CLEVER ENOUGH...
"...HOW YOU COULD HAVE MASTERED HIM..."

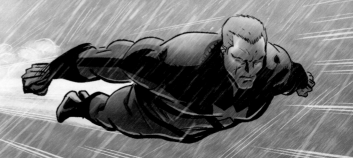

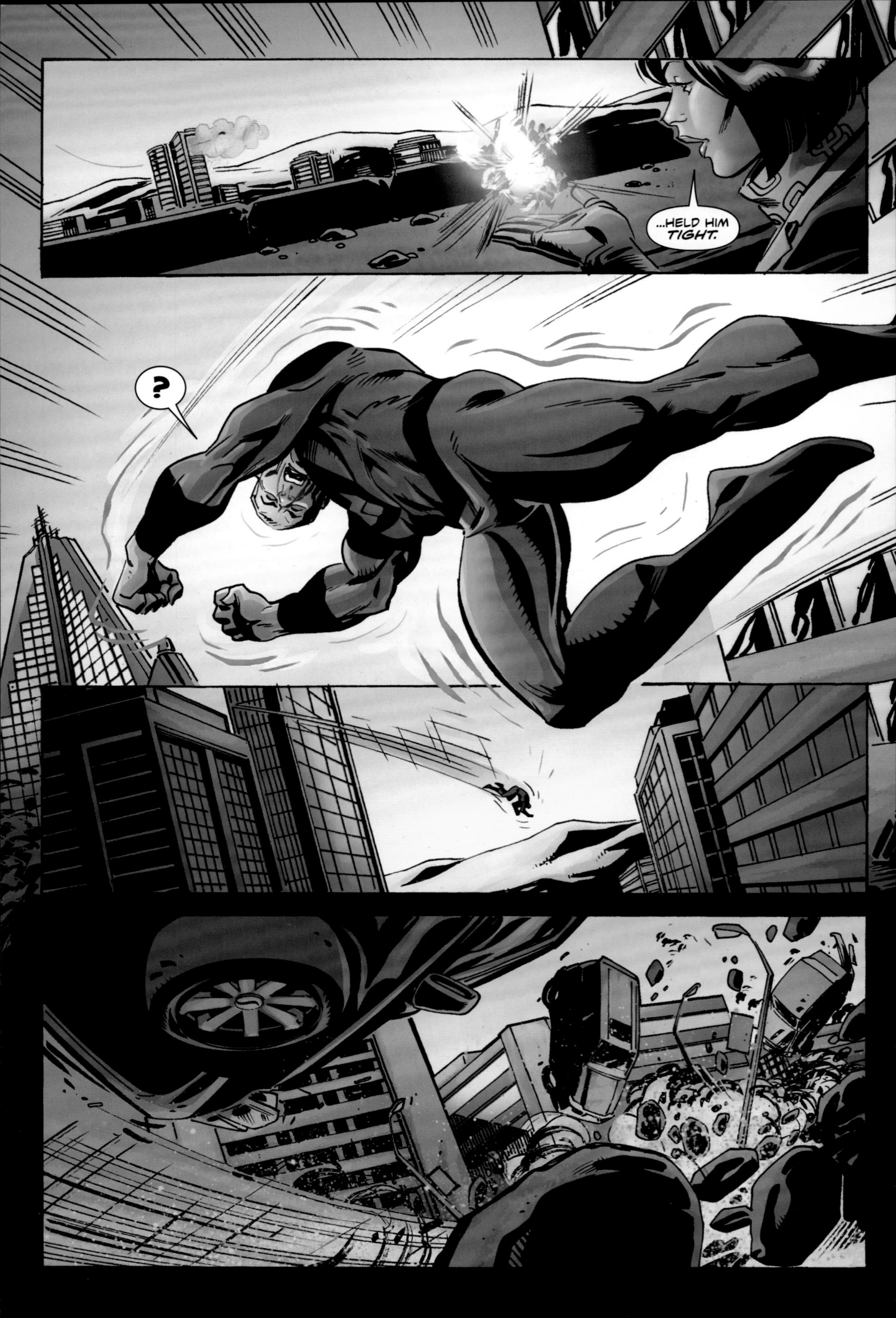
...HELD HIM TIGHT.
?

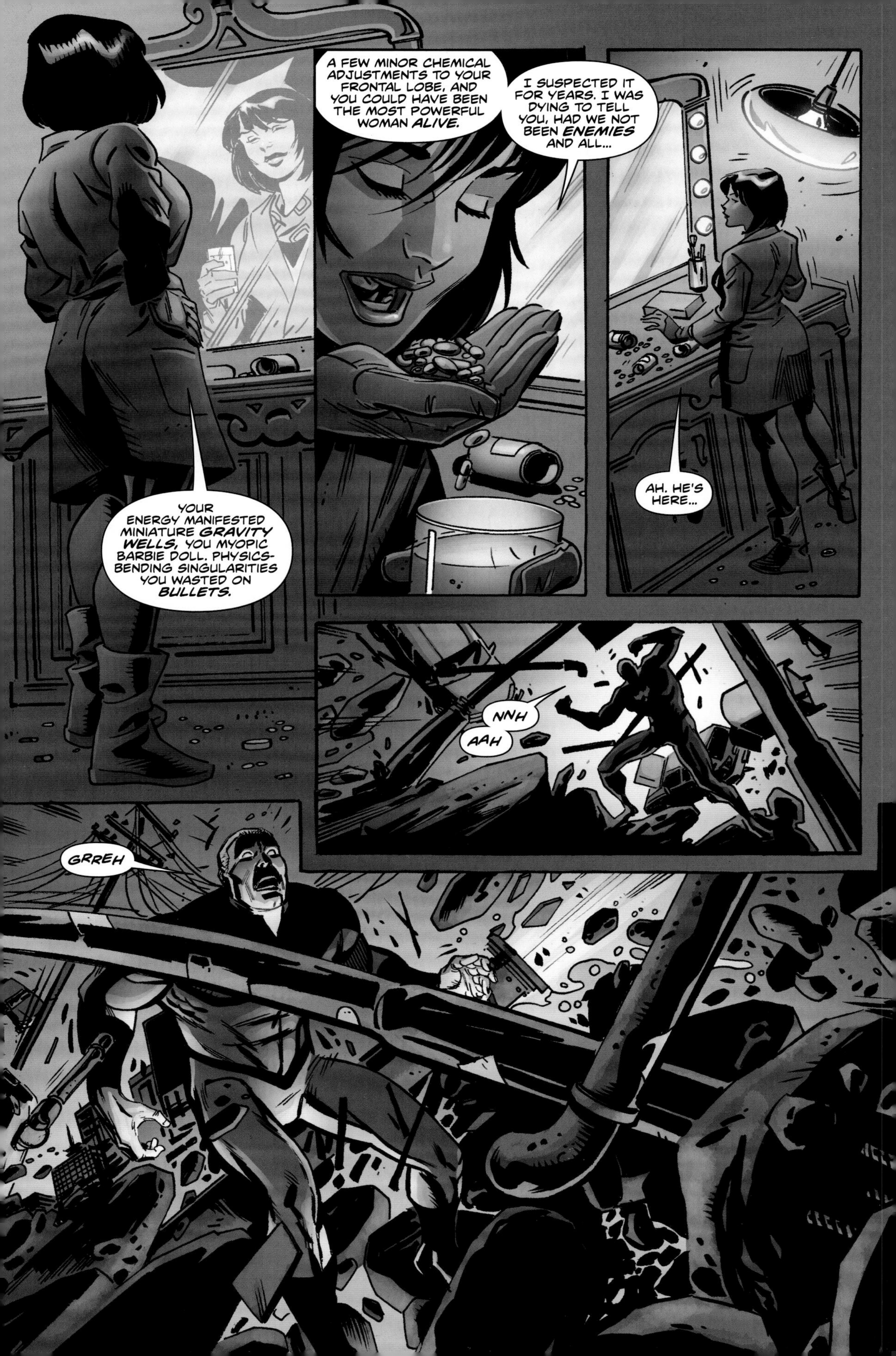
A FEW MINOR CHEMICAL ADJUSTMENTS TO YOUR FRONTAL LOBE, AND YOU COULD HAVE BEEN THE MOST POWERFUL WOMAN ALIVE.
I SUSPECTED IT FOR YEARS. I WAS DYING TO TELL YOU, HAD WE NOT BEEN ENEMIES AND ALL...
YOUR ENERGY MANIFESTED MINIATURE GRAVITY WELLS, YOU MYOPIC BARBIE DOLL. PHYSICS-BENDING SINGULARITIES YOU WASTED ON BULLETS.
AH. HE'S HERE...
NNH
AAH
GRREH

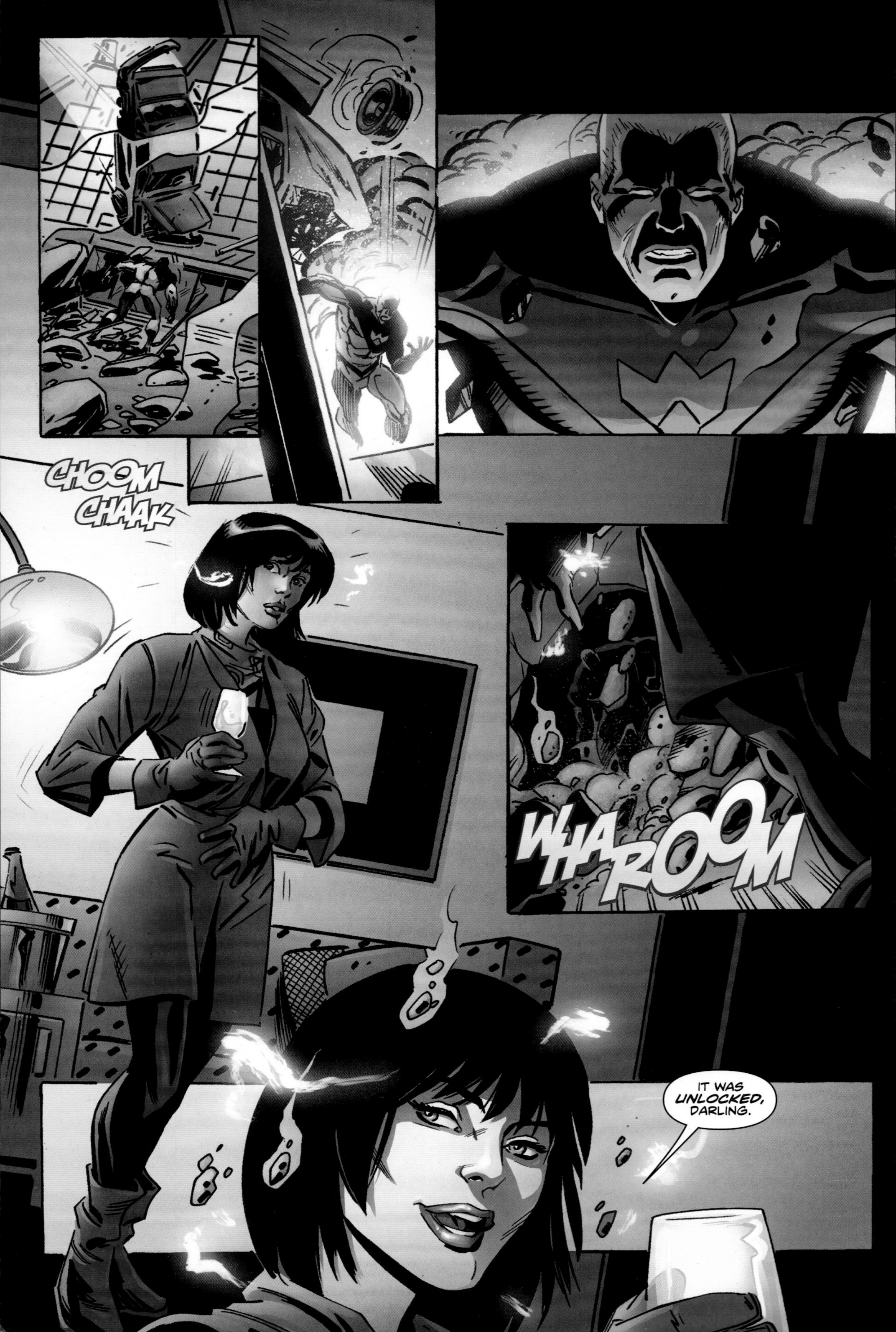
CHOOM
CHAAK
WHAROOM
IT WAS UNLOCKED, DARLING.

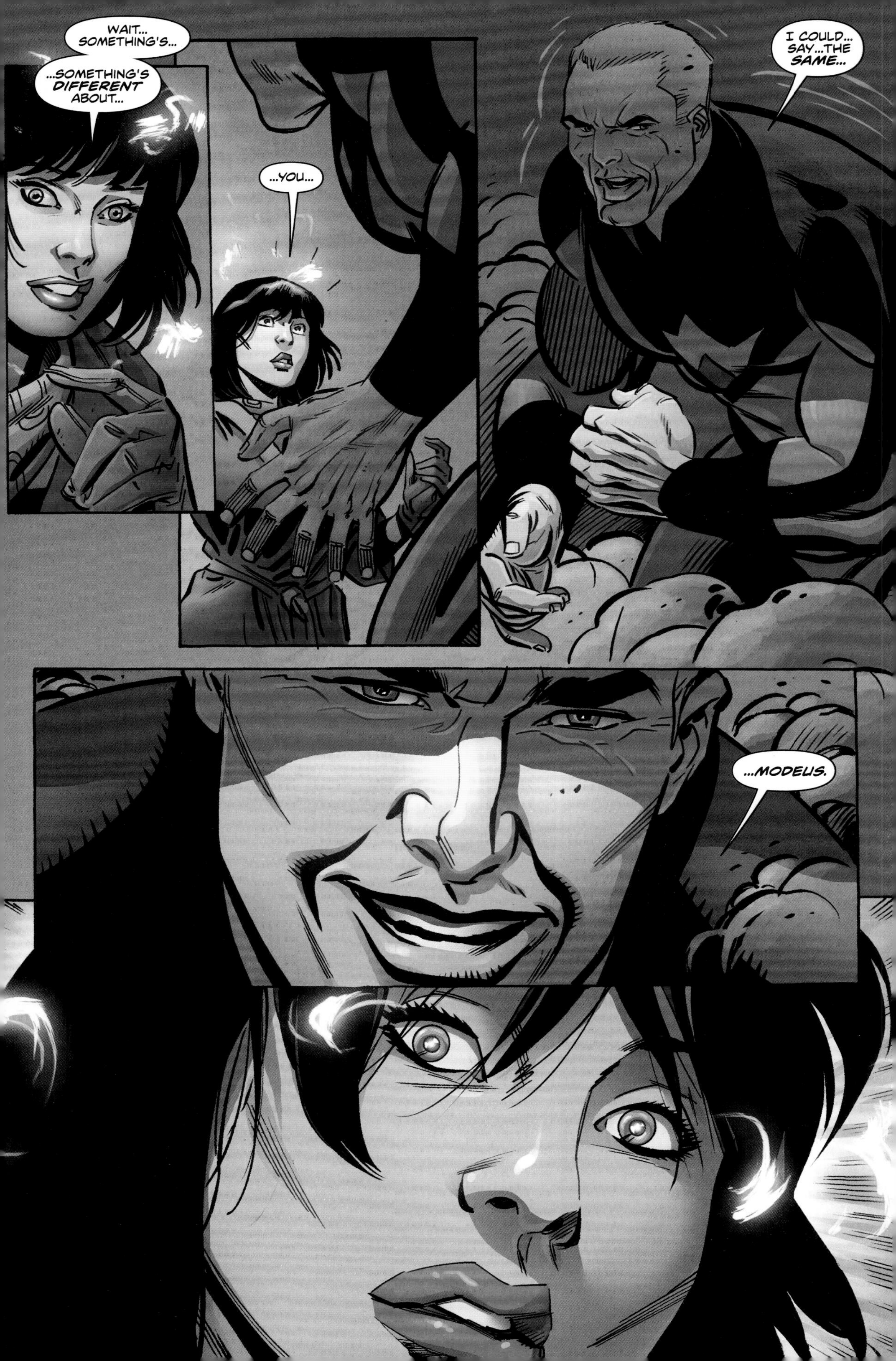
WAIT... SOMETHING'S...
...SOMETHING'S DIFFERENT ABOUT...
...YOU...
I COULD... SAY...THE SAME...
...MODEUS.

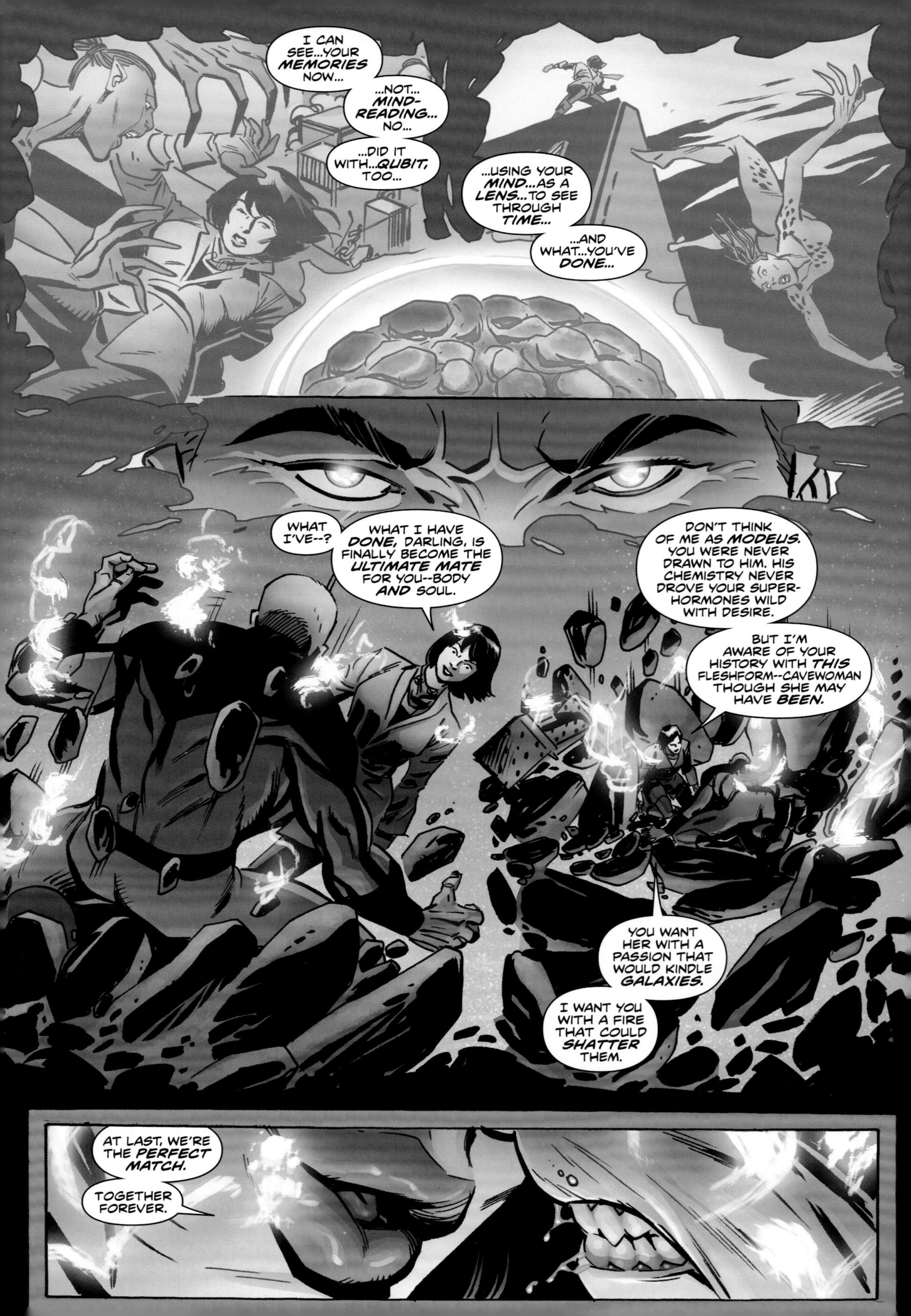
I CAN SEE...YOUR MEMORIES NOW...
...NOT... MIND-READING... NO...
...DID IT WITH...QUBIT, TOO...
...USING YOUR MIND...AS A LENS...TO SEE THROUGH TIME...
...AND WHAT...YOU'VE DONE...
WHAT I'VE--?
WHAT I HAVE DONE, DARLING, IS FINALLY BECOME THE ULTIMATE MATE FOR YOU--BODY AND SOUL.
DON'T THINK OF ME AS MODEUS. YOU WERE NEVER DRAWN TO HIM. HIS CHEMISTRY NEVER DROVE YOUR SUPER-HORMONES WILD WITH DESIRE.
BUT I'M AWARE OF YOUR HISTORY WITH THIS FLESHFORM--CAVEWOMAN THOUGH SHE MAY HAVE BEEN.
YOU WANT HER WITH A PASSION THAT WOULD KINDLE GALAXIES.
I WANT YOU WITH A FIRE THAT COULD SHATTER THEM.
AT LAST, WE'RE THE PERFECT MATCH.
TOGETHER FOREVER.

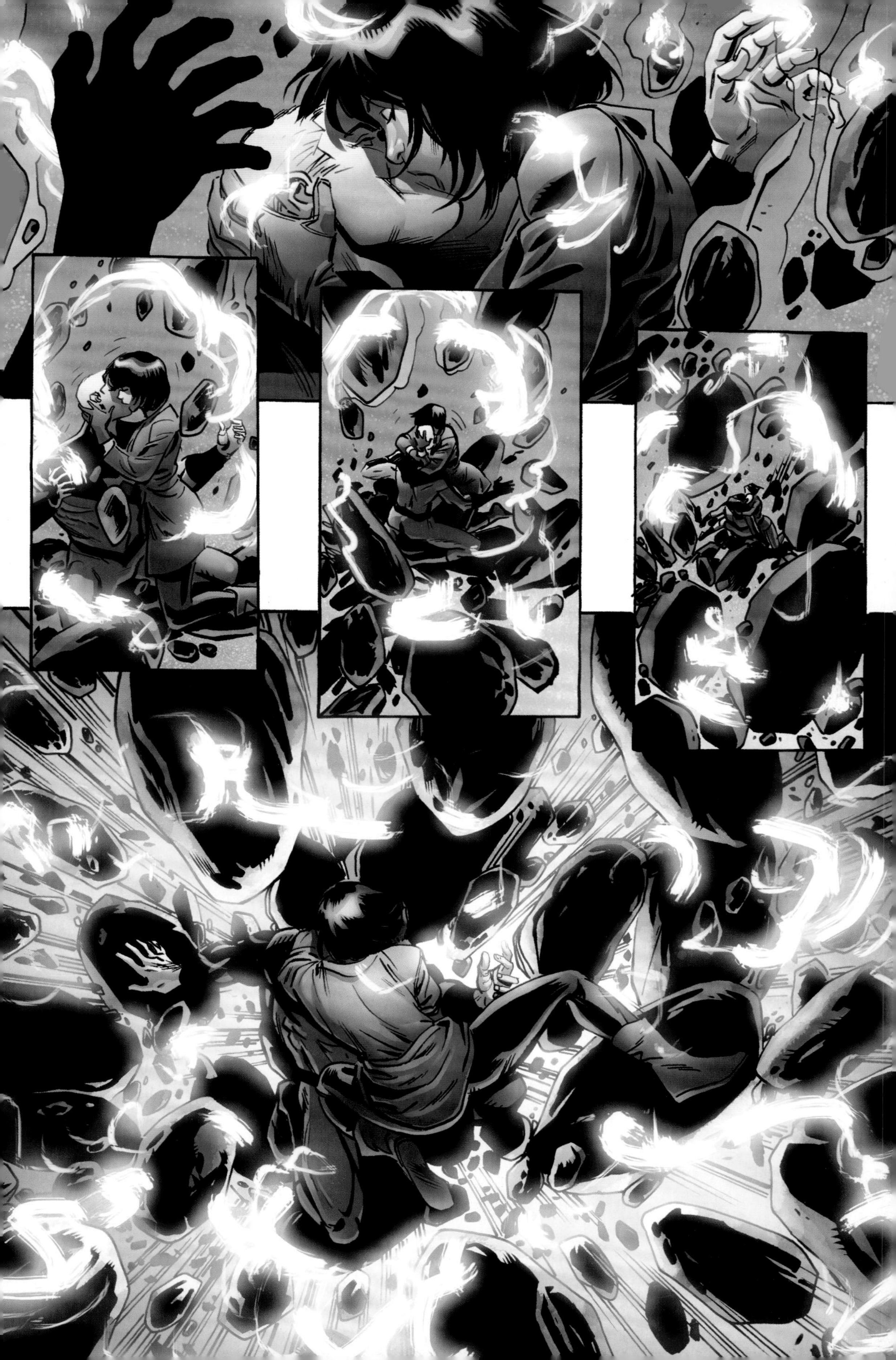

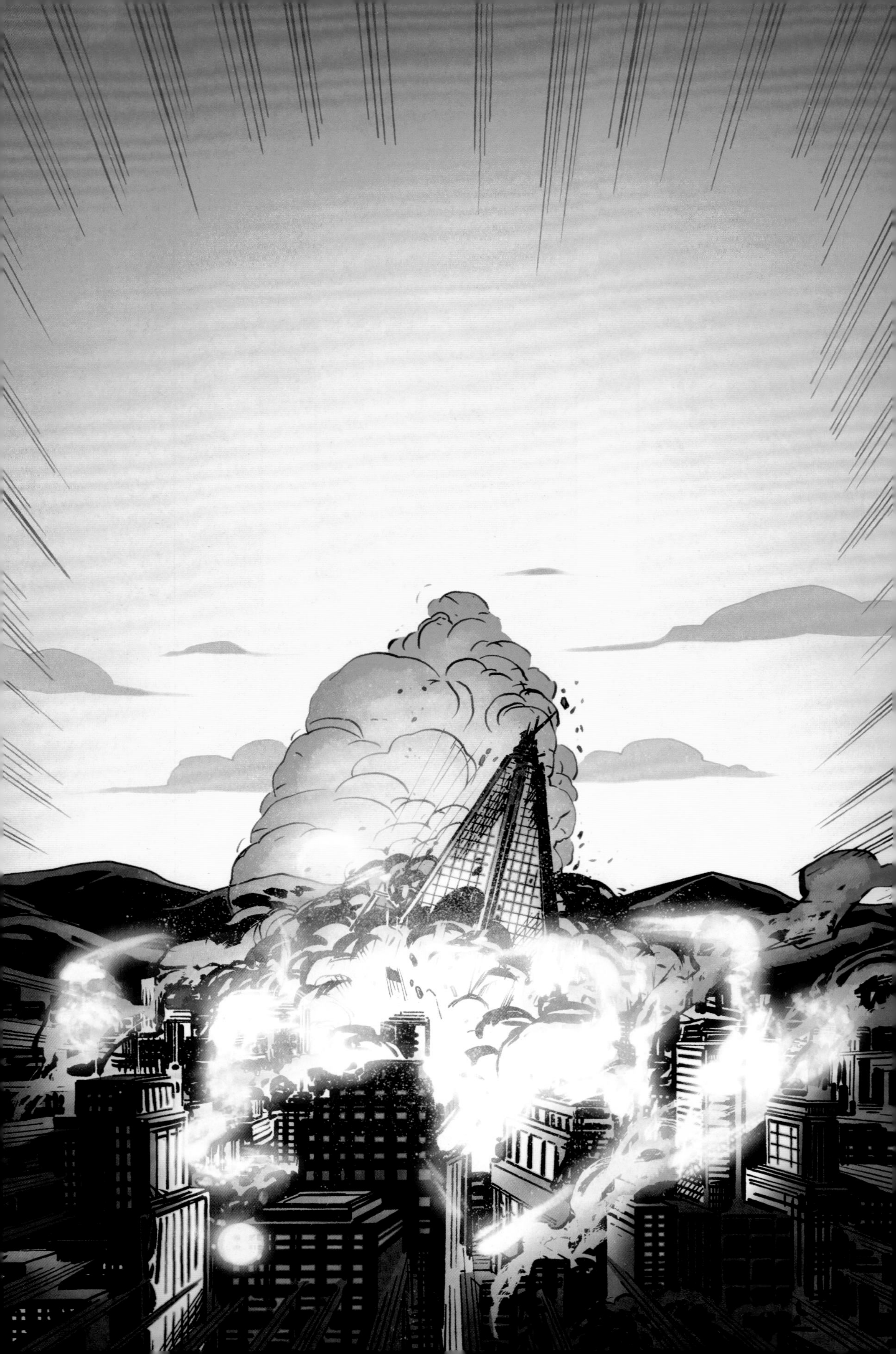

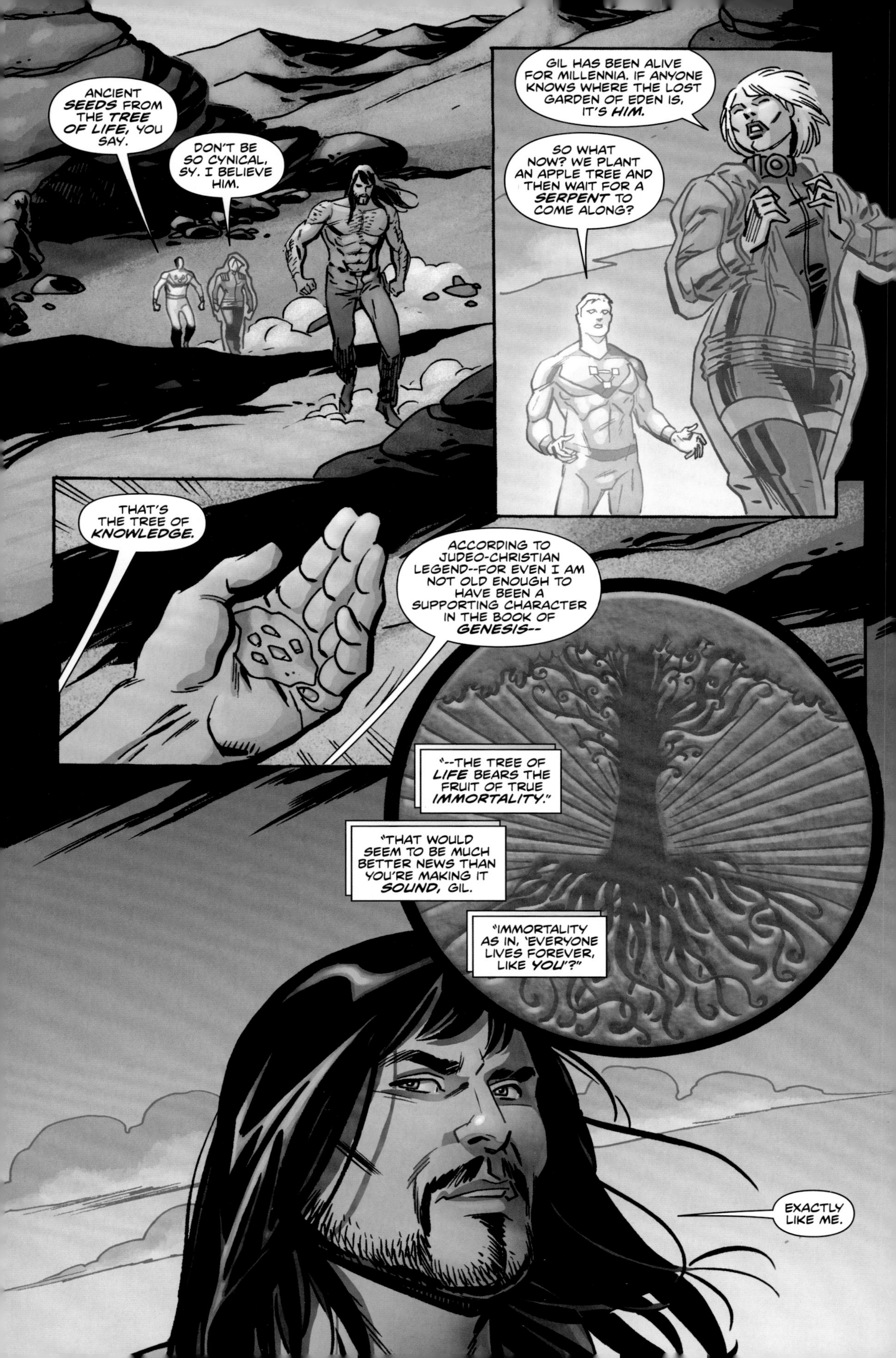
ANCIENT SEEDS FROM THE TREE OF LIFE, YOU SAY.
DON'T BE SO CYNICAL, SY. I BELIEVE HIM.
GIL HAS BEEN ALIVE FOR MILLENNIA. IF ANYONE KNOWS WHERE THE LOST GARDEN OF EDEN IS, IT'S HIM.
SO WHAT NOW? WE PLANT AN APPLE TREE AND THEN WAIT FOR A SERPENT TO COME ALONG?
THAT'S THE TREE OF KNOWLEDGE.
ACCORDING TO JUDEO-CHRISTIAN LEGEND--FOR EVEN I AM NOT OLD ENOUGH TO HAVE BEEN A SUPPORTING CHARACTER IN THE BOOK OF GENESIS--
"--THE TREE OF LIFE BEARS THE FRUIT OF TRUE IMMORTALITY."
"THAT WOULD SEEM TO BE MUCH BETTER NEWS THAN YOU'RE MAKING IT SOUND, GIL.
"IMMORTALITY AS IN, 'EVERYONE LIVES FOREVER, LIKE YOU'?"
EXACTLY LIKE ME.

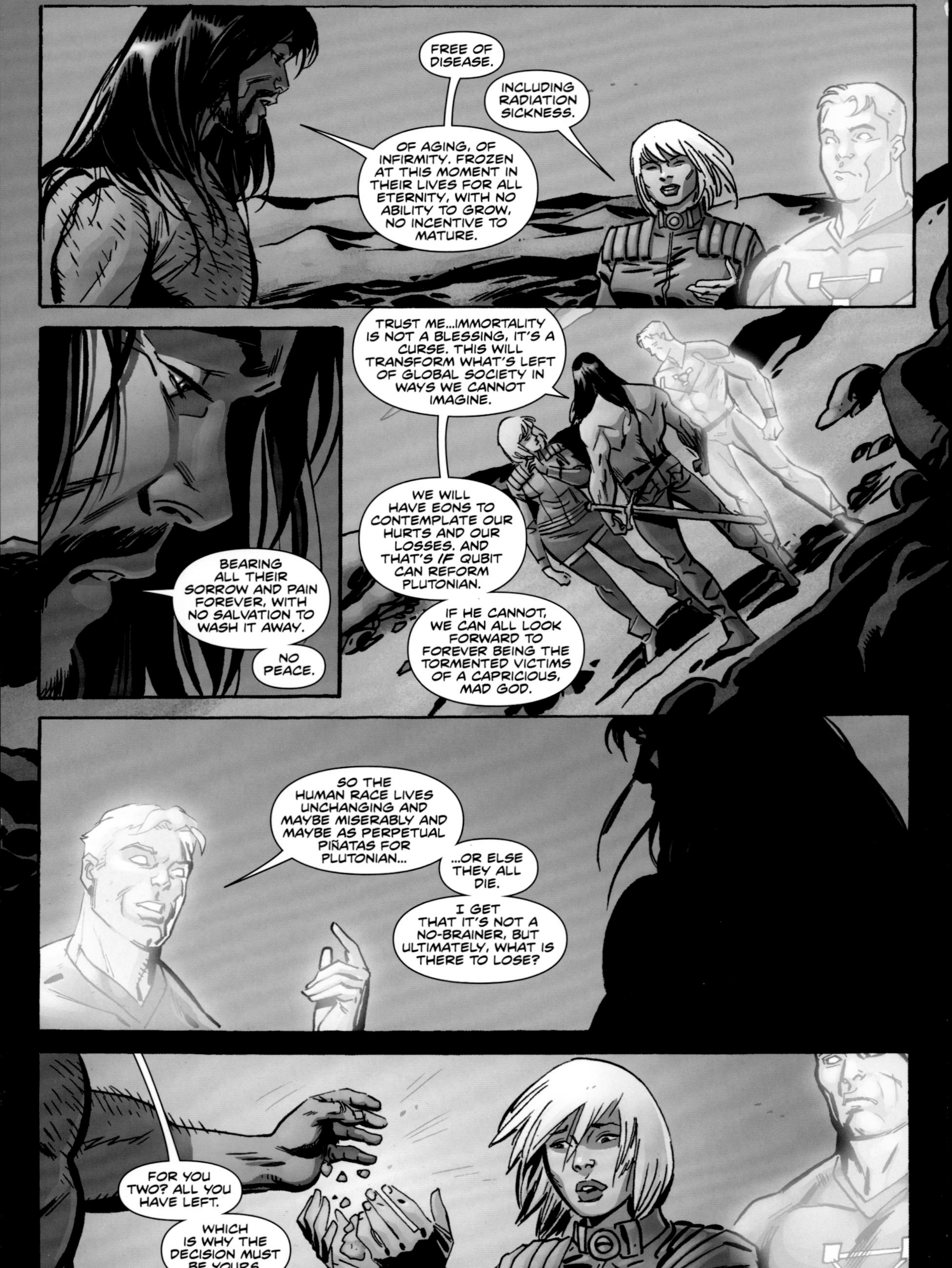
FREE OF DISEASE.
INCLUDING RADIATION SICKNESS.
OF AGING, OF INFIRMITY. FROZEN AT THIS MOMENT IN THEIR LIVES FOR ALL ETERNITY, WITH NO ABILITY TO GROW, NO INCENTIVE TO MATURE.
BEARING ALL THEIR SORROW AND PAIN FOREVER, WITH NO SALVATION TO WASH IT AWAY.
NO PEACE.
TRUST ME...IMMORTALITY IS NOT A BLESSING, IT'S A CURSE. THIS WILL TRANSFORM WHAT'S LEFT OF GLOBAL SOCIETY IN WAYS WE CANNOT IMAGINE.
WE WILL HAVE EONS TO CONTEMPLATE OUR HURTS AND OUR LOSSES. AND THAT'S IF QUBIT CAN REFORM PLUTONIAN.
IF HE CANNOT, WE CAN ALL LOOK FORWARD TO FOREVER BEING THE TORMENTED VICTIMS OF A CAPRICIOUS, MAD GOD.
SO THE HUMAN RACE LIVES UNCHANGING AND MAYBE MISERABLY AND MAYBE AS PERPETUAL PIÑATAS FOR PLUTONIAN...
...OR ELSE THEY ALL DIE.
I GET THAT IT'S NOT A NO-BRAINER, BUT ULTIMATELY, WHAT IS THERE TO LOSE?
FOR YOU TWO? ALL YOU HAVE LEFT.
WHICH IS WHY THE DECISION MUST BE YOURS.

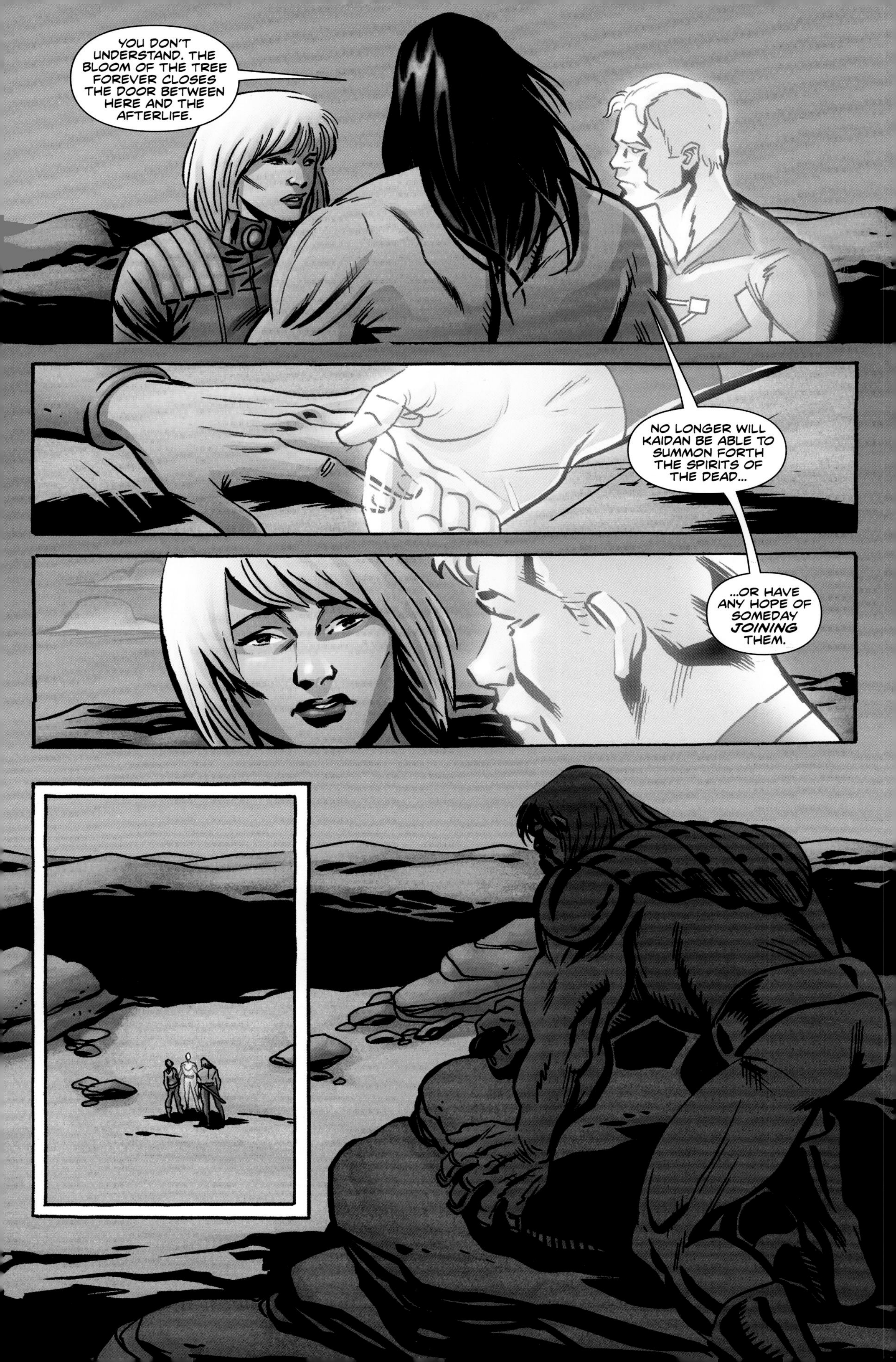
YOU DON'T UNDERSTAND. THE BLOOM OF THE TREE FOREVER CLOSES THE DOOR BETWEEN HERE AND THE AFTERLIFE.
NO LONGER WILL KAIDAN BE ABLE TO SUMMON FORTH THE SPIRITS OF THE DEAD...
...OR HAVE ANY HOPE OF SOMEDAY JOINING THEM.

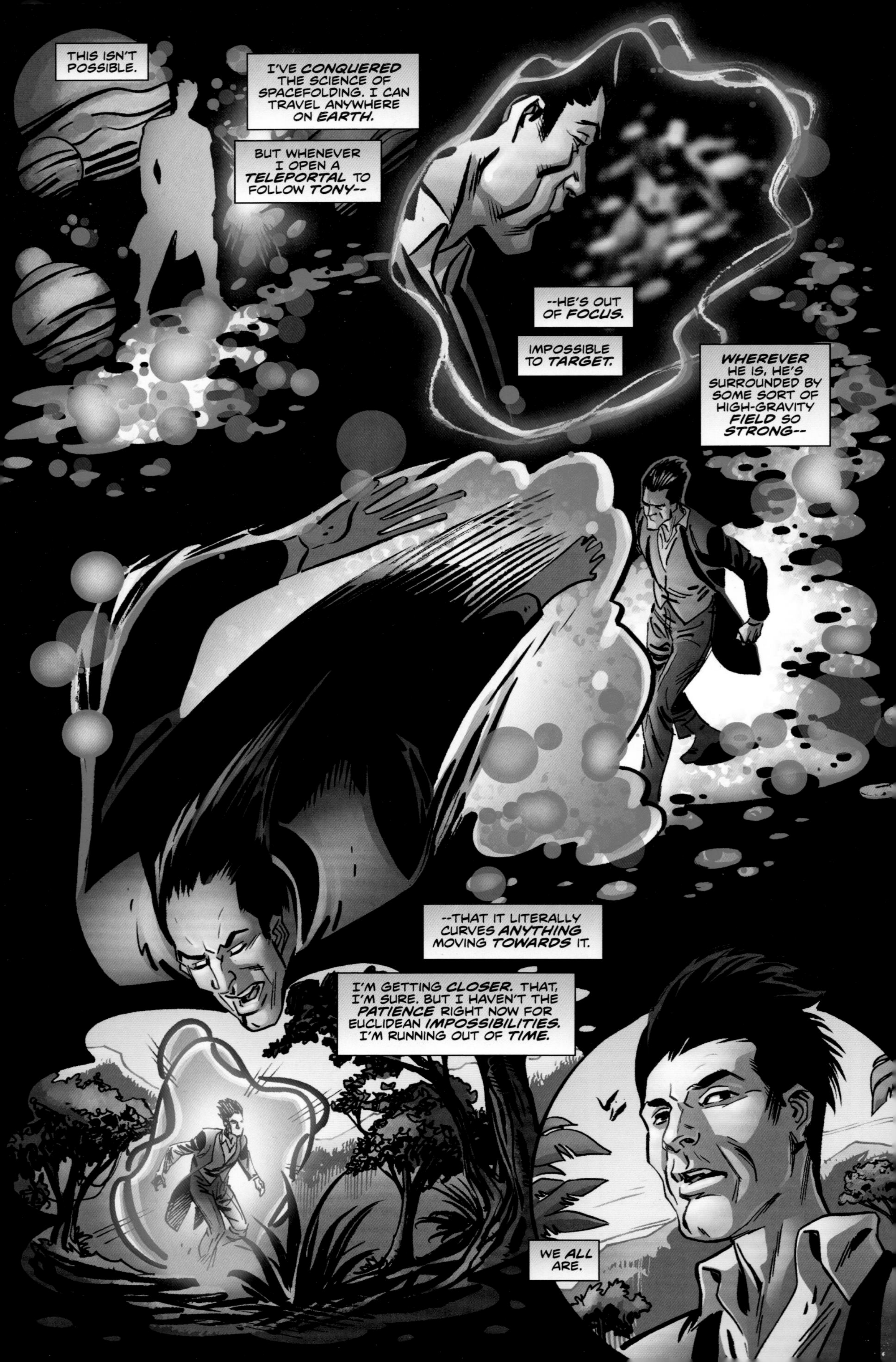

THIS ISN'T POSSIBLE.
I'VE CONQUERED THE SCIENCE OF SPACEFOLDING. I CAN TRAVEL ANYWHERE ON EARTH.
BUT WHENEVER I OPEN A TELEPORTAL TO FOLLOW TONY--
--HE'S OUT OF FOCUS.
IMPOSSIBLE TO TARGET.
WHEREVER HE IS, HE'S SURROUNDED BY SOME SORT OF HIGH-GRAVITY FIELD SO STRONG--
--THAT IT LITERALLY CURVES ANYTHING MOVING TOWARDS IT.
I'M GETTING CLOSER. THAT, I'M SURE. BUT I HAVEN'T THE PATIENCE RIGHT NOW FOR EUCLIDEAN IMPOSSIBILITIES. I'M RUNNING OUT OF TIME.
WE ALL ARE.

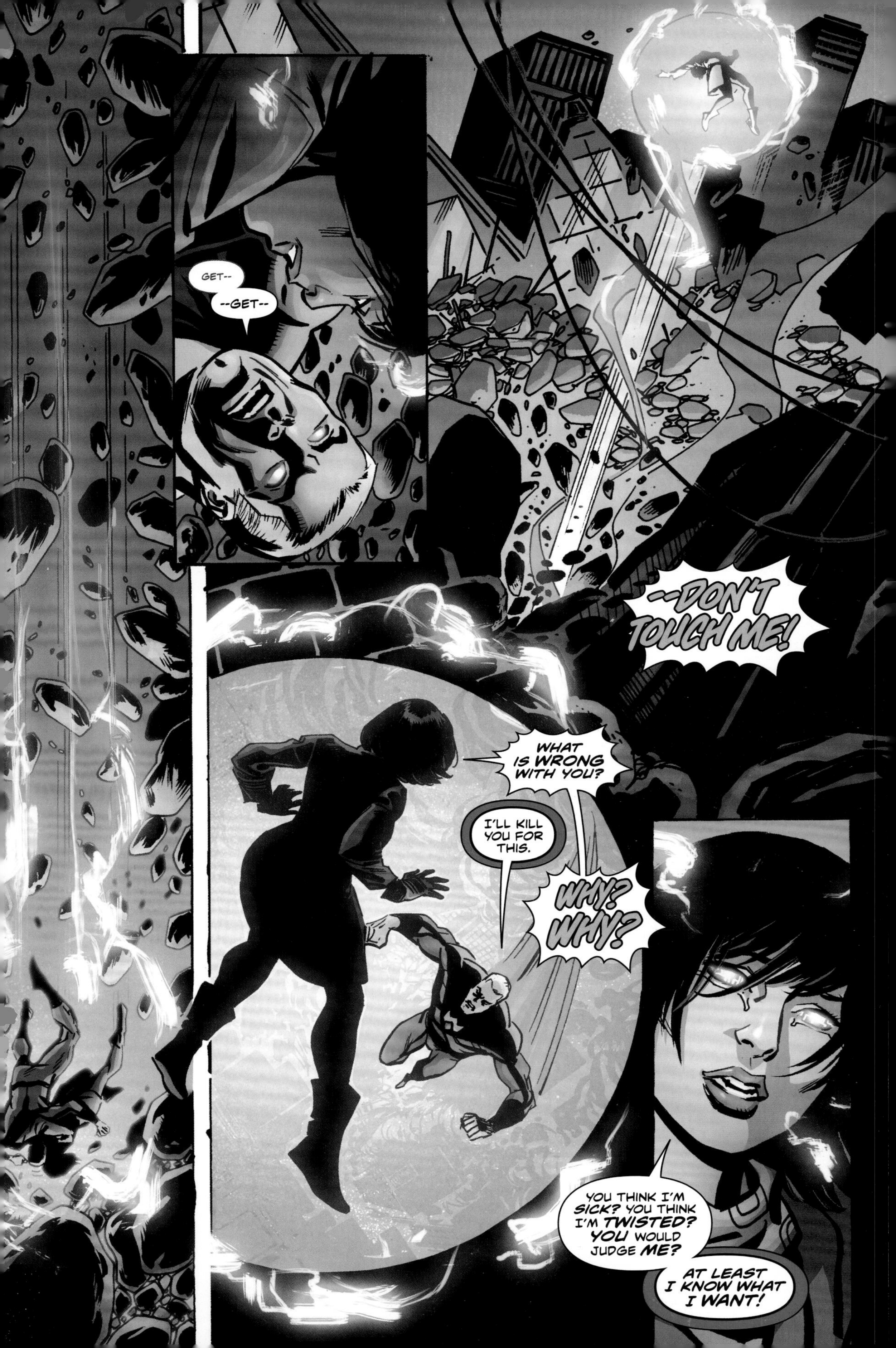
GET--
--GET--
--DON'T TOUCH ME!
WHAT IS WRONG WITH YOU?
I'LL KILL YOU FOR THIS.
WHY? WHY?
YOU THINK I'M SICK? YOU THINK I'M TWISTED? YOU WOULD JUDGE ME?
AT LEAST I KNOW WHAT I WANT!

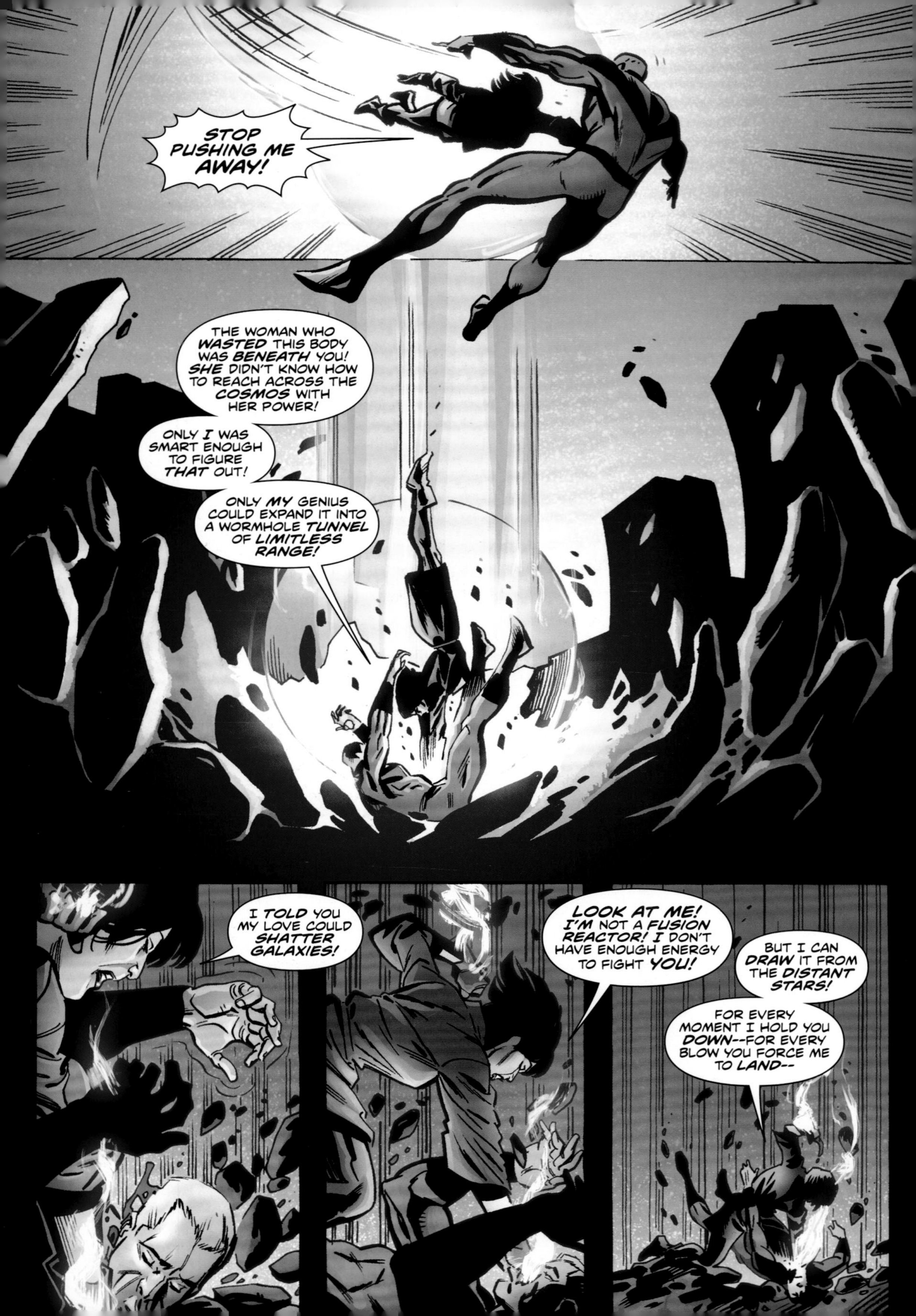
STOP PUSHING ME AWAY!
THE WOMAN WHO WASTED THIS BODY WAS BENEATH YOU! SHE DIDN'T KNOW HOW TO REACH ACROSS THE COSMOS WITH HER POWER!
ONLY I WAS SMART ENOUGH TO FIGURE THAT OUT!
ONLY MY GENIUS COULD EXPAND IT INTO A WORMHOLE TUNNEL OF LIMITLESS RANGE!
I TOLD YOU MY LOVE COULD SHATTER GALAXIES!
LOOK AT ME! I'M NOT A FUSION REACTOR! I DON'T HAVE ENOUGH ENERGY TO FIGHT YOU!
BUT I CAN DRAW IT FROM THE DISTANT STARS!
FOR EVERY MOMENT I HOLD YOU DOWN--FOR EVERY BLOW YOU FORCE ME TO LAND--

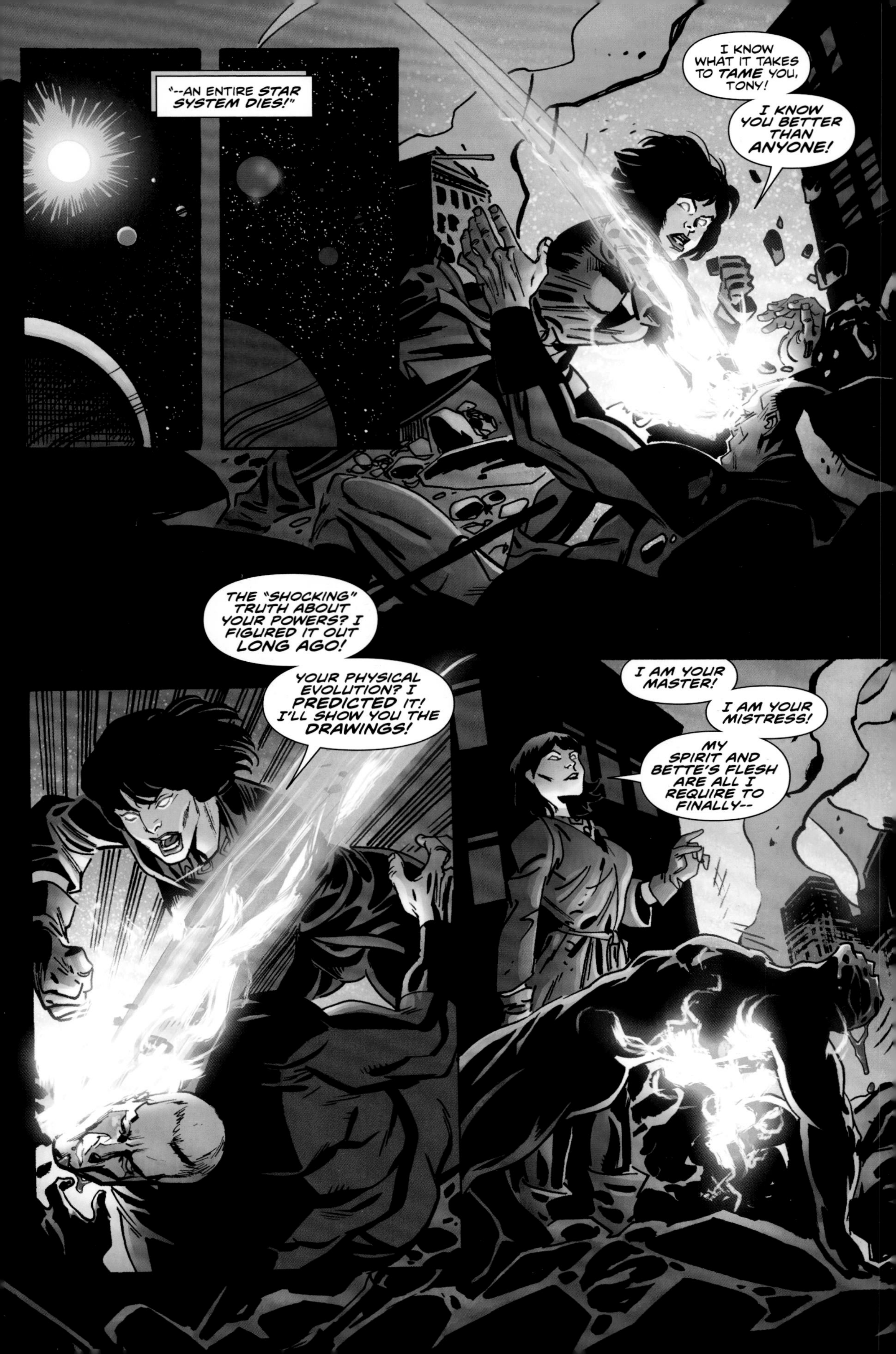
"--AN ENTIRE STAR SYSTEM DIES!"
I KNOW WHAT IT TAKES TO TAME YOU, TONY!
I KNOW YOU BETTER THAN ANYONE!
THE "SHOCKING" TRUTH ABOUT YOUR POWERS? I FIGURED IT OUT LONG AGO!
YOUR PHYSICAL EVOLUTION? I PREDICTED IT! I'LL SHOW YOU THE DRAWINGS!
I AM YOUR MASTER!
I AM YOUR MISTRESS!
MY SPIRIT AND BETTE'S FLESH ARE ALL I REQUIRE TO FINALLY--

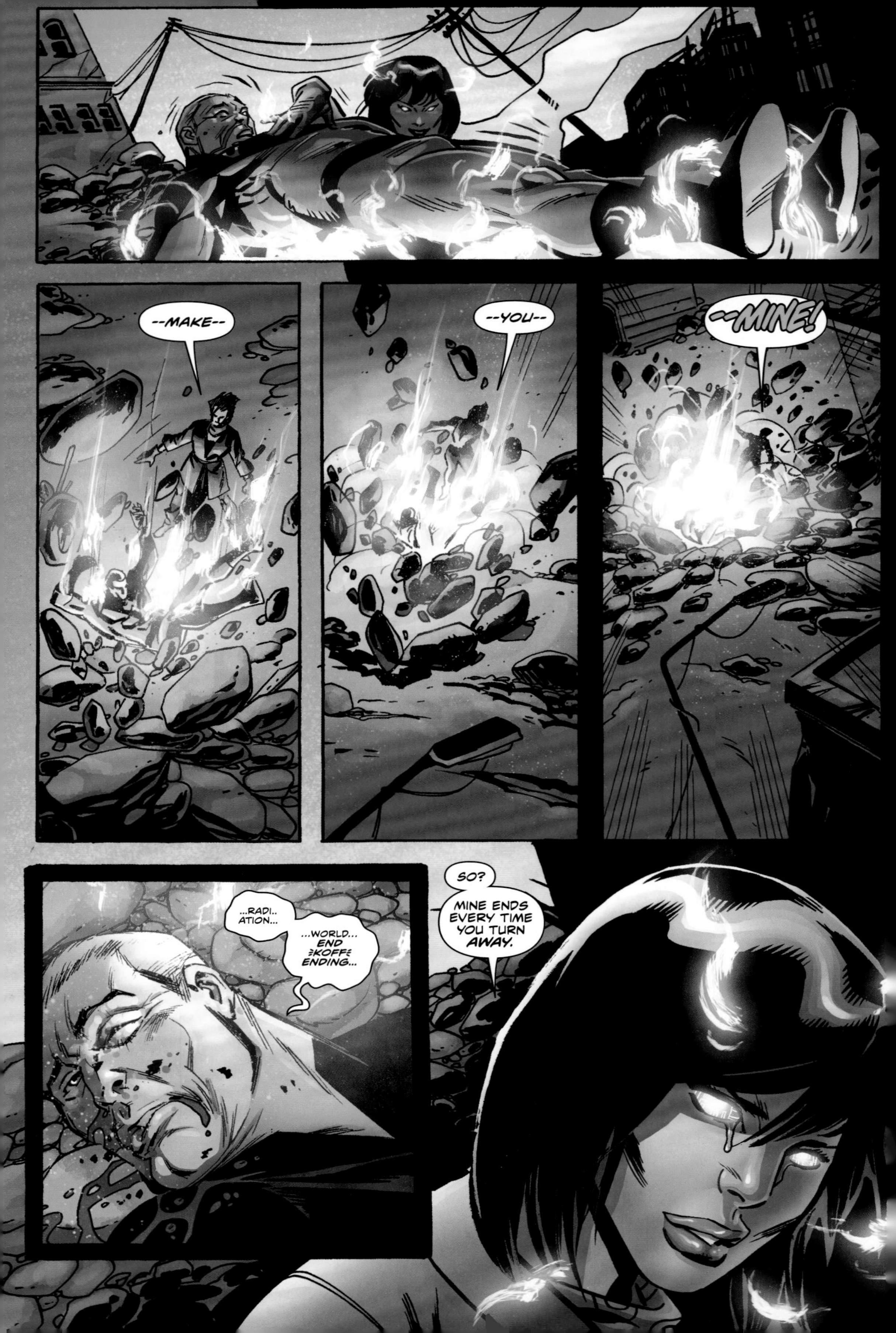
--MAKE--
--YOU--
--MINE!
...RADI.. ATION...
...WORLD... END KOFF ENDING...
SO?
MINE ENDS EVERY TIME YOU TURN AWAY.

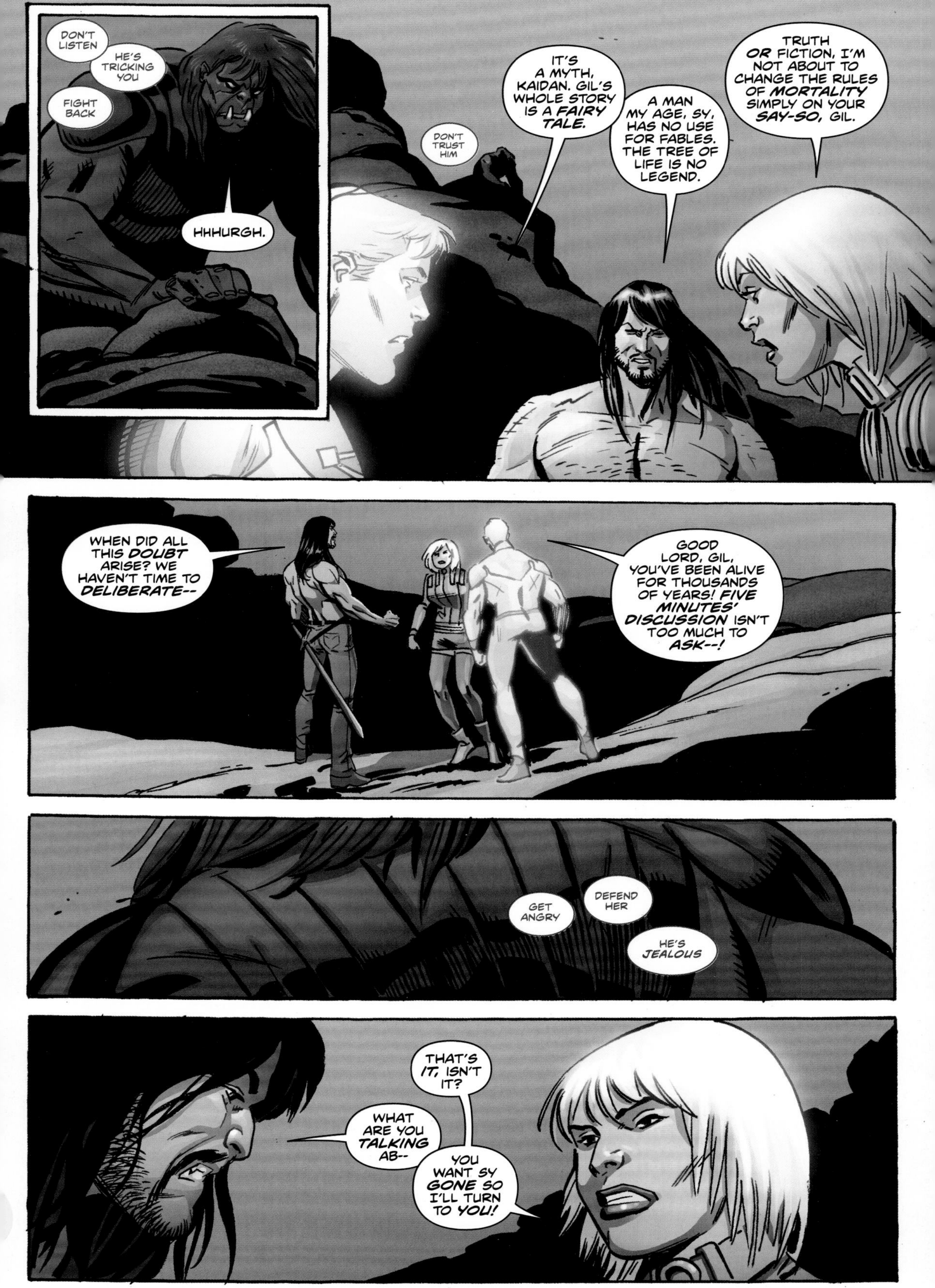
DON'T LISTEN
HE'S TRICKING YOU
FIGHT BACK
HHHURGH.
DON'T TRUST HIM
IT'S A MYTH, KAIDAN. GIL'S WHOLE STORY IS A FAIRY TALE.
A MAN MY AGE, SY, HAS NO USE FOR FABLES. THE TREE OF LIFE IS NO LEGEND.
TRUTH OR FICTION, I'M NOT ABOUT TO CHANGE THE RULES OF MORTALITY SIMPLY ON YOUR SAY-SO, GIL.
WHEN DID ALL THIS DOUBT ARISE? WE HAVEN'T TIME TO DELIBERATE--
GOOD LORD, GIL, YOU'VE BEEN ALIVE FOR THOUSANDS OF YEARS! FIVE MINUTES' DISCUSSION ISN'T TOO MUCH TO ASK--!
GET ANGRY
DEFEND HER
HE'S JEALOUS
THAT'S IT, ISN'T IT?
WHAT ARE YOU TALKING AB--
YOU WANT SY GONE SO I'LL TURN TO YOU!

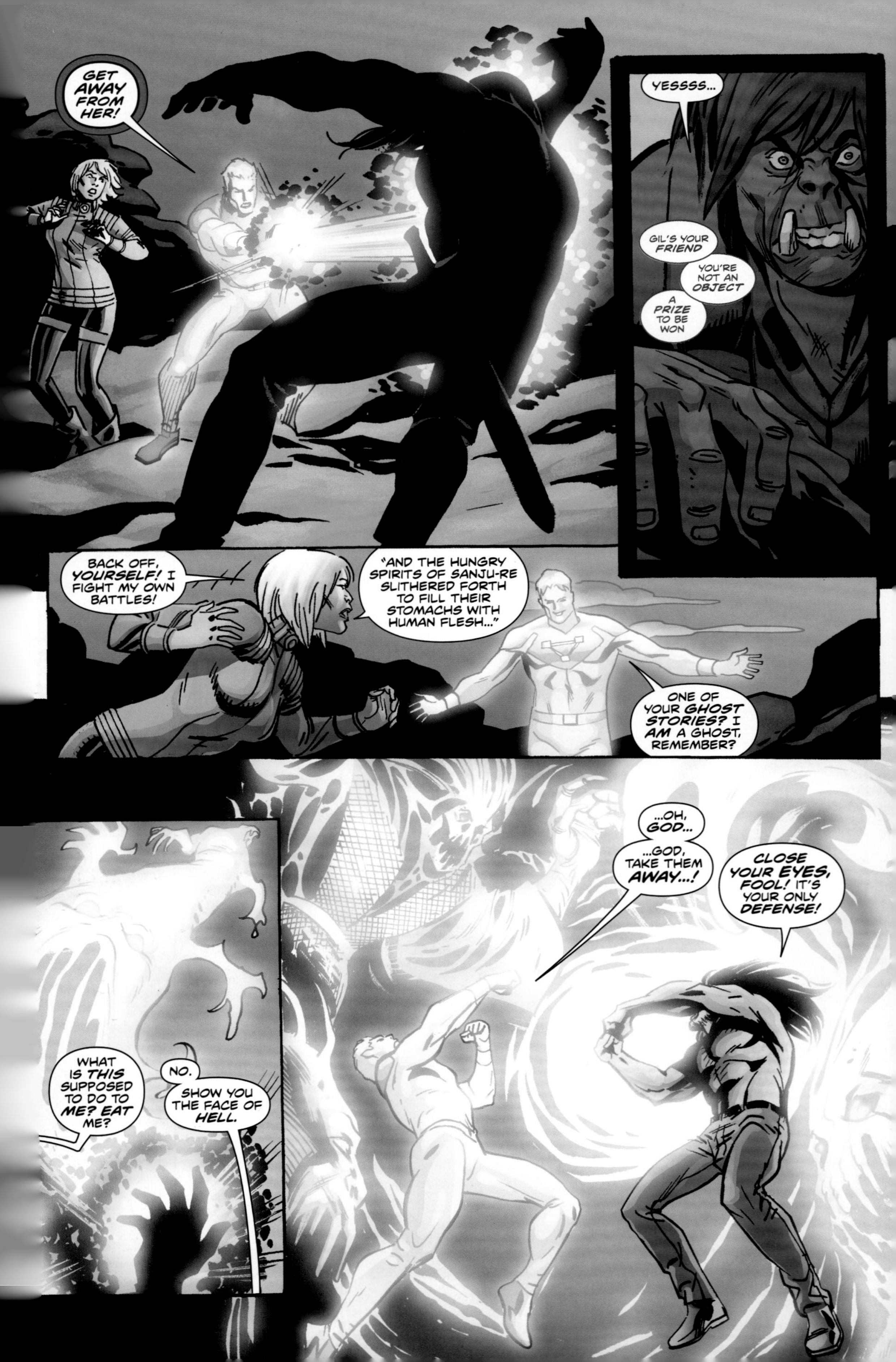
GET AWAY FROM HER!
YESSSS...
GIL'S YOUR FRIEND
YOU'RE NOT AN OBJECT
A PRIZE TO BE WON
BACK OFF, YOURSELF! I FIGHT MY OWN BATTLES!
"AND THE HUNGRY SPIRITS OF SANJU-RE SLITHERED FORTH TO FILL THEIR STOMACHS WITH HUMAN FLESH..."
ONE OF YOUR GHOST STORIES? I AM A GHOST, REMEMBER?
WHAT IS THIS SUPPOSED TO DO TO ME? EAT ME?
NO.
SHOW YOU THE FACE OF HELL.
...OH, GOD...
...GOD, TAKE THEM AWAY...!
CLOSE YOUR EYES, FOOL! IT'S YOUR ONLY DEFENSE!

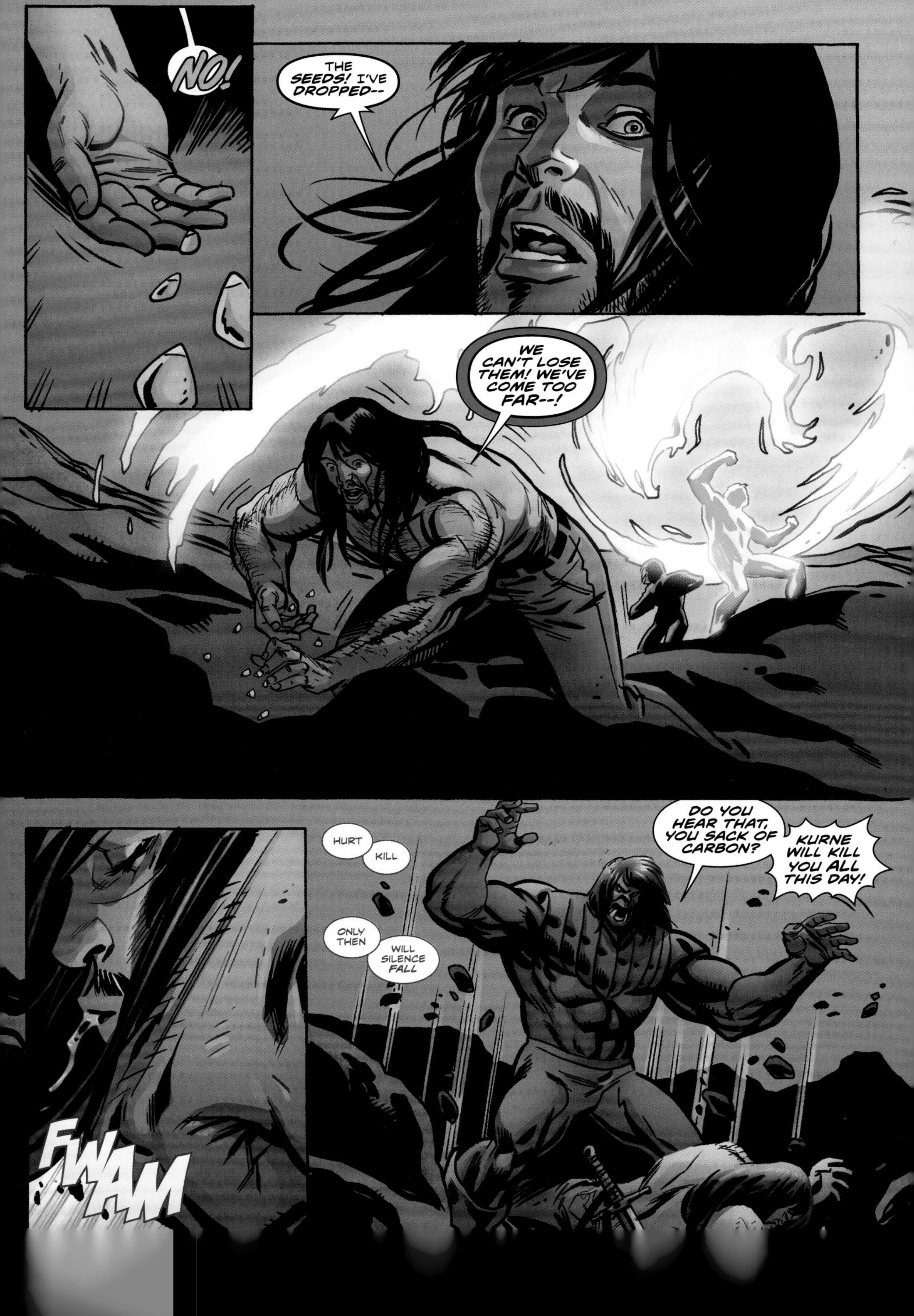
NO!
THE SEEDS! I'VE DROPPED--
WE CAN'T LOSE THEM! WE'VE COME TOO FAR--!
FWAM
HURT
KILL
ONLY THEN
WILL SILENCE FALL
DO YOU HEAR THAT, YOU SACK OF CARBON?
KURNE WILL KILL YOU ALL THIS DAY!

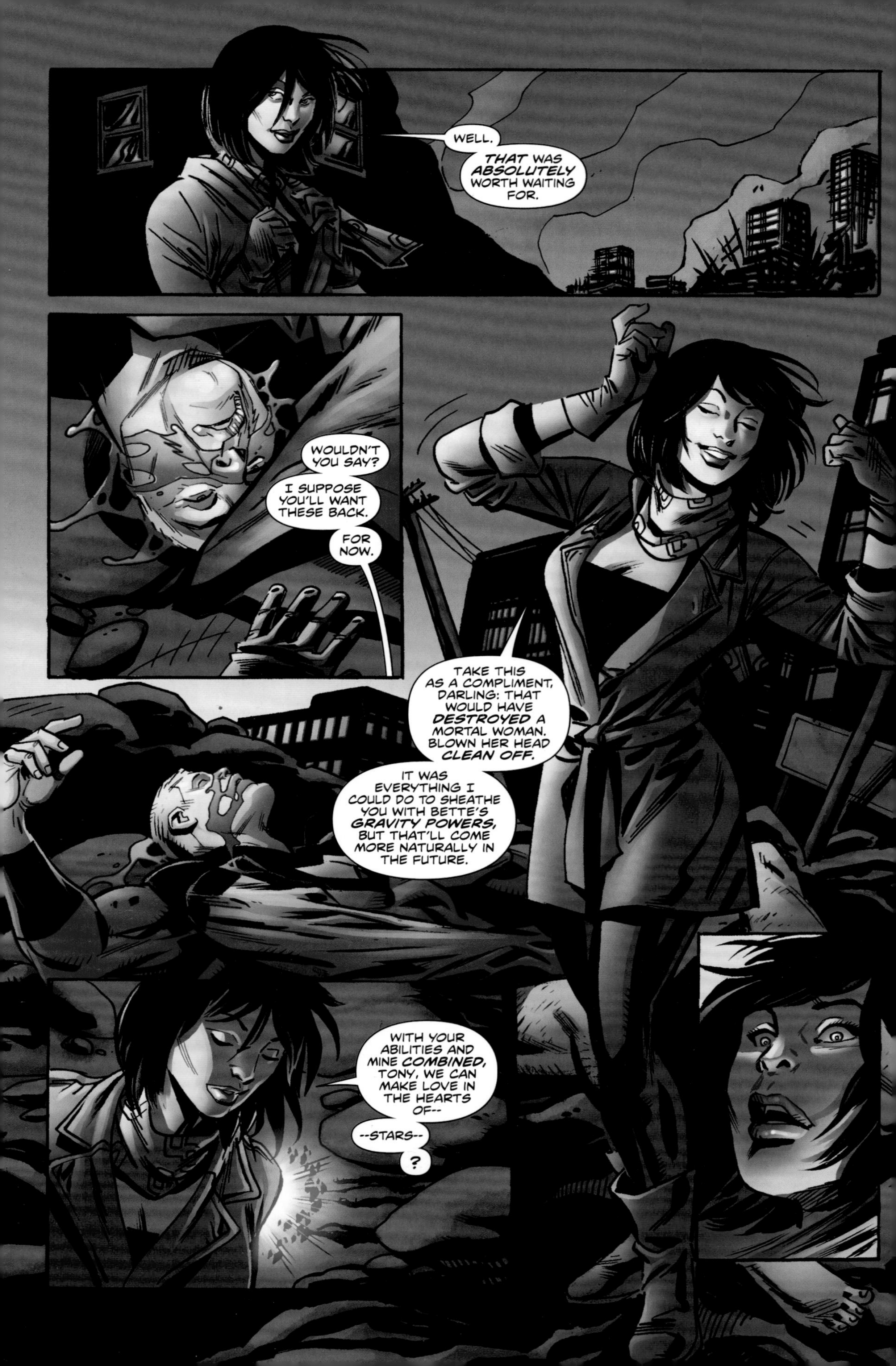
WELL.
THAT WAS ABSOLUTELY WORTH WAITING FOR.
WOULDN'T YOU SAY?
I SUPPOSE YOU'LL WANT THESE BACK.
FOR NOW.
TAKE THIS AS A COMPLIMENT, DARLING: THAT WOULD HAVE DESTROYED A MORTAL WOMAN. BLOWN HER HEAD CLEAN OFF.
IT WAS EVERYTHING I COULD DO TO SHEATHE YOU WITH BETTE'S GRAVITY POWERS, BUT THAT'LL COME MORE NATURALLY IN THE FUTURE.
WITH YOUR ABILITIES AND MINE COMBINED, TONY, WE CAN MAKE LOVE IN THE HEARTS OF--
--STARS--
?

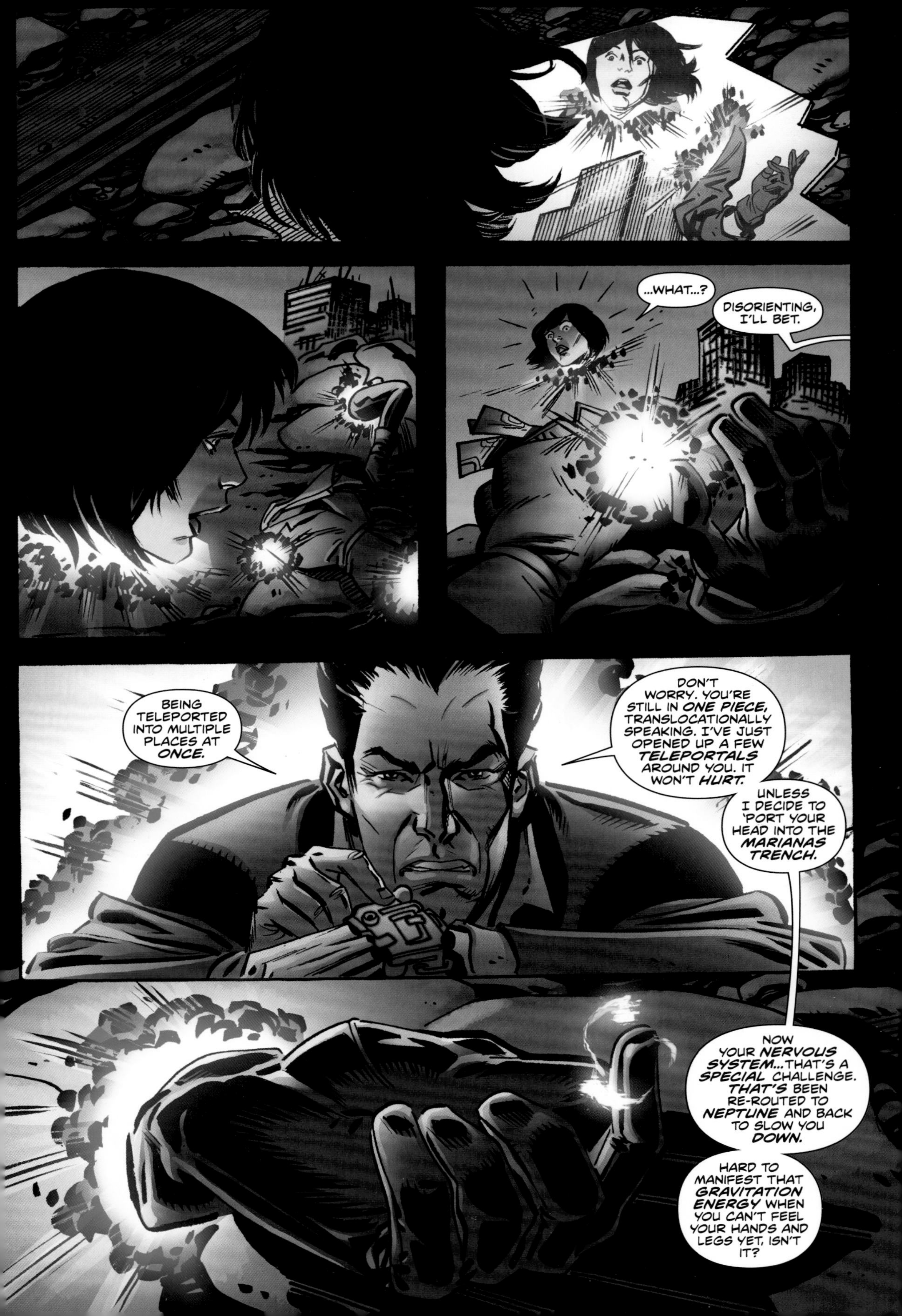

...WHAT...?
DISORIENTING, I'LL BET.
BEING TELEPORTED INTO MULTIPLE PLACES AT ONCE.
DON'T WORRY. YOU'RE STILL IN ONE PIECE, TRANSLOCATIONALLY SPEAKING. I'VE JUST OPENED UP A FEW TELEPORTALS AROUND YOU. IT WON'T HURT.
UNLESS I DECIDE TO 'PORT YOUR HEAD INTO THE MARIANAS TRENCH.
NOW YOUR NERVOUS SYSTEM...THAT'S A SPECIAL CHALLENGE. THAT'S BEEN RE-ROUTED TO NEPTUNE AND BACK TO SLOW YOU DOWN.
HARD TO MANIFEST THAT GRAVITATION ENERGY WHEN YOU CAN'T FEEL YOUR HANDS AND LEGS YET, ISN'T IT?

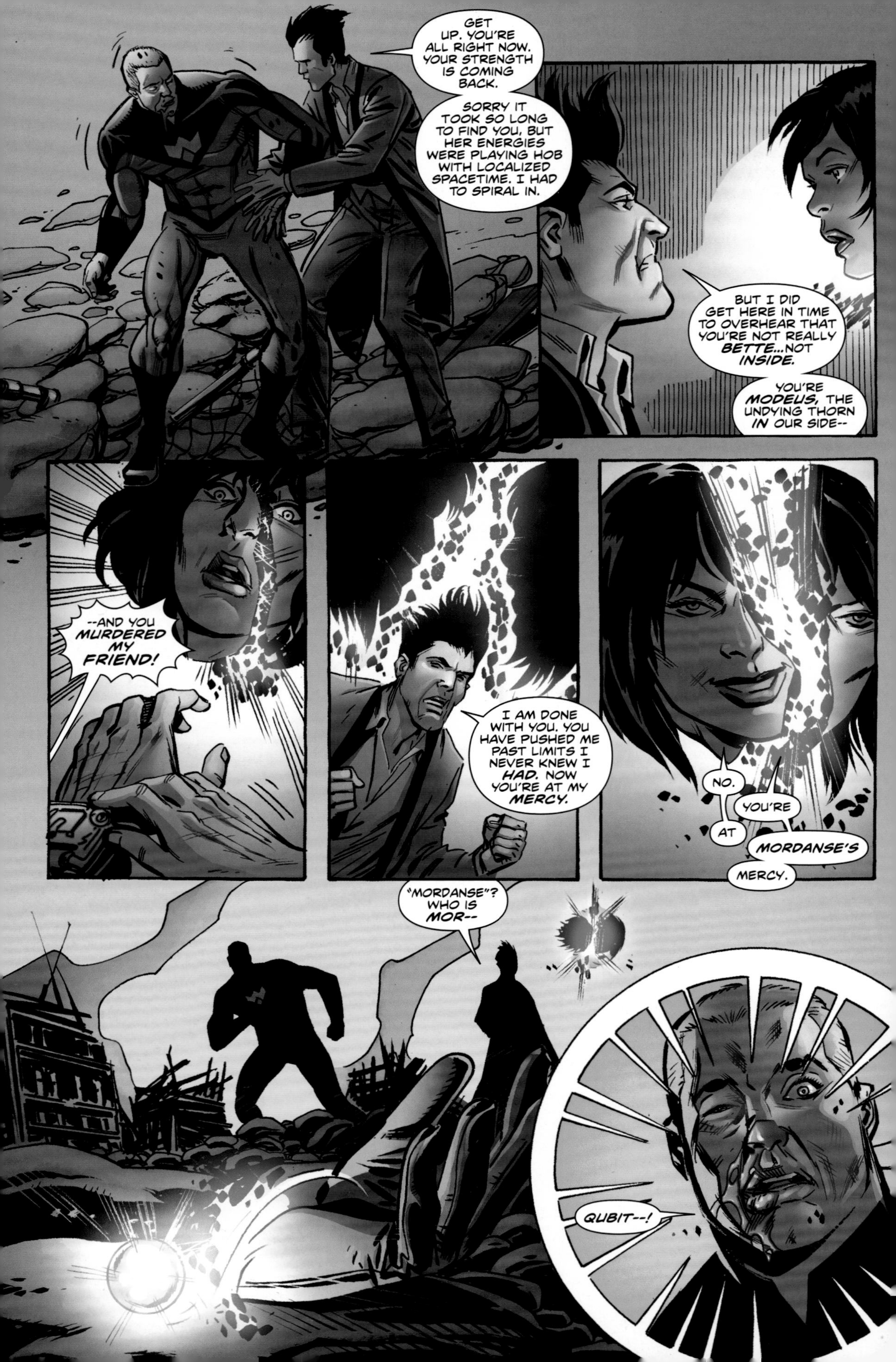
GET UP. YOU'RE ALL RIGHT NOW. YOUR STRENGTH IS COMING BACK.
SORRY IT TOOK SO LONG TO FIND YOU, BUT HER ENERGIES WERE PLAYING HOB WITH LOCALIZED SPACETIME. I HAD TO SPIRAL IN.
BUT I DID GET HERE IN TIME TO OVERHEAR THAT YOU'RE NOT REALLY BETTE...NOT INSIDE.
YOU'RE MODEUS, THE UNDYING THORN IN OUR SIDE--
--AND YOU MURDERED MY FRIEND!
I AM DONE WITH YOU. YOU HAVE PUSHED ME PAST LIMITS I NEVER KNEW I HAD. NOW YOU'RE AT MY MERCY.
NO.
YOU'RE
AT
MORDANSE'S
MERCY.
"MORDANSE"? WHO IS MOR--
QUBIT--!

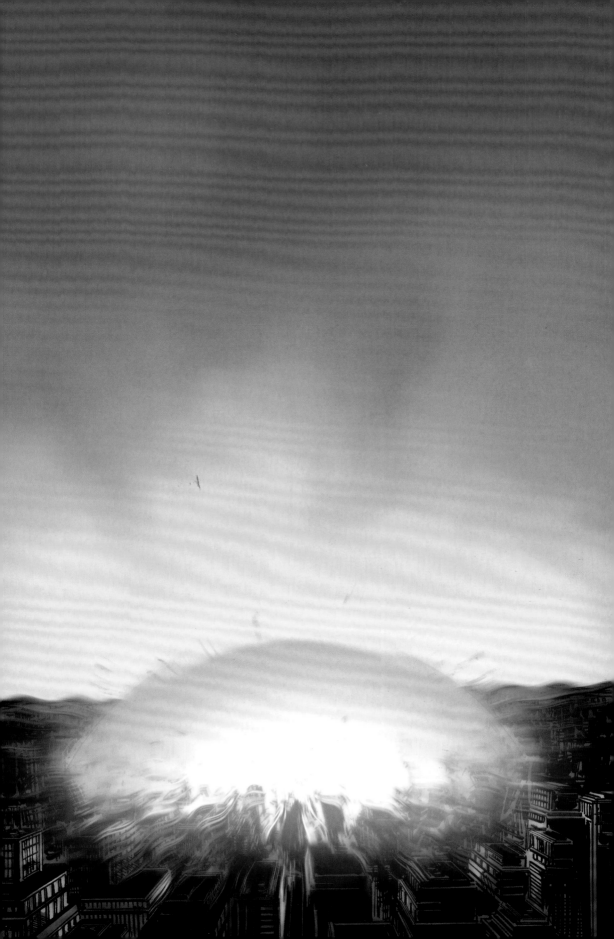

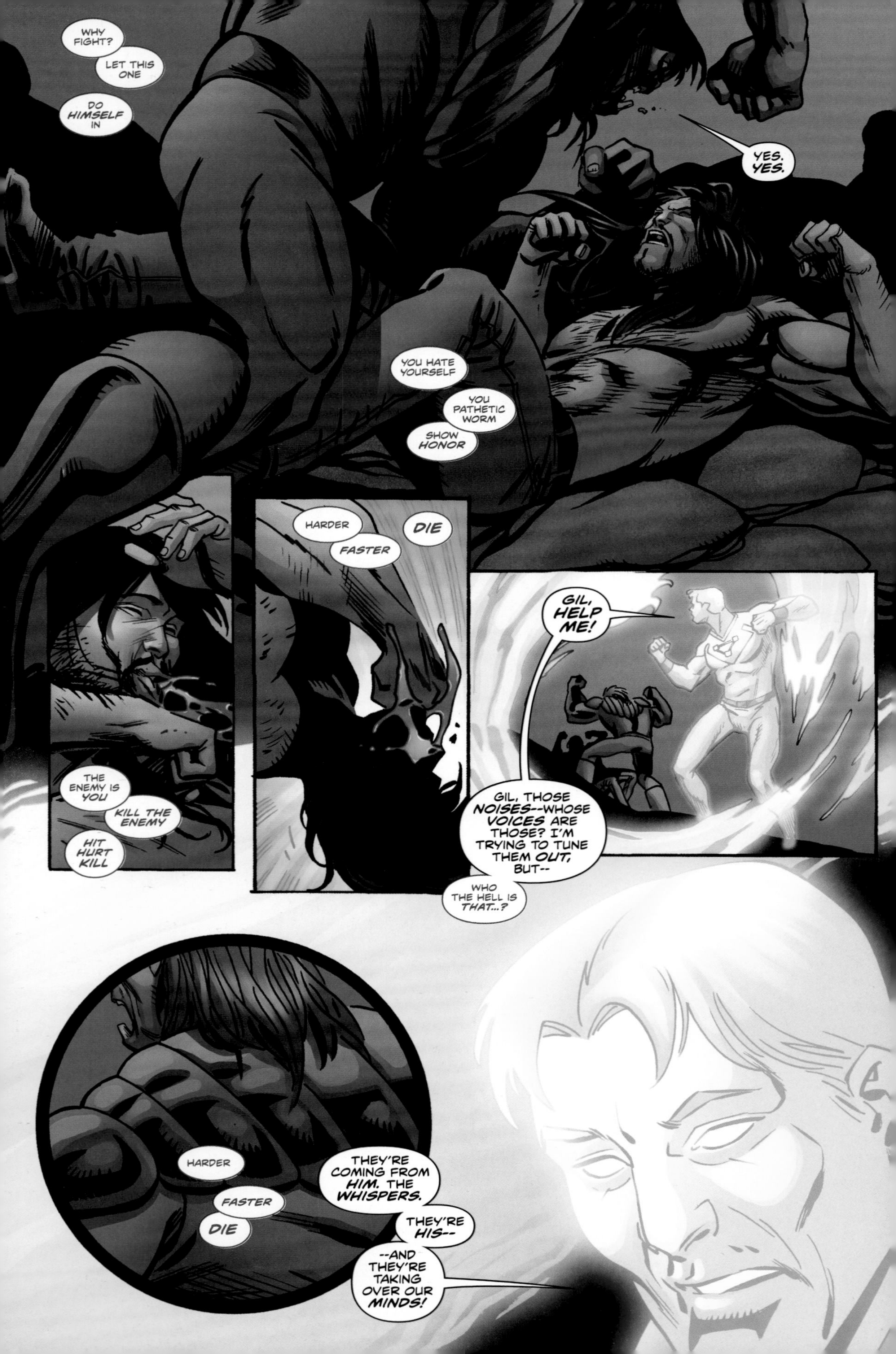

WHY FIGHT?
LET THIS ONE
DO HIMSELF IN
YES. YES.
YOU HATE YOURSELF
YOU PATHETIC WORM
SHOW HONOR
THE ENEMY IS YOU
KILL THE ENEMY
HIT HURT KILL
HARDER
FASTER
DIE
GIL, HELP ME!
GIL, THOSE NOISES--WHOSE VOICES ARE THOSE? I'M TRYING TO TUNE THEM OUT, BUT--
WHO THE HELL IS THAT...?
HARDER
FASTER
DIE
THEY'RE COMING FROM HIM. THE WHISPERS.
THEY'RE HIS--
--AND THEY'RE TAKING OVER OUR MINDS!

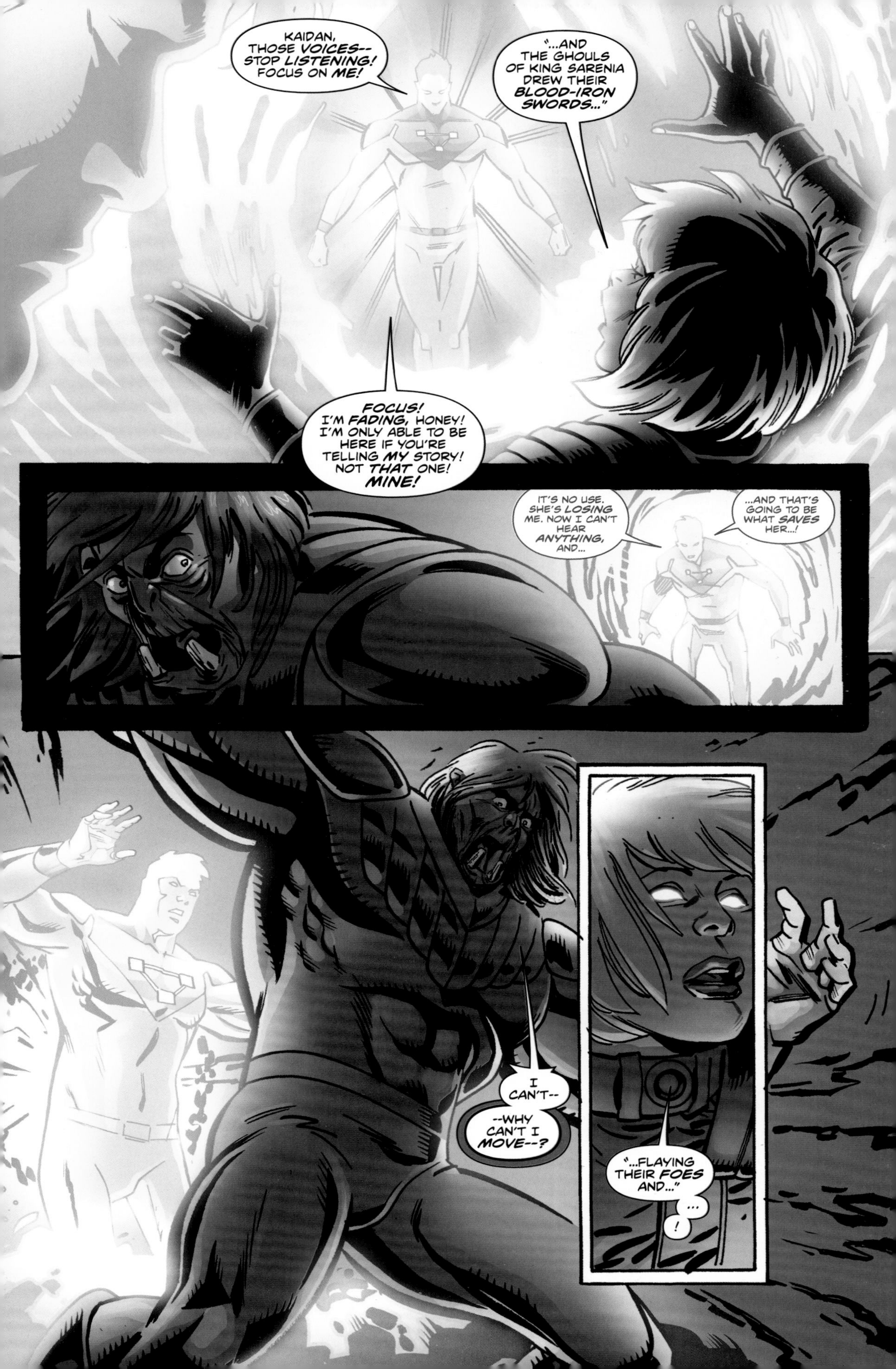
KAIDAN, THOSE VOICES-- STOP LISTENING! FOCUS ON ME!
"...AND THE GHOULS OF KING SARENIA DREW THEIR BLOOD-IRON SWORDS..."
FOCUS! I'M FADING, HONEY! I'M ONLY ABLE TO BE HERE IF YOU'RE TELLING MY STORY! NOT THAT ONE! MINE!
IT'S NO USE. SHE'S LOSING ME. NOW I CAN'T HEAR ANYTHING, AND...
...AND THAT'S GOING TO BE WHAT SAVES HER...!
I CAN'T--
--WHY CAN'T I MOVE--?
"...FLAYING THEIR FOES AND..."
...
!

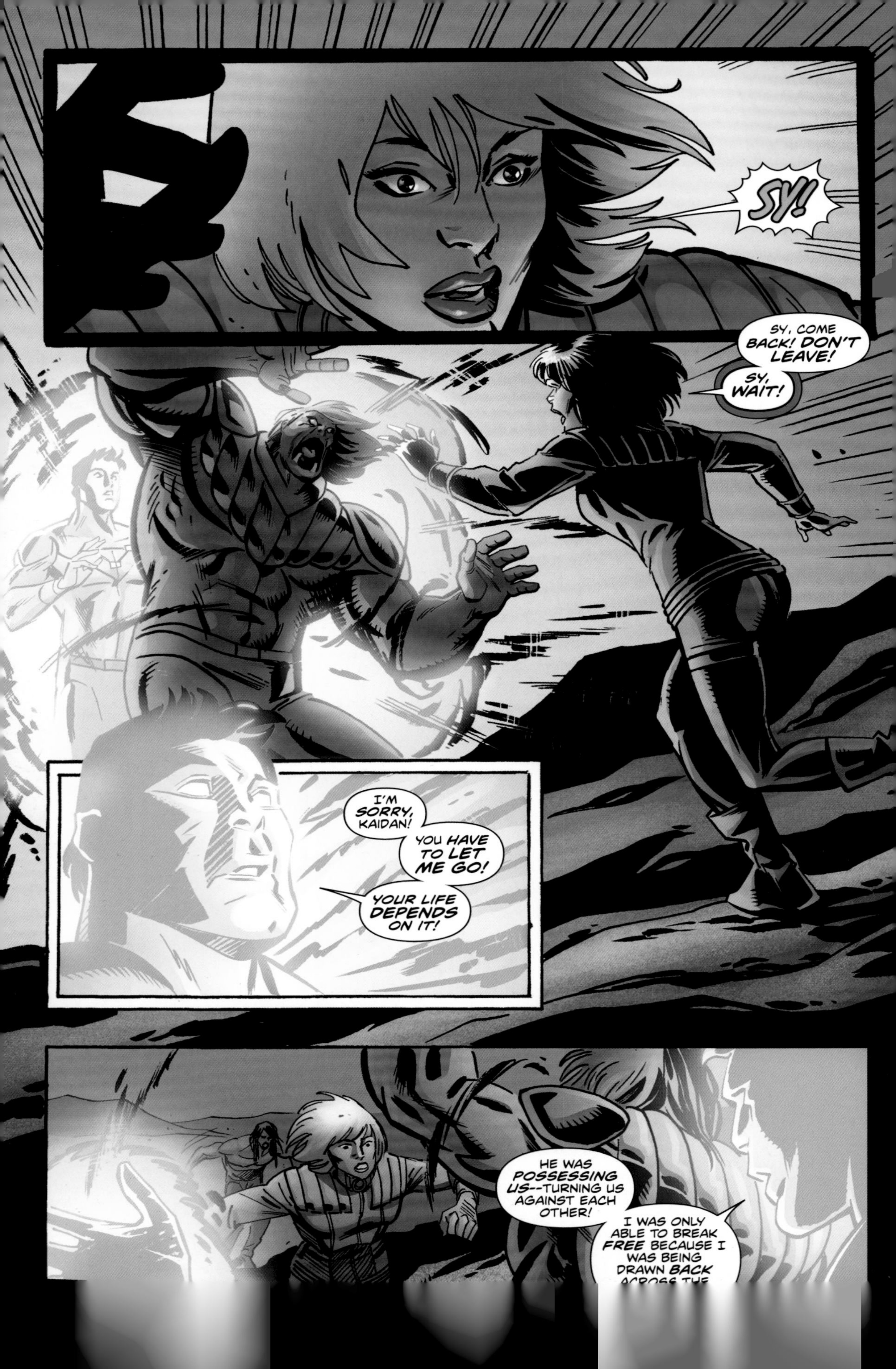
SY!
SY, COME BACK! DON'T LEAVE!
SY, WAIT!
I'M SORRY, KAIDAN!
YOU HAVE TO LET ME GO!
YOUR LIFE DEPENDS ON IT!
HE WAS POSSESSING US--TURNING US AGAINST EACH OTHER!
I WAS ONLY ABLE TO BREAK FREE BECAUSE I WAS BEING DRAWN BACK

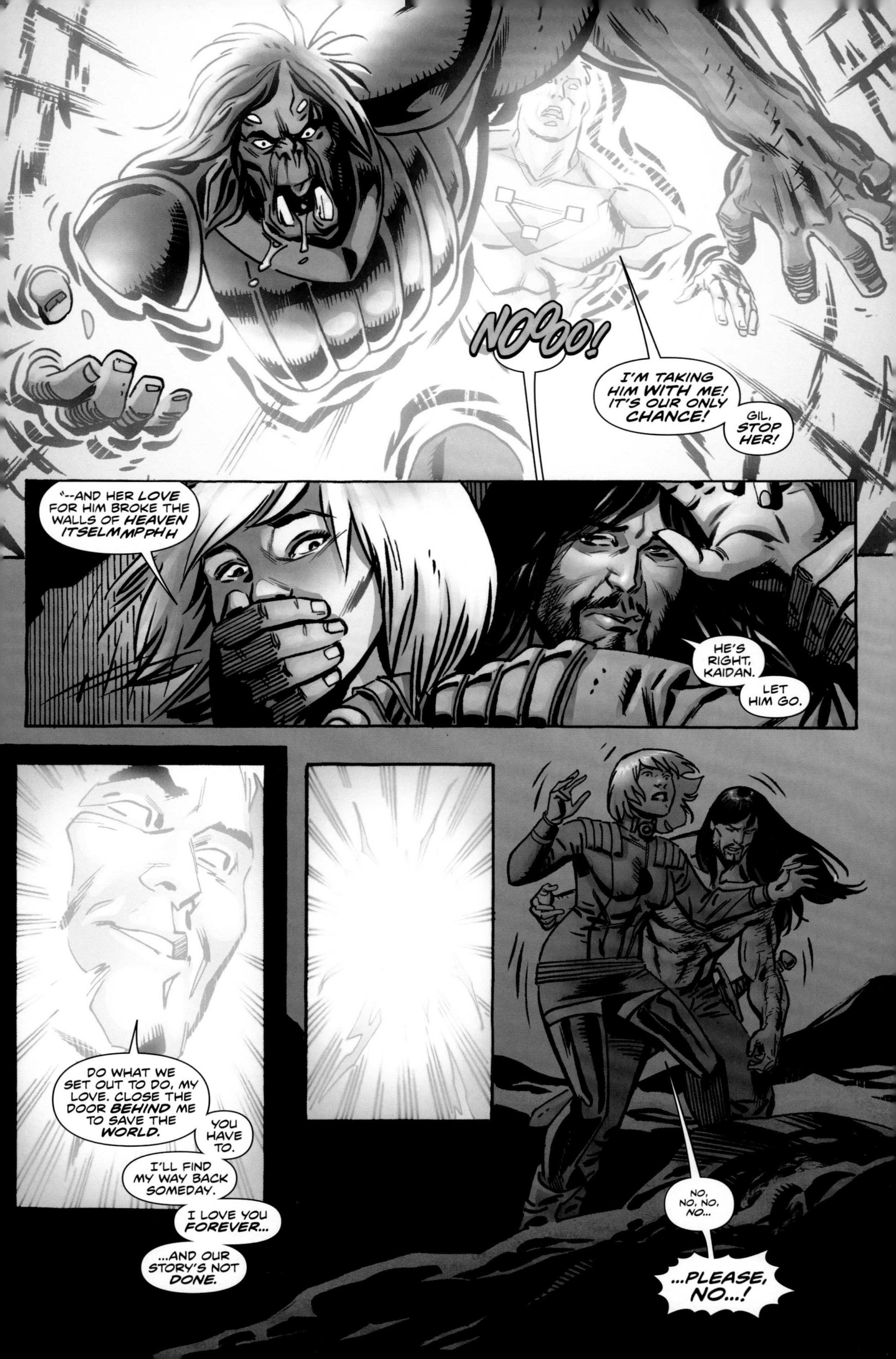
NOOOO!
I'M TAKING HIM WITH ME! IT'S OUR ONLY CHANCE!
GIL, STOP HER!
"--AND HER LOVE FOR HIM BROKE THE WALLS OF HEAVEN ITSELMMPPHH
HE'S RIGHT, KAIDAN.
LET HIM GO.
DO WHAT WE SET OUT TO DO, MY LOVE. CLOSE THE DOOR BEHIND ME TO SAVE THE WORLD.
YOU HAVE TO.
I'LL FIND MY WAY BACK SOMEDAY.
I LOVE YOU FOREVER...
...AND OUR STORY'S NOT DONE.
NO, NO, NO, NO...
...PLEASE, NO...!

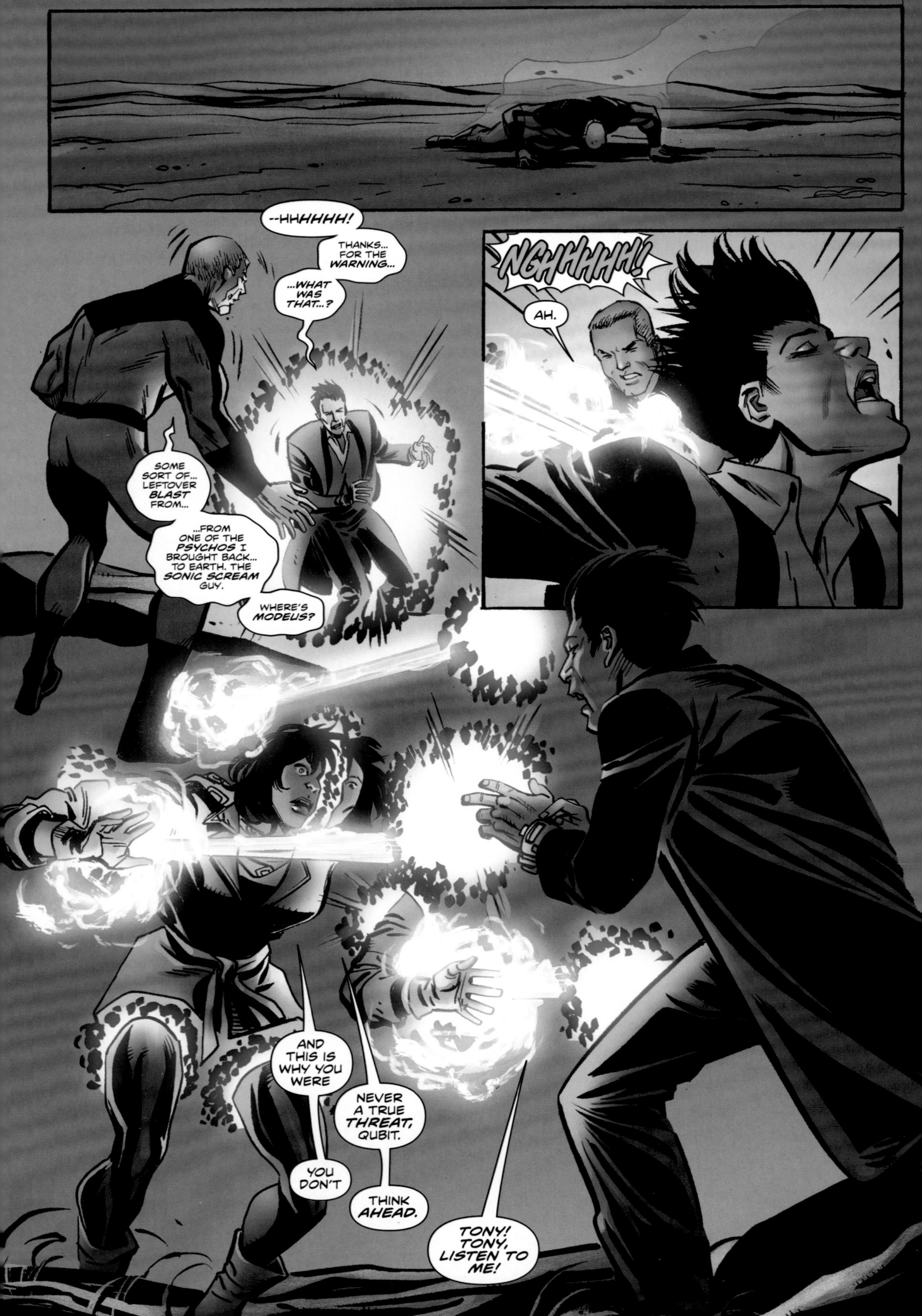
--HHHHHH!
THANKS... FOR THE WARNING...
...WHAT WAS THAT...?
NGHHHHH!
AH.
SOME SORT OF... LEFTOVER BLAST FROM...
...FROM ONE OF THE PSYCHOS I BROUGHT BACK... TO EARTH. THE SONIC SCREAM GUY.
WHERE'S MODEUS?
AND THIS IS WHY YOU WERE
NEVER A TRUE THREAT, QUBIT.
YOU DON'T
THINK AHEAD.
TONY! TONY, LISTEN TO ME!

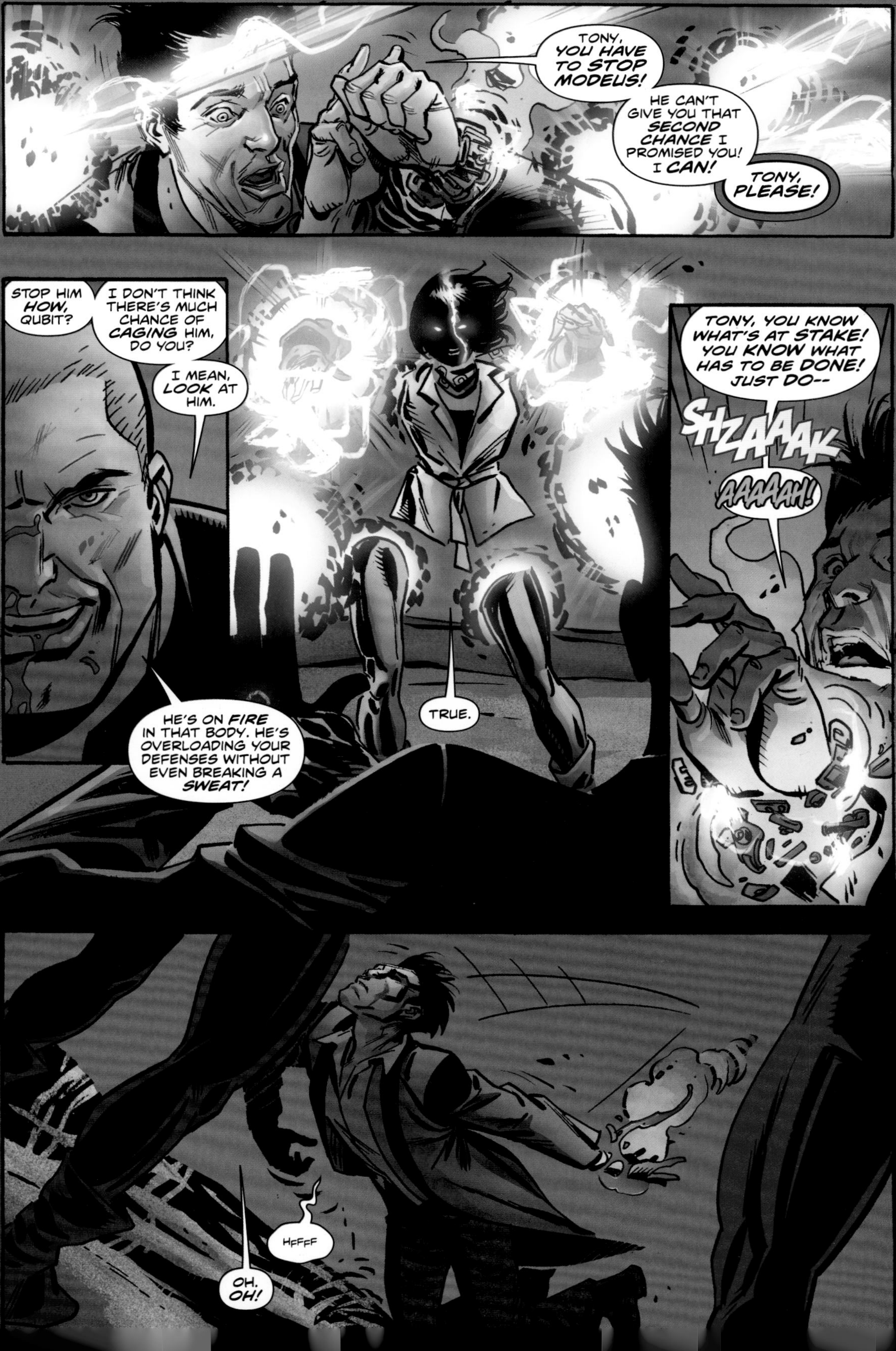
TONY, YOU HAVE TO STOP MODEUS!
HE CAN'T GIVE YOU THAT SECOND CHANCE I PROMISED YOU! I CAN!
TONY, PLEASE!
STOP HIM HOW, QUBIT?
I DON'T THINK THERE'S MUCH CHANCE OF CAGING HIM, DO YOU?
I MEAN, LOOK AT HIM.
HE'S ON FIRE IN THAT BODY. HE'S OVERLOADING YOUR DEFENSES WITHOUT EVEN BREAKING A SWEAT!
TRUE.
TONY, YOU KNOW WHAT'S AT STAKE! YOU KNOW WHAT HAS TO BE DONE! JUST DO--
SHZAAAK
AAAAAH!
HFFFF
OH. OH!

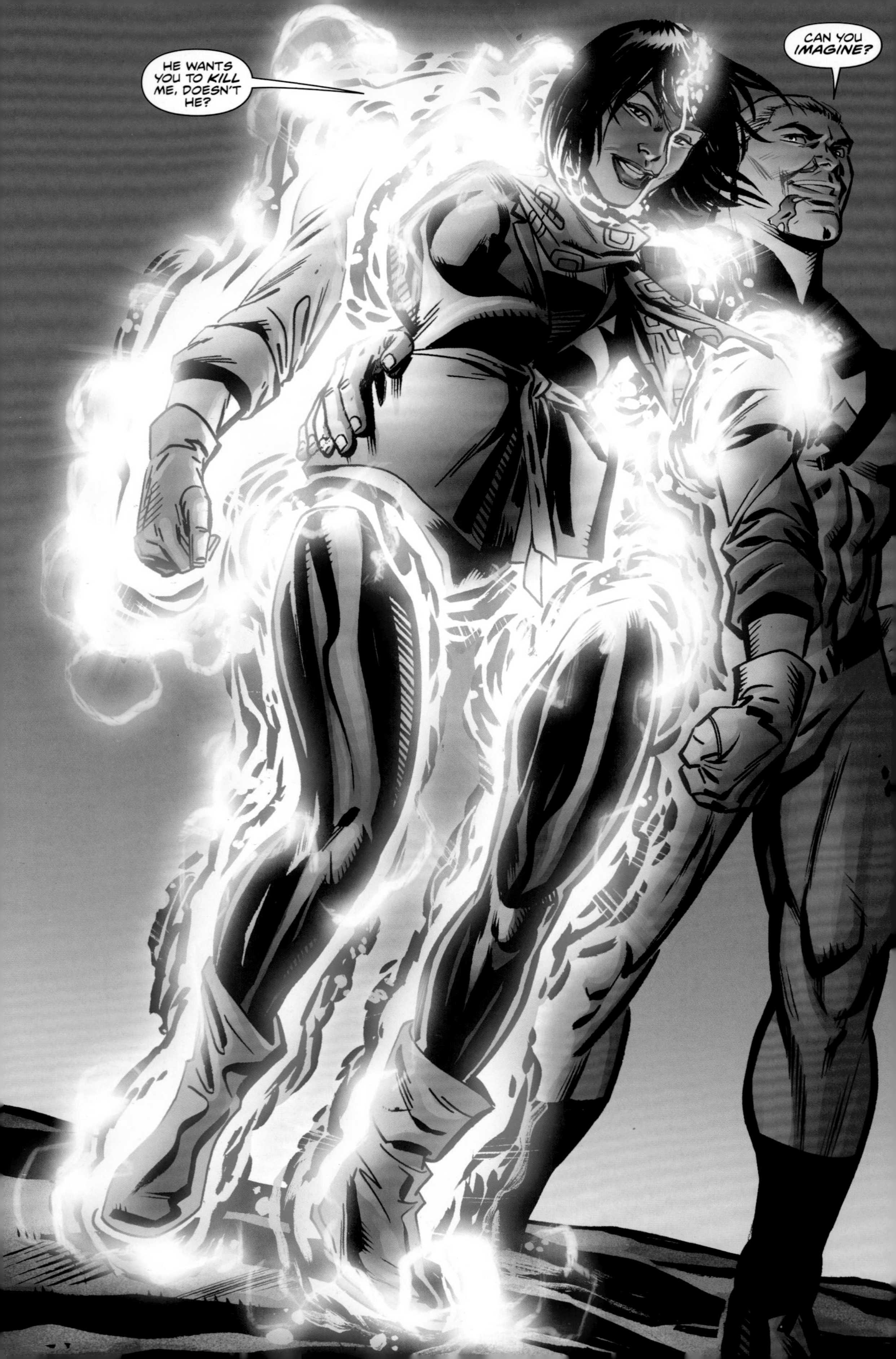
HE WANTS YOU TO KILL ME, DOESN'T HE?
CAN YOU IMAGINE?

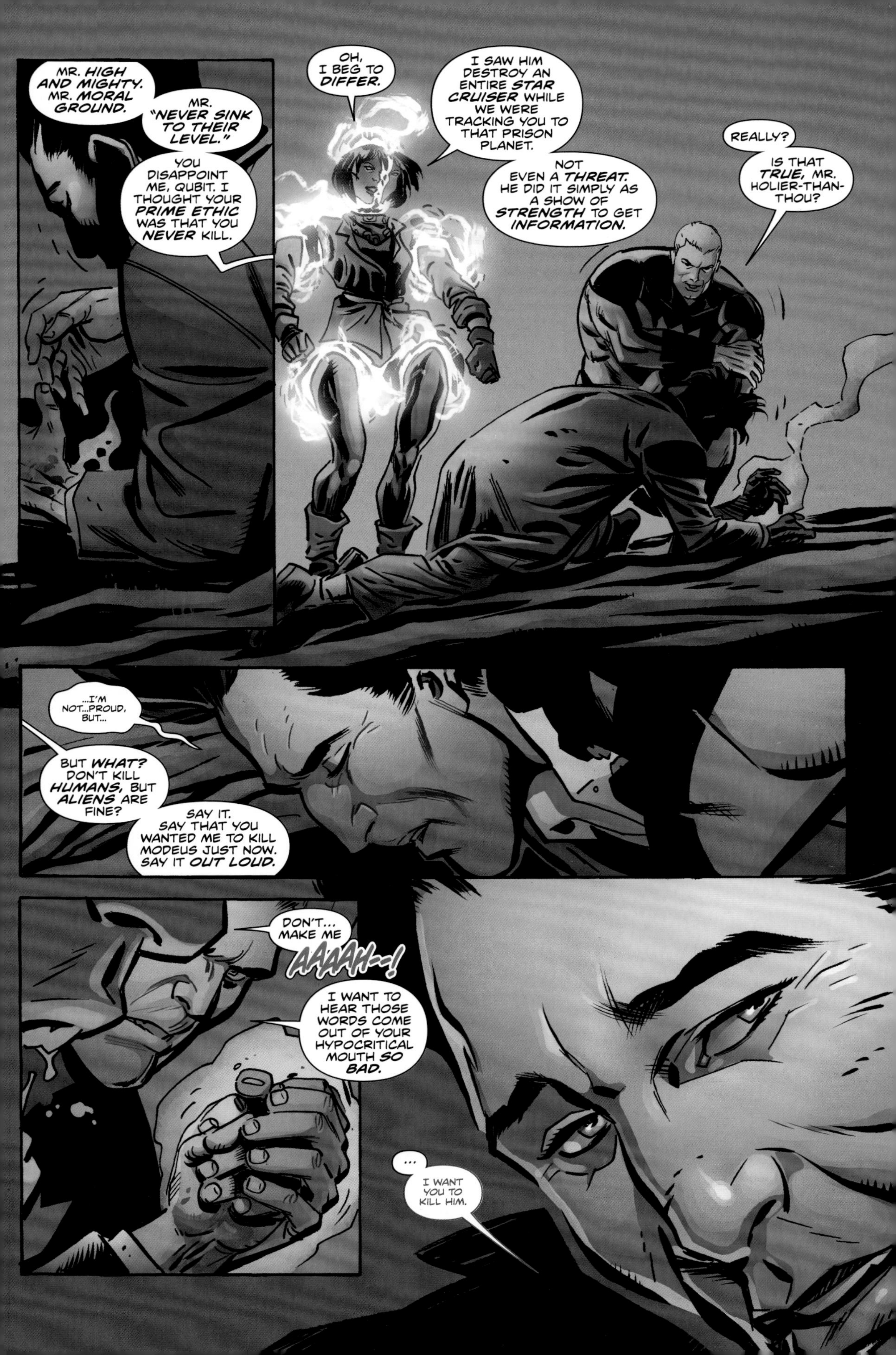
MR. HIGH AND MIGHTY. MR. MORAL GROUND.
MR. "NEVER SINK TO THEIR LEVEL."
YOU DISAPPOINT ME, QUBIT. I THOUGHT YOUR PRIME ETHIC WAS THAT YOU NEVER KILL.
OH, I BEG TO DIFFER.
I SAW HIM DESTROY AN ENTIRE STAR CRUISER WHILE WE WERE TRACKING YOU TO THAT PRISON PLANET.
NOT EVEN A THREAT. HE DID IT SIMPLY AS A SHOW OF STRENGTH TO GET INFORMATION.
REALLY?
IS THAT TRUE, MR. HOLIER-THAN-THOU?
...I'M NOT...PROUD, BUT...
BUT WHAT? DON'T KILL HUMANS, BUT ALIENS ARE FINE?
SAY IT. SAY THAT YOU WANTED ME TO KILL MODEUS JUST NOW. SAY IT OUT LOUD.
DON'T... MAKE ME
AAAAH--!
I WANT TO HEAR THOSE WORDS COME OUT OF YOUR HYPOCRITICAL MOUTH SO BAD.
...
I WANT YOU TO KILL HIM.

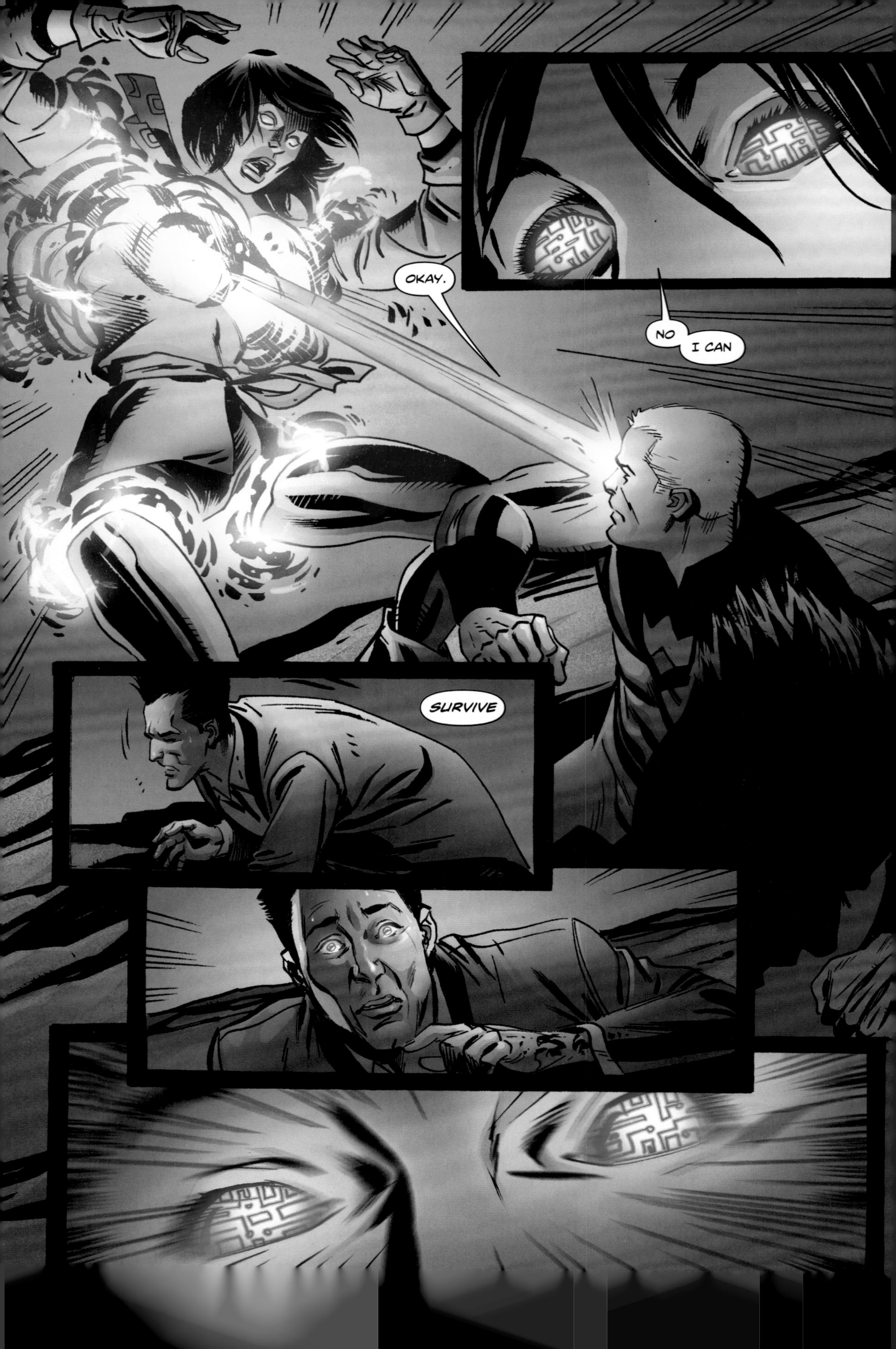
OKAY.
NO
I CAN
SURVIVE

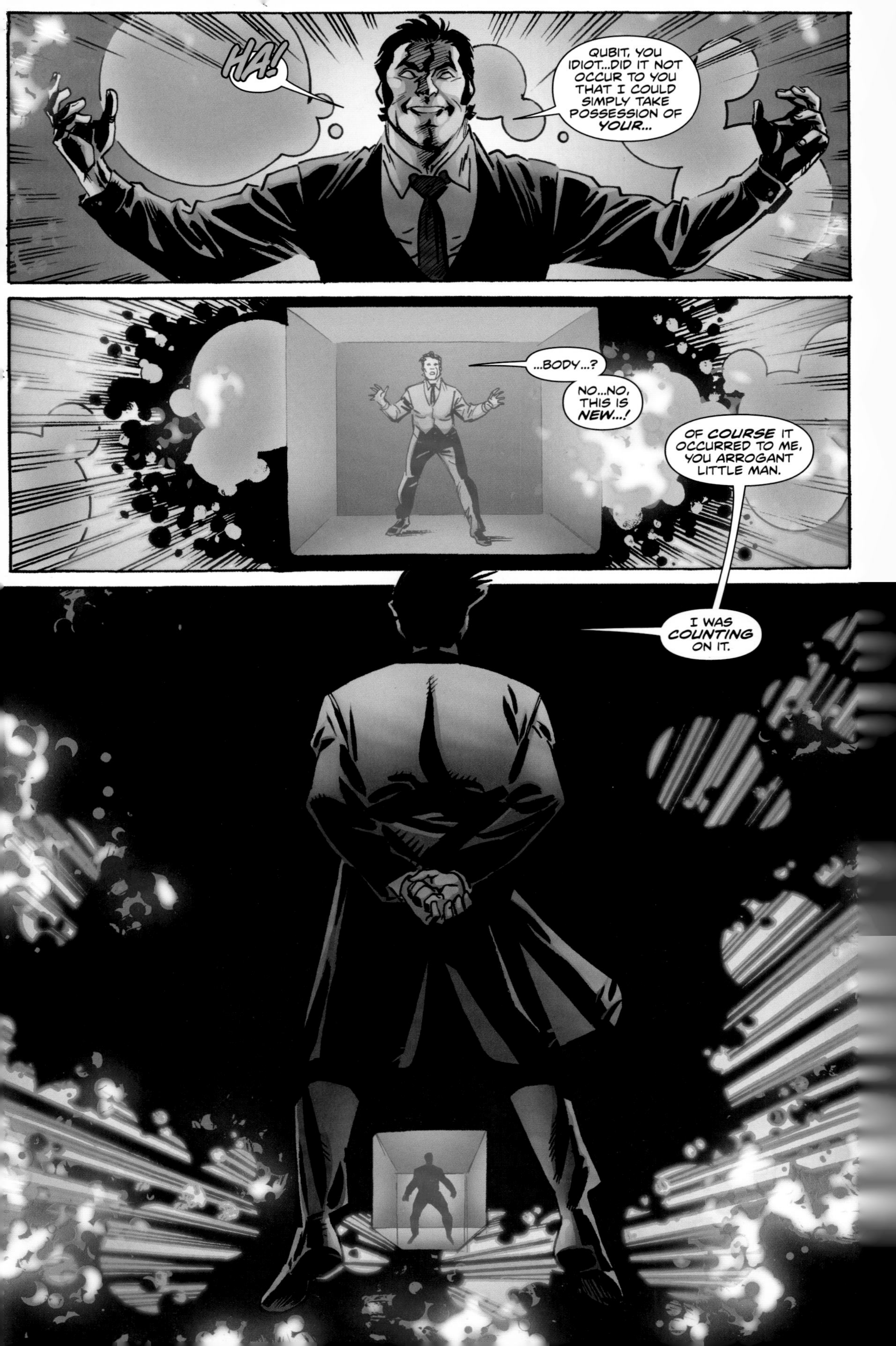
HA!
QUBIT, YOU IDIOT...DID IT NOT OCCUR TO YOU THAT I COULD SIMPLY TAKE POSSESSION OF YOUR...
...BODY...?
NO...NO, THIS IS NEW...!
OF COURSE IT OCCURRED TO ME, YOU ARROGANT LITTLE MAN.
I WAS COUNTING ON IT.

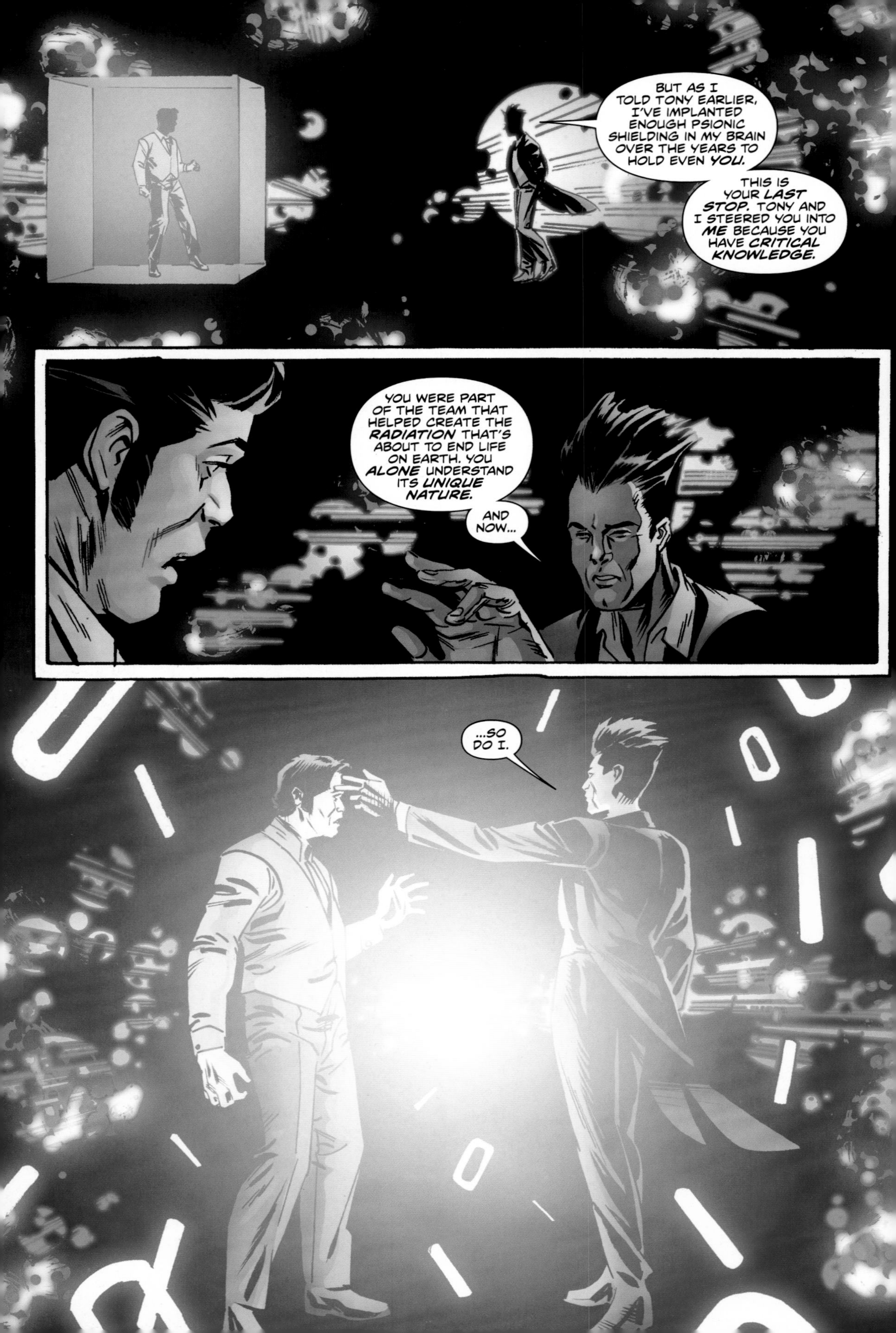
BUT AS I TOLD TONY EARLIER, I'VE IMPLANTED ENOUGH PSIONIC SHIELDING IN MY BRAIN OVER THE YEARS TO HOLD EVEN YOU.
THIS IS YOUR LAST STOP. TONY AND I STEERED YOU INTO ME BECAUSE YOU HAVE CRITICAL KNOWLEDGE.
YOU WERE PART OF THE TEAM THAT HELPED CREATE THE RADIATION THAT'S ABOUT TO END LIFE ON EARTH. YOU ALONE UNDERSTAND ITS UNIQUE NATURE.
AND NOW...
...SO DO I.

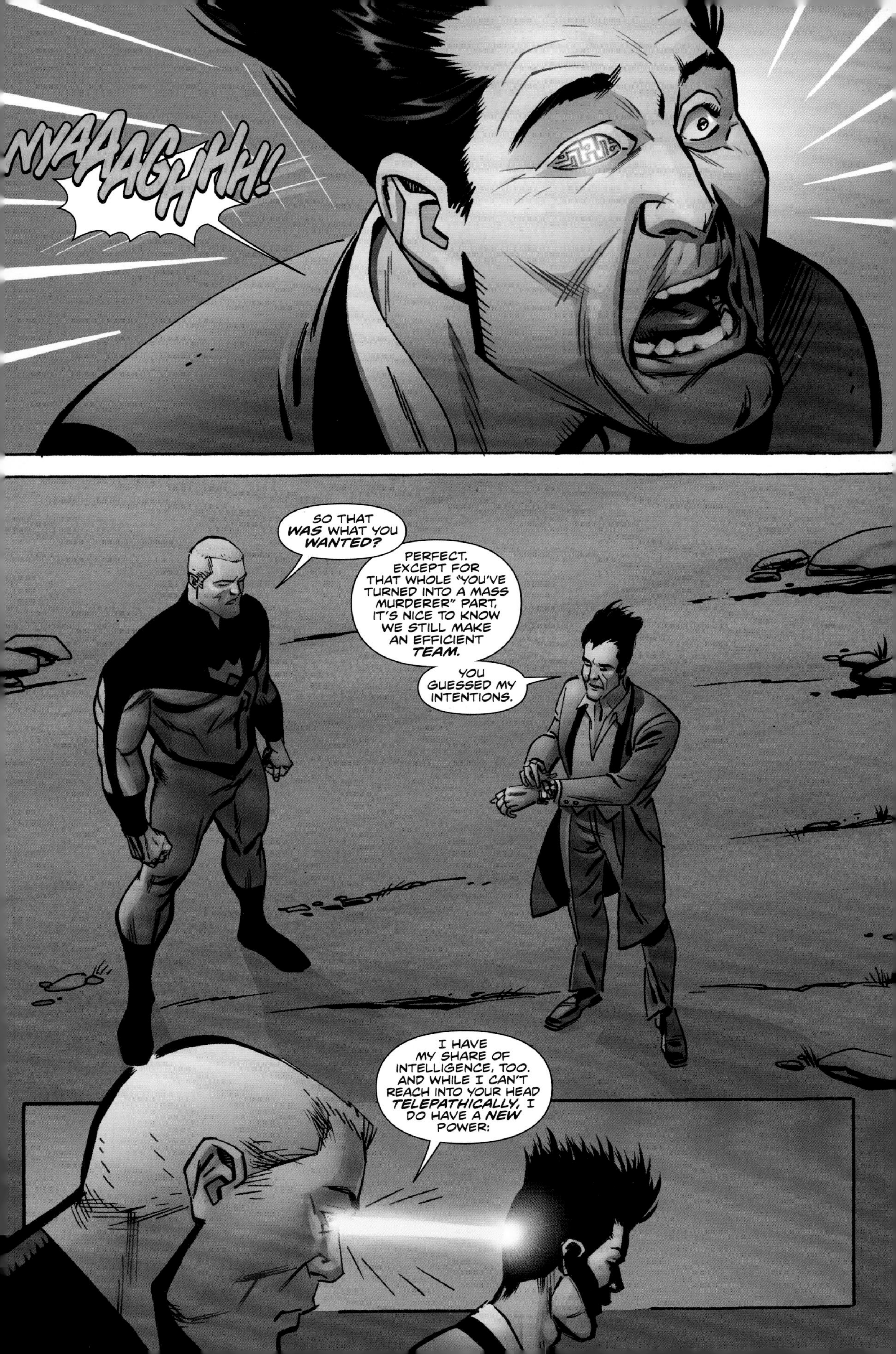
NYAAAAGHHH!
SO THAT WAS WHAT YOU WANTED?
PERFECT. EXCEPT FOR THAT WHOLE "YOU'VE TURNED INTO A MASS MURDERER" PART, IT'S NICE TO KNOW WE STILL MAKE AN EFFICIENT TEAM.
YOU GUESSED MY INTENTIONS.
I HAVE MY SHARE OF INTELLIGENCE, TOO. AND WHILE I CAN'T REACH INTO YOUR HEAD TELEPATHICALLY, I DO HAVE A NEW POWER:

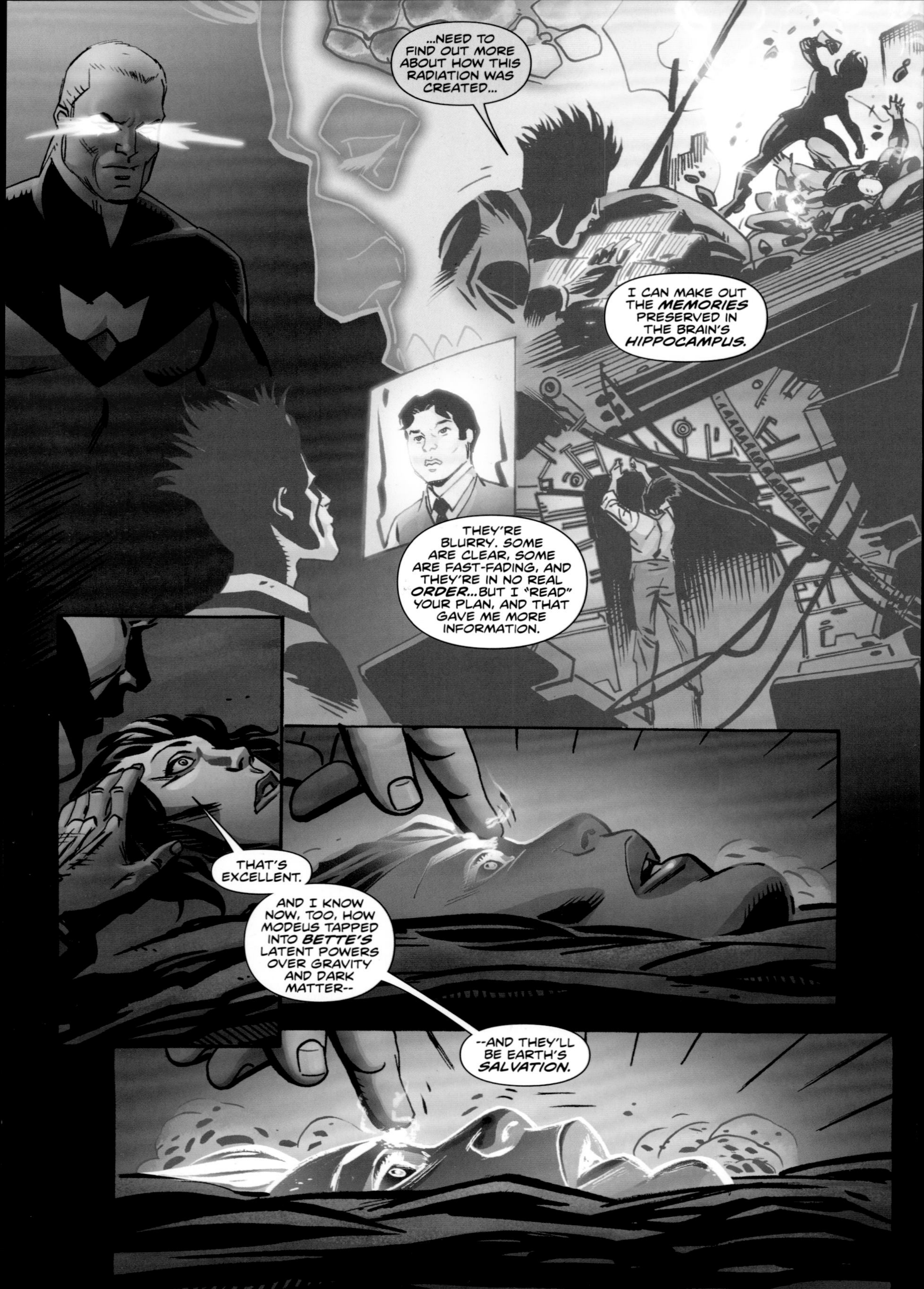
...NEED TO FIND OUT MORE ABOUT HOW THIS RADIATION WAS CREATED...
I CAN MAKE OUT THE MEMORIES PRESERVED IN THE BRAIN'S HIPPOCAMPUS.
THEY'RE BLURRY. SOME ARE CLEAR, SOME ARE FAST-FADING, AND THEY'RE IN NO REAL ORDER...BUT I "READ" YOUR PLAN, AND THAT GAVE ME MORE INFORMATION.
THAT'S EXCELLENT.
AND I KNOW NOW, TOO, HOW MODEUS TAPPED INTO BETTE'S LATENT POWERS OVER GRAVITY AND DARK MATTER--
--AND THEY'LL BE EARTH'S SALVATION.

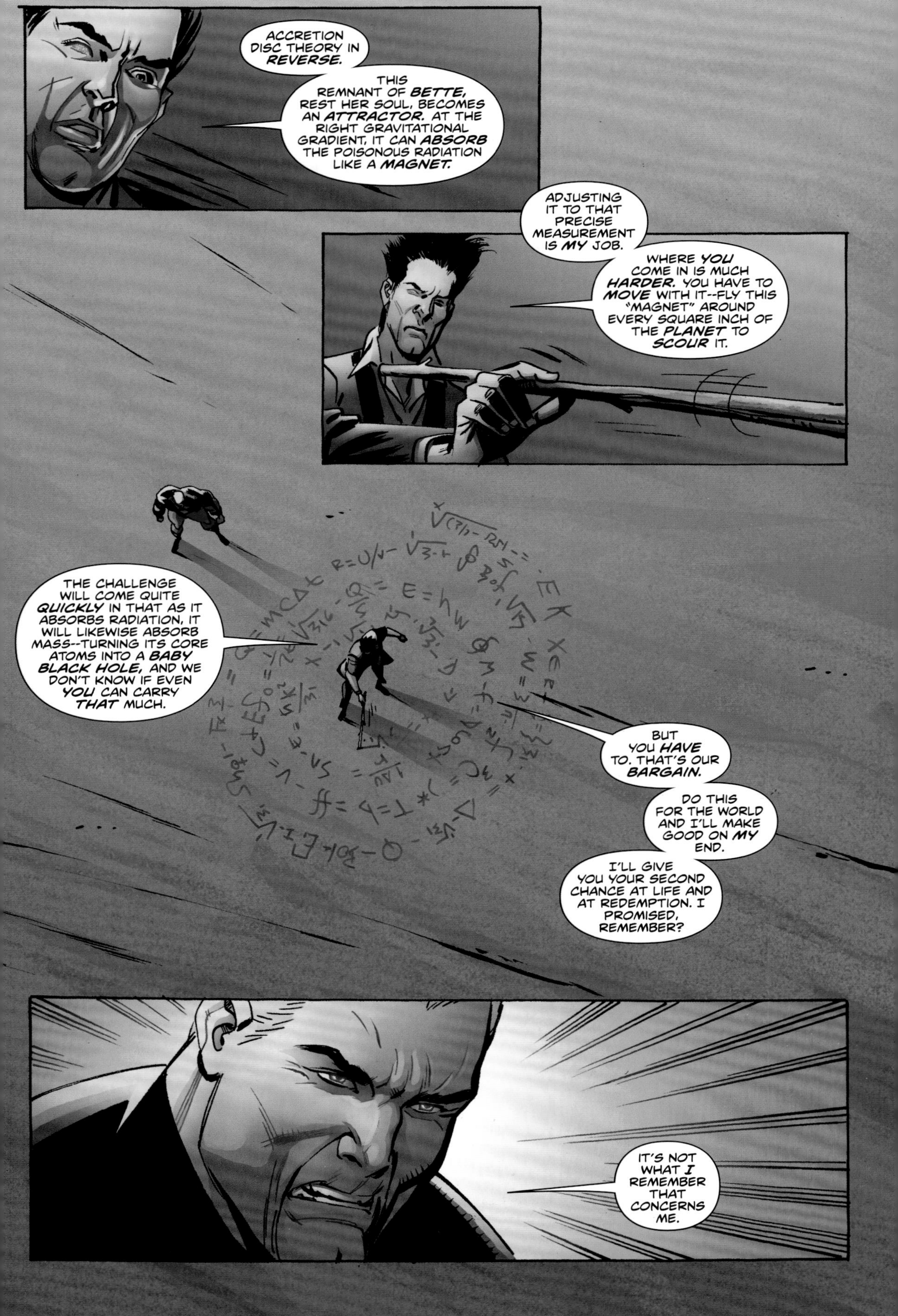
ACCRETION DISC THEORY IN REVERSE.
THIS REMNANT OF BETTE, REST HER SOUL, BECOMES AN ATTRACTOR. AT THE RIGHT GRAVITATIONAL GRADIENT, IT CAN ABSORB THE POISONOUS RADIATION LIKE A MAGNET.
ADJUSTING IT TO THAT PRECISE MEASUREMENT IS MY JOB.
WHERE YOU COME IN IS MUCH HARDER. YOU HAVE TO MOVE WITH IT--FLY THIS "MAGNET" AROUND EVERY SQUARE INCH OF THE PLANET TO SCOUR IT.
THE CHALLENGE WILL COME QUITE QUICKLY IN THAT AS IT ABSORBS RADIATION, IT WILL LIKEWISE ABSORB MASS--TURNING ITS CORE ATOMS INTO A BABY BLACK HOLE, AND WE DON'T KNOW IF EVEN YOU CAN CARRY THAT MUCH.
BUT YOU HAVE TO. THAT'S OUR BARGAIN.
DO THIS FOR THE WORLD AND I'LL MAKE GOOD ON MY END.
I'LL GIVE YOU YOUR SECOND CHANCE AT LIFE AND AT REDEMPTION. I PROMISED, REMEMBER?
IT'S NOT WHAT I REMEMBER THAT CONCERNS ME.

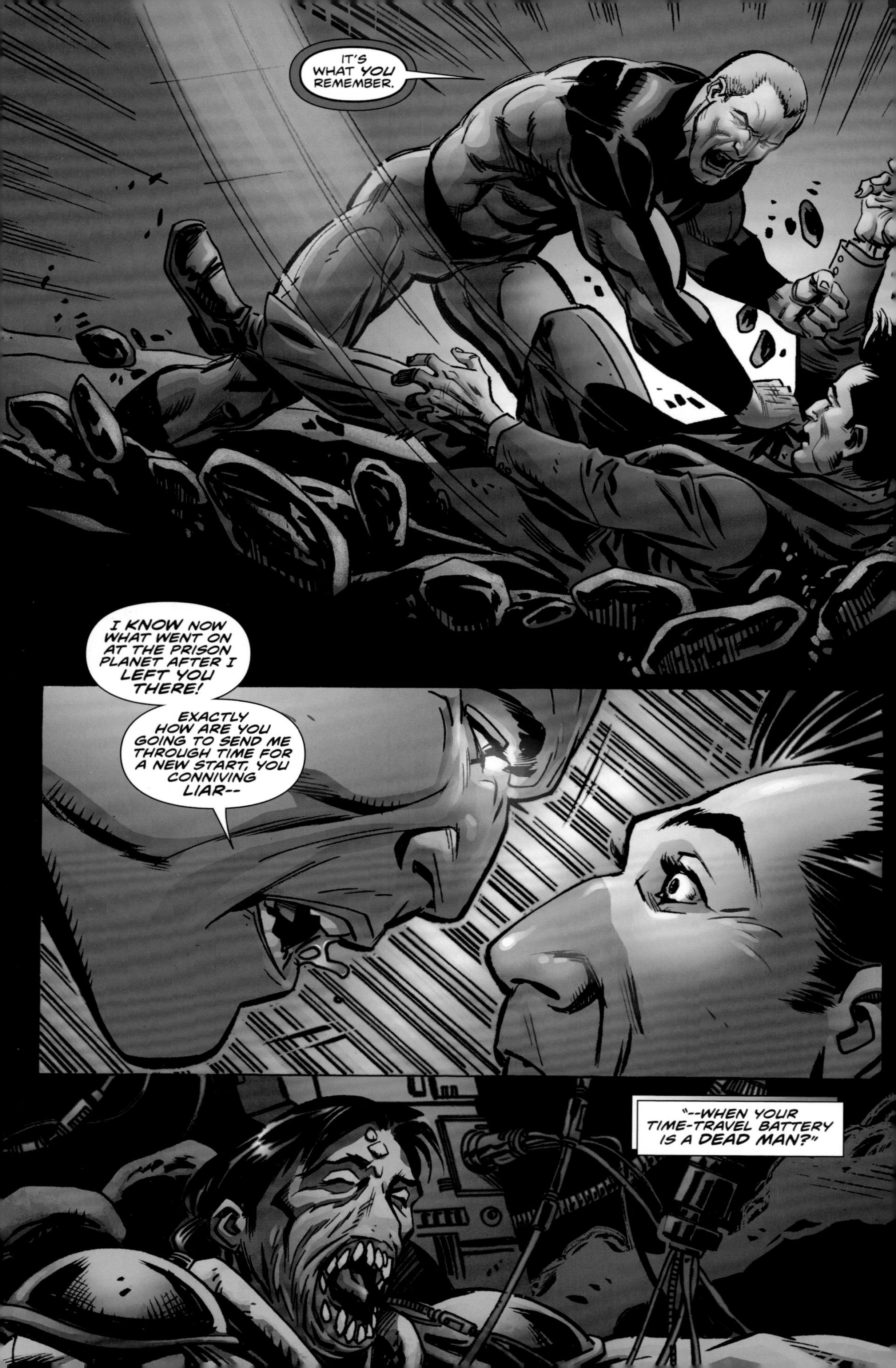
IT'S WHAT YOU REMEMBER.
I KNOW NOW WHAT WENT ON AT THE PRISON PLANET AFTER I LEFT YOU THERE!
EXACTLY HOW ARE YOU GOING TO SEND ME THROUGH TIME FOR A NEW START, YOU CONNIVING LIAR--
"--WHEN YOUR TIME-TRAVEL BATTERY IS A DEAD MAN?"

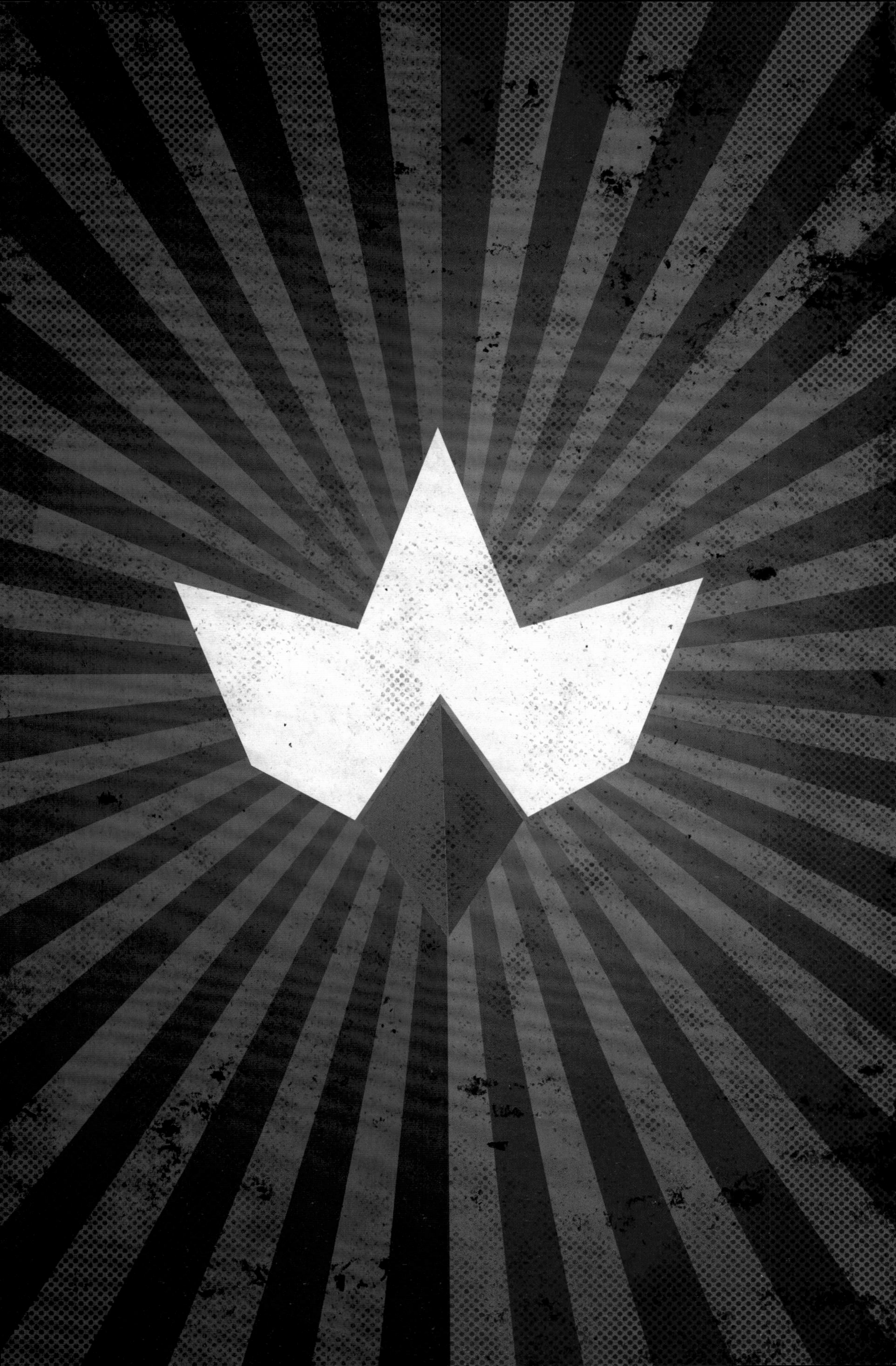

CHAPTER 37

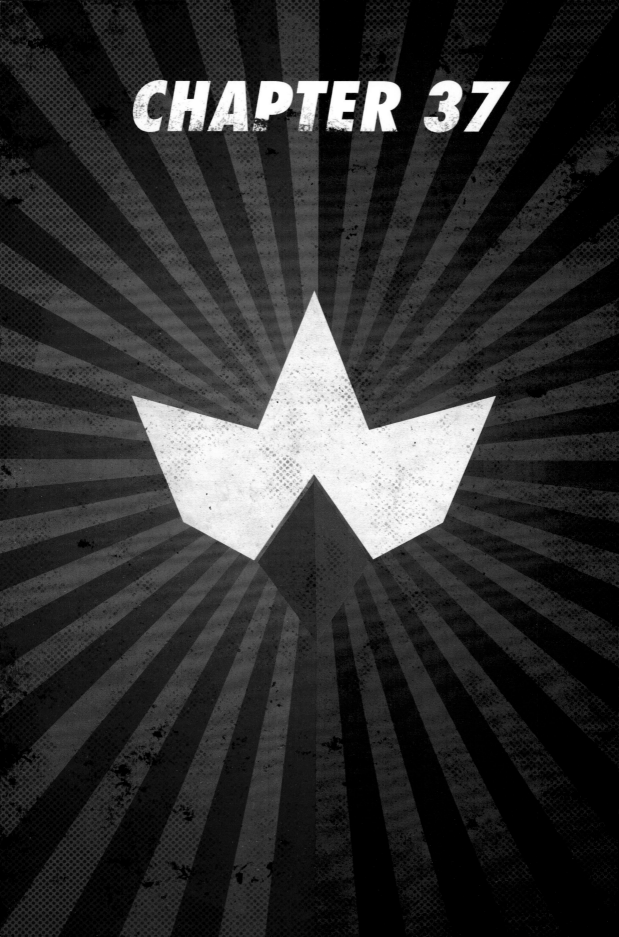

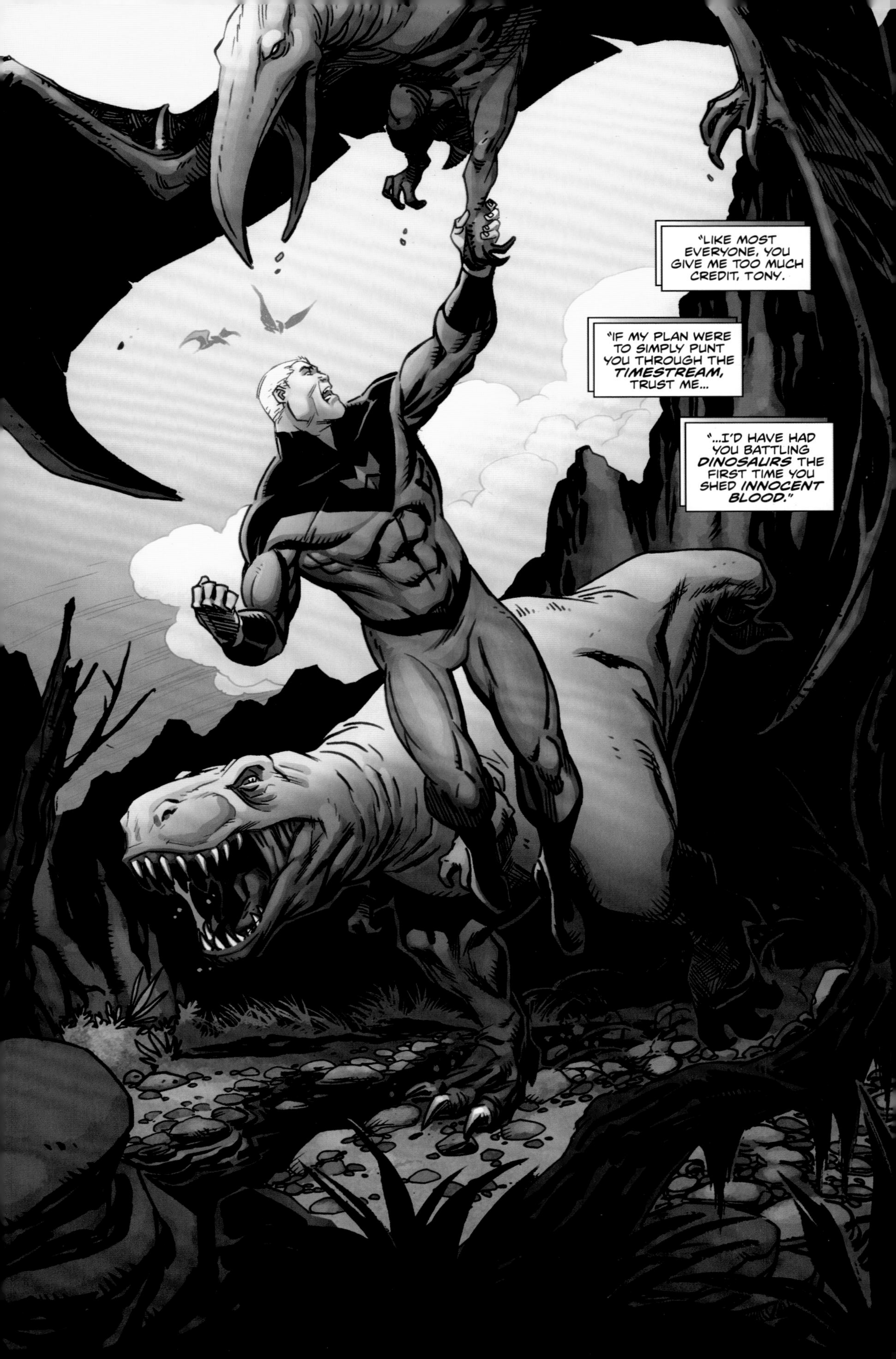
"LIKE MOST EVERYONE, YOU GIVE ME TOO MUCH CREDIT, TONY.
"IF MY PLAN WERE TO SIMPLY PUNT YOU THROUGH THE *TIMESTREAM,* TRUST ME...
"...I'D HAVE HAD YOU BATTLING *DINOSAURS* THE FIRST TIME YOU SHED *INNOCENT BLOOD."*

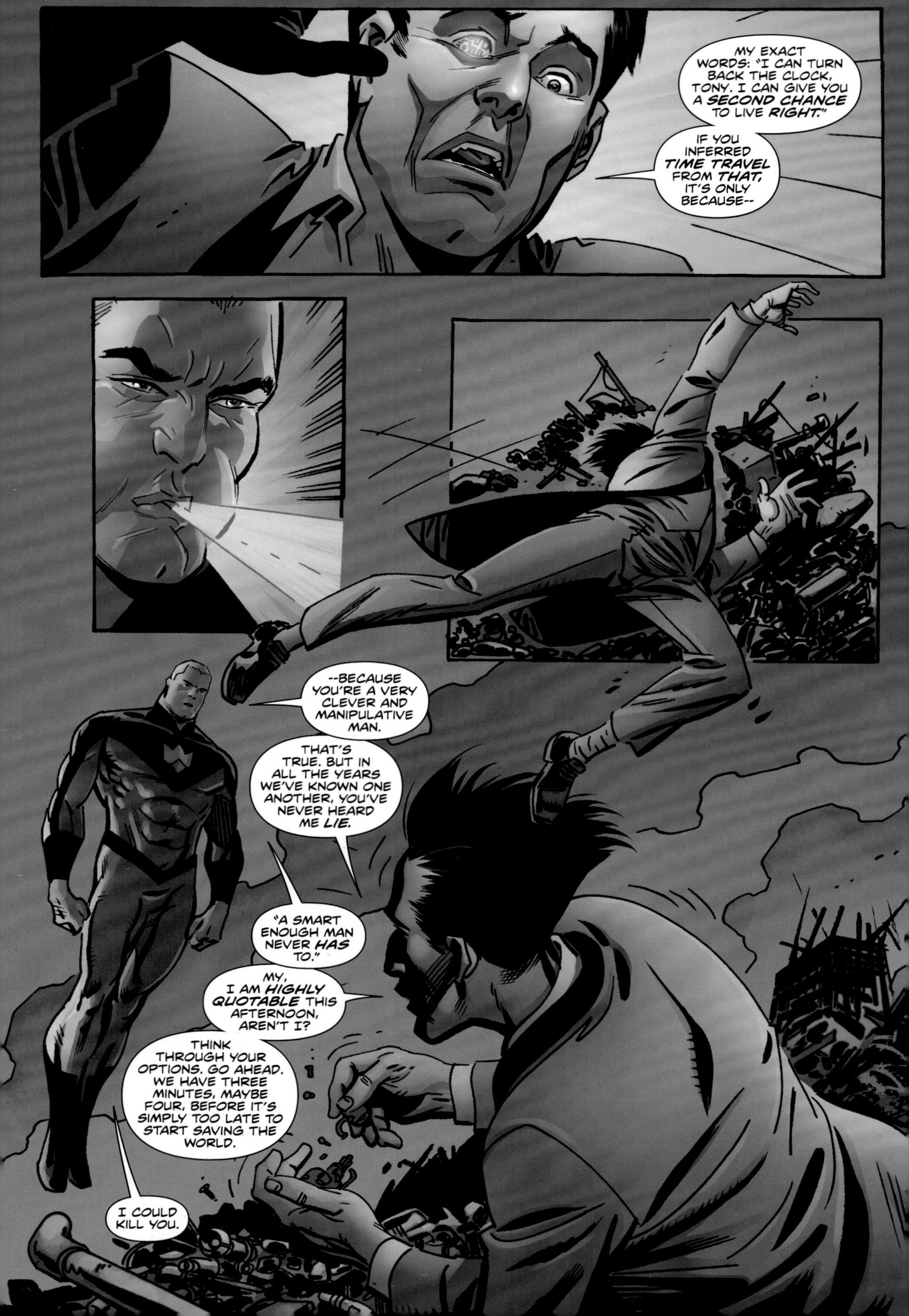

MY EXACT WORDS: "I CAN TURN BACK THE CLOCK, TONY. I CAN GIVE YOU A SECOND CHANCE TO LIVE RIGHT."
IF YOU INFERRED TIME TRAVEL FROM THAT, IT'S ONLY BECAUSE--
--BECAUSE YOU'RE A VERY CLEVER AND MANIPULATIVE MAN.
THAT'S TRUE. BUT IN ALL THE YEARS WE'VE KNOWN ONE ANOTHER, YOU'VE NEVER HEARD ME LIE.
"A SMART ENOUGH MAN NEVER HAS TO."
MY, I AM HIGHLY QUOTABLE THIS AFTERNOON, AREN'T I?
THINK THROUGH YOUR OPTIONS. GO AHEAD. WE HAVE THREE MINUTES, MAYBE FOUR, BEFORE IT'S SIMPLY TOO LATE TO START SAVING THE WORLD.
I COULD KILL YOU.

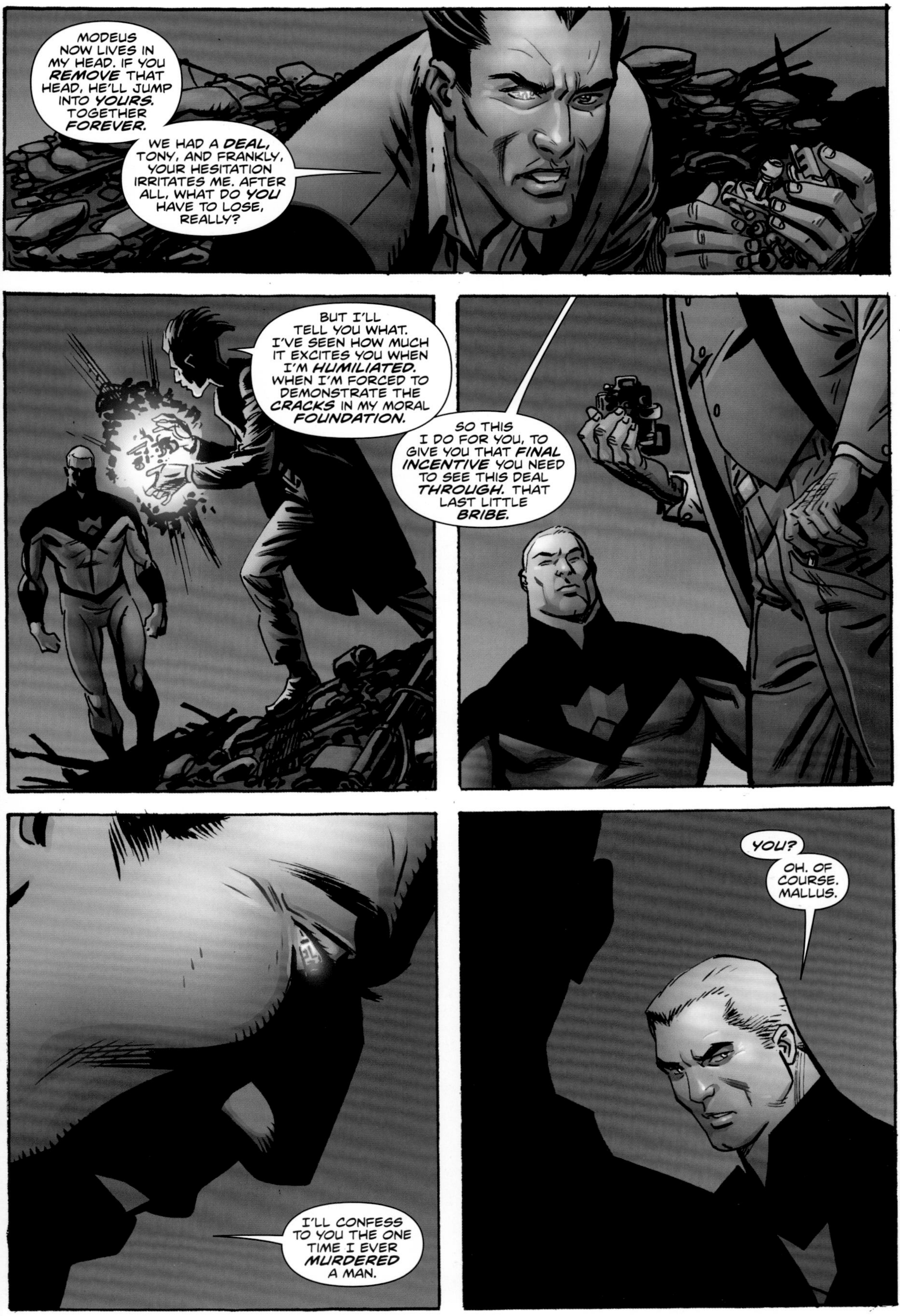
MODEUS NOW LIVES IN MY HEAD. IF YOU REMOVE THAT HEAD, HE'LL JUMP INTO YOURS. TOGETHER FOREVER.
WE HAD A DEAL, TONY, AND FRANKLY, YOUR HESITATION IRRITATES ME. AFTER ALL, WHAT DO YOU HAVE TO LOSE, REALLY?
BUT I'LL TELL YOU WHAT. I'VE SEEN HOW MUCH IT EXCITES YOU WHEN I'M HUMILIATED. WHEN I'M FORCED TO DEMONSTRATE THE CRACKS IN MY MORAL FOUNDATION.
SO THIS I DO FOR YOU, TO GIVE YOU THAT FINAL INCENTIVE YOU NEED TO SEE THIS DEAL THROUGH. THAT LAST LITTLE BRIBE.
I'LL CONFESS TO YOU THE ONE TIME I EVER MURDERED A MAN.
YOU?
OH. OF COURSE. MALLUS.

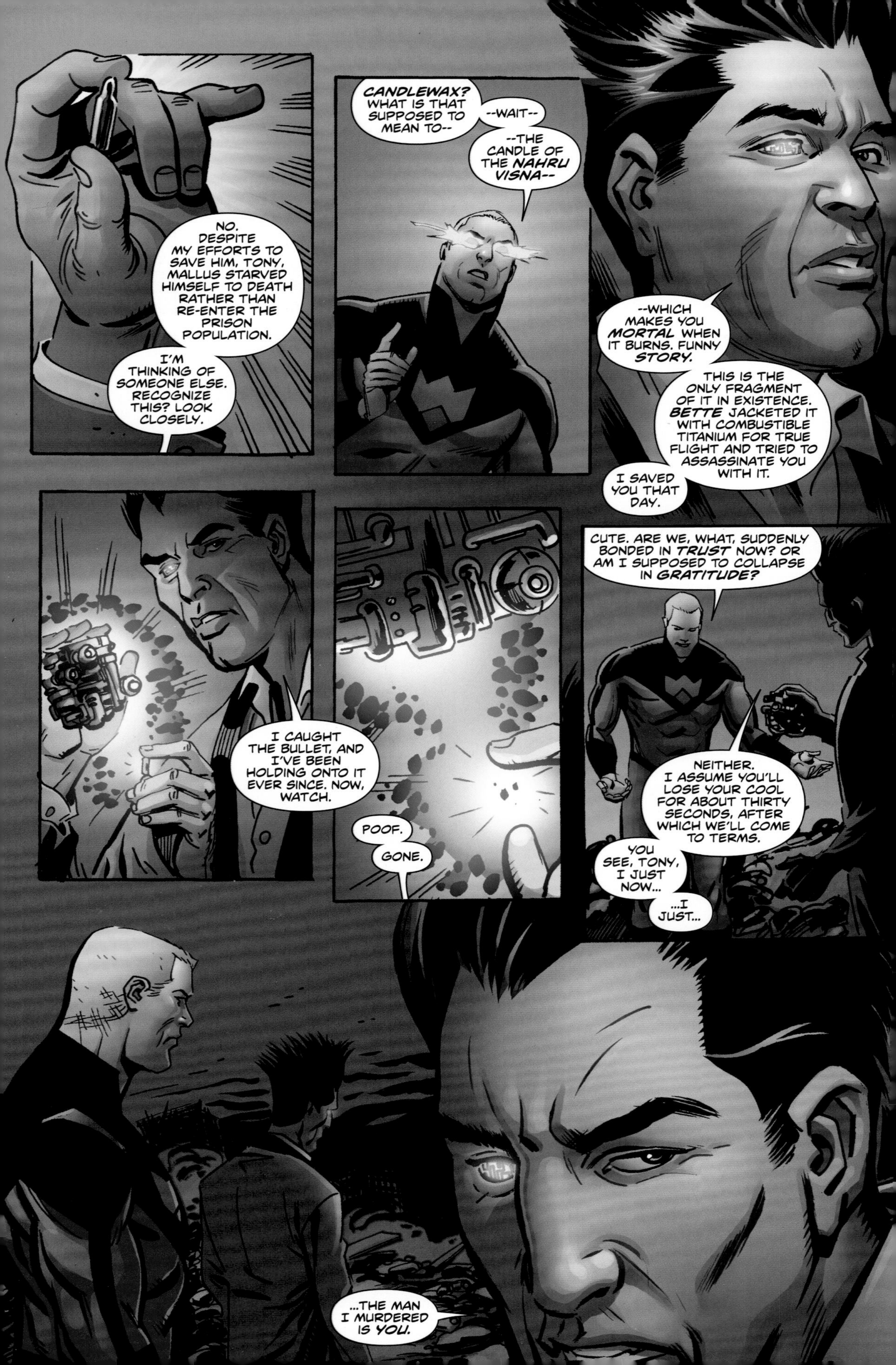

NO. DESPITE MY EFFORTS TO SAVE HIM, TONY, MALLUS STARVED HIMSELF TO DEATH RATHER THAN RE-ENTER THE PRISON POPULATION.
I'M THINKING OF SOMEONE ELSE. RECOGNIZE THIS? LOOK CLOSELY.
CANDLEWAX? WHAT IS THAT SUPPOSED TO MEAN TO--
--WAIT--
--THE CANDLE OF THE NAHRU VISNA--
--WHICH MAKES YOU MORTAL WHEN IT BURNS. FUNNY STORY.
THIS IS THE ONLY FRAGMENT OF IT IN EXISTENCE. BETTE JACKETED IT WITH COMBUSTIBLE TITANIUM FOR TRUE FLIGHT AND TRIED TO ASSASSINATE YOU WITH IT.
I SAVED YOU THAT DAY.
I CAUGHT THE BULLET, AND I'VE BEEN HOLDING ONTO IT EVER SINCE. NOW, WATCH.
POOF.
GONE.
CUTE. ARE WE, WHAT, SUDDENLY BONDED IN TRUST NOW? OR AM I SUPPOSED TO COLLAPSE IN GRATITUDE?
NEITHER. I ASSUME YOU'LL LOSE YOUR COOL FOR ABOUT THIRTY SECONDS, AFTER WHICH WE'LL COME TO TERMS.
YOU SEE, TONY, I JUST NOW...
...I JUST...
...THE MAN I MURDERED IS YOU.

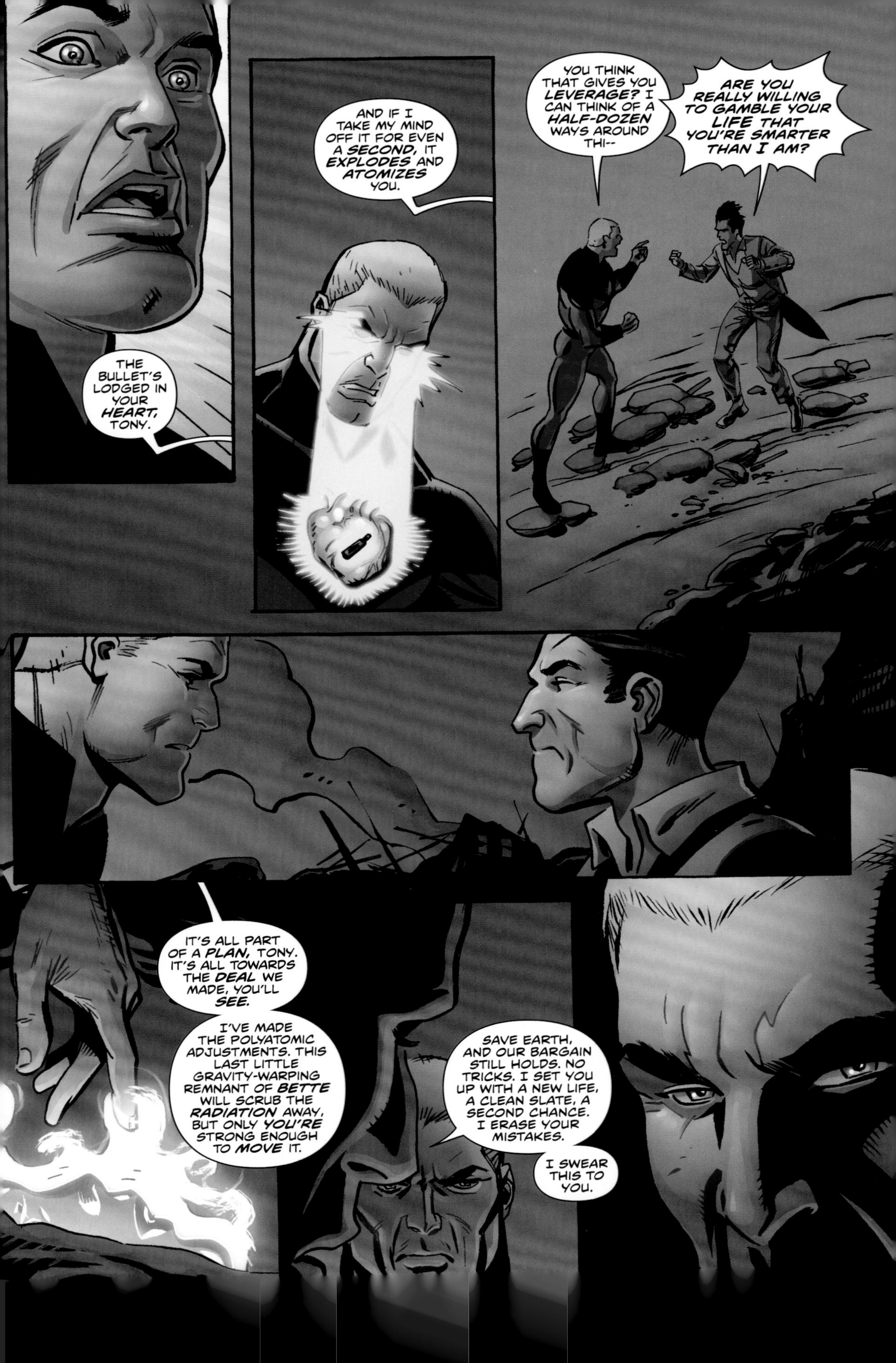
THE BULLET'S LODGED IN YOUR HEART, TONY.
AND IF I TAKE MY MIND OFF IT FOR EVEN A SECOND, IT EXPLODES AND ATOMIZES YOU.
YOU THINK THAT GIVES YOU LEVERAGE? I CAN THINK OF A HALF-DOZEN WAYS AROUND THI--
ARE YOU REALLY WILLING TO GAMBLE YOUR LIFE THAT YOU'RE SMARTER THAN I AM?
IT'S ALL PART OF A PLAN, TONY. IT'S ALL TOWARDS THE DEAL WE MADE, YOU'LL SEE.
I'VE MADE THE POLYATOMIC ADJUSTMENTS. THIS LAST LITTLE GRAVITY-WARPING REMNANT OF BETTE WILL SCRUB THE RADIATION AWAY, BUT ONLY YOU'RE STRONG ENOUGH TO MOVE IT.
SAVE EARTH, AND OUR BARGAIN STILL HOLDS. NO TRICKS. I SET YOU UP WITH A NEW LIFE, A CLEAN SLATE, A SECOND CHANCE. I ERASE YOUR MISTAKES.
I SWEAR THIS TO YOU.

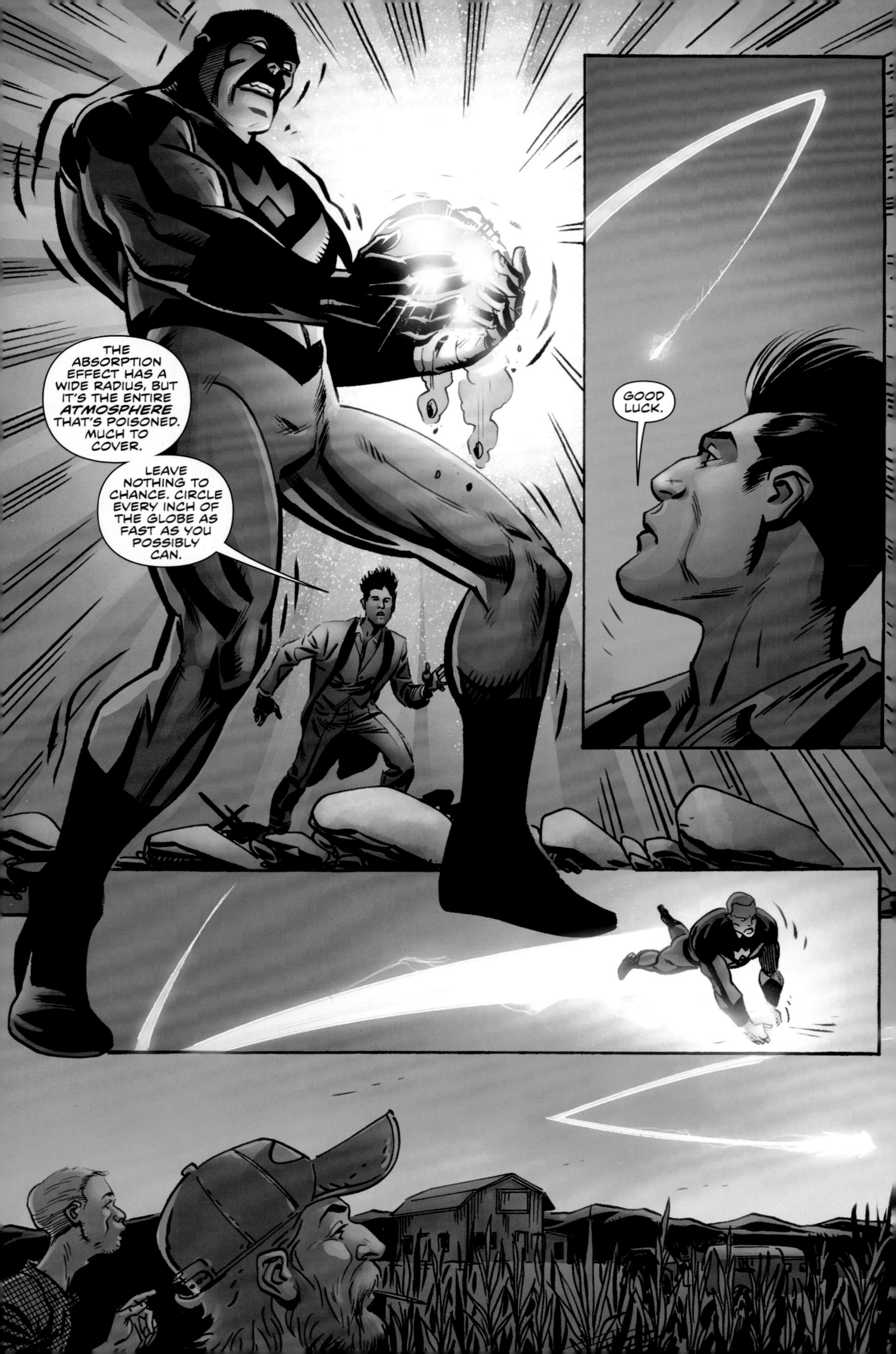
THE ABSORPTION EFFECT HAS A WIDE RADIUS, BUT IT'S THE ENTIRE *ATMOSPHERE* THAT'S POISONED. MUCH TO COVER.
LEAVE NOTHING TO CHANCE. CIRCLE EVERY INCH OF THE GLOBE AS FAST AS YOU POSSIBLY CAN.
GOOD LUCK.

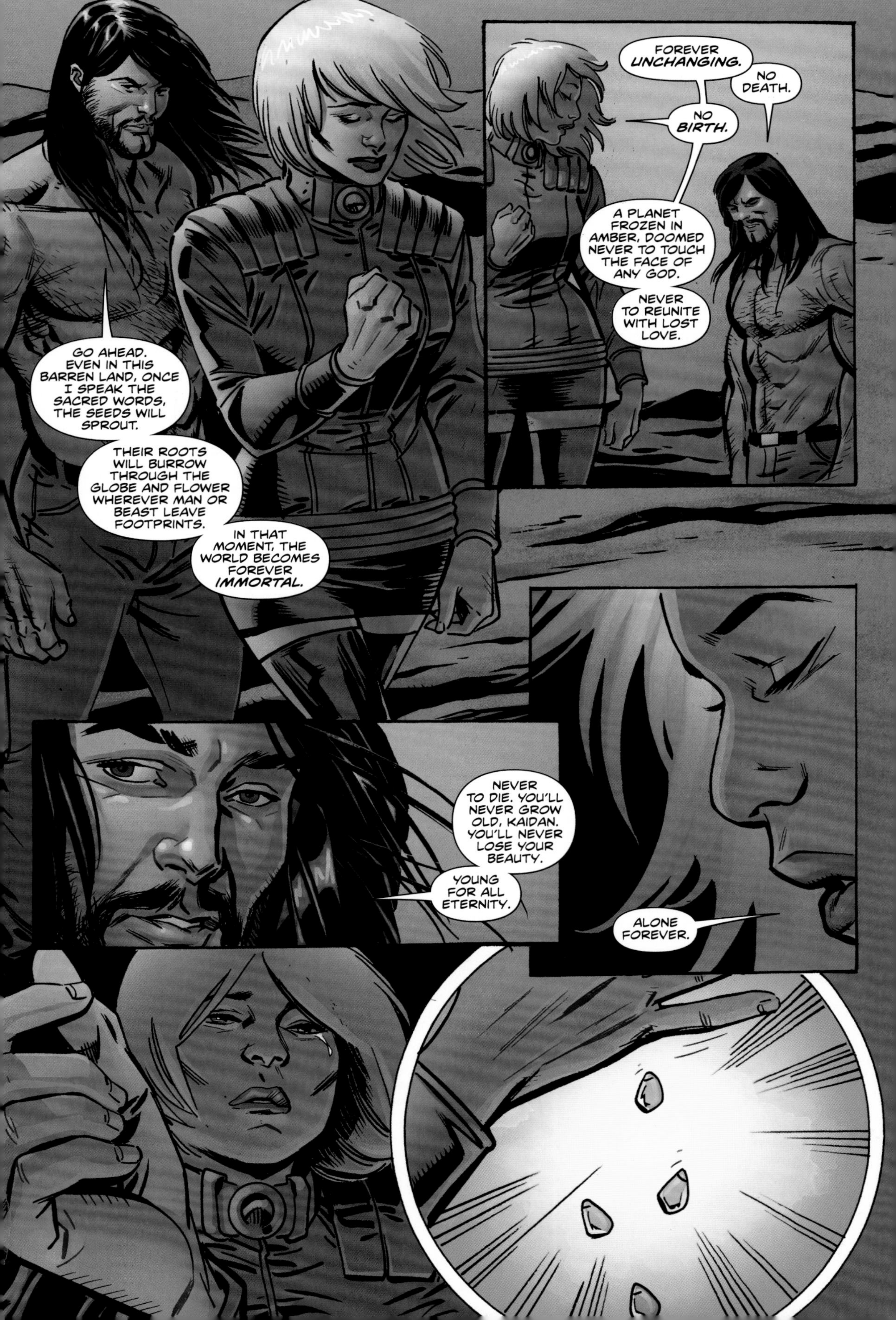
GO AHEAD. EVEN IN THIS BARREN LAND, ONCE I SPEAK THE SACRED WORDS, THE SEEDS WILL SPROUT.
THEIR ROOTS WILL BURROW THROUGH THE GLOBE AND FLOWER WHEREVER MAN OR BEAST LEAVE FOOTPRINTS.
IN THAT MOMENT, THE WORLD BECOMES FOREVER *IMMORTAL*.
FOREVER ***UNCHANGING.***
NO DEATH.
NO ***BIRTH.***
A PLANET FROZEN IN AMBER, DOOMED NEVER TO TOUCH THE FACE OF ANY GOD.
NEVER TO REUNITE WITH LOST LOVE.
NEVER TO DIE. YOU'LL NEVER GROW OLD, KAIDAN. YOU'LL NEVER LOSE YOUR BEAUTY.
YOUNG FOR ALL ETERNITY.
ALONE FOREVER.

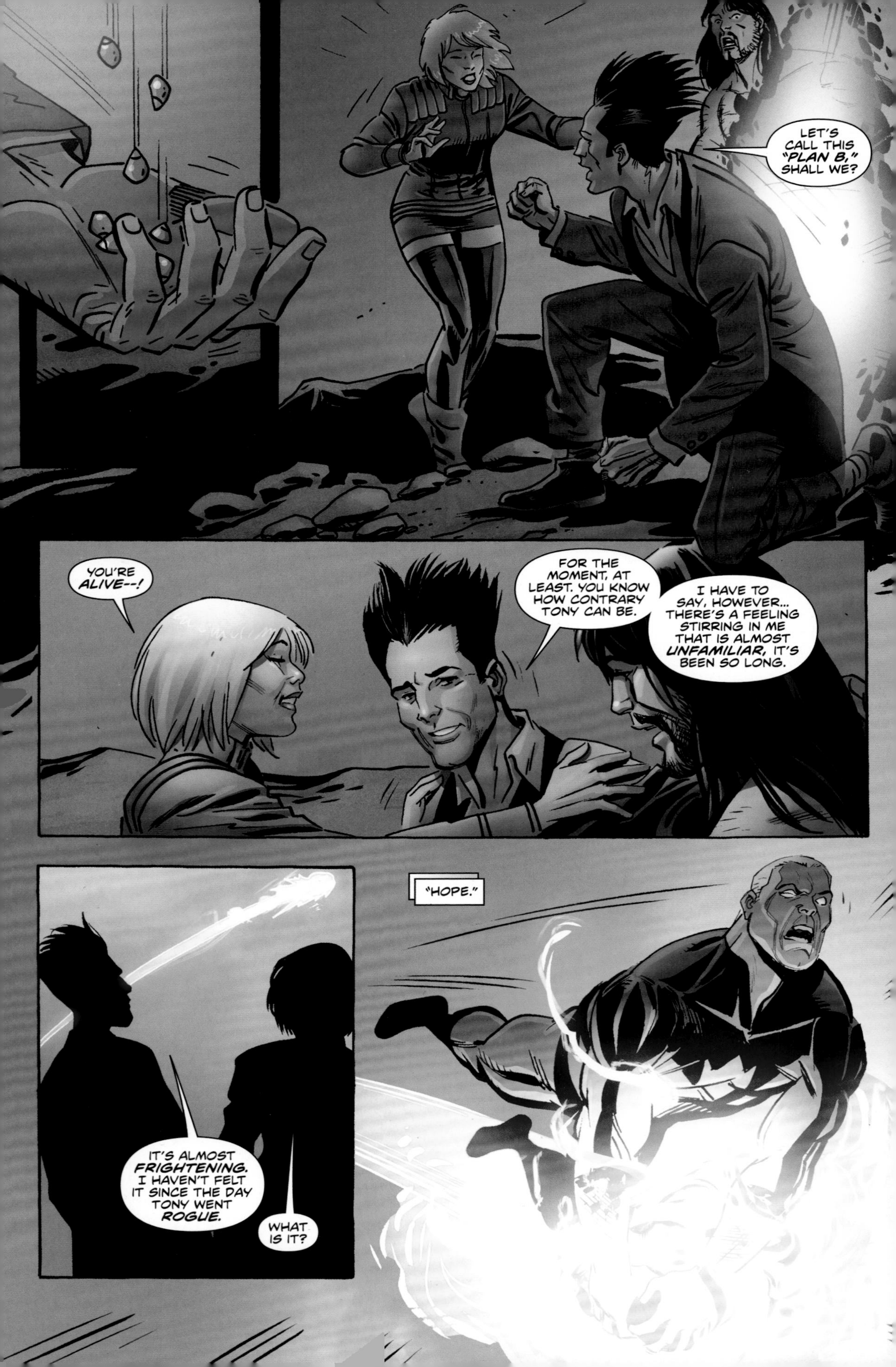
LET'S CALL THIS "PLAN B," SHALL WE?
YOU'RE ALIVE--!
FOR THE MOMENT, AT LEAST. YOU KNOW HOW CONTRARY TONY CAN BE.
I HAVE TO SAY, HOWEVER... THERE'S A FEELING STIRRING IN ME THAT IS ALMOST UNFAMILIAR, IT'S BEEN SO LONG.
IT'S ALMOST FRIGHTENING. I HAVEN'T FELT IT SINCE THE DAY TONY WENT ROGUE.
WHAT IS IT?
"HOPE."

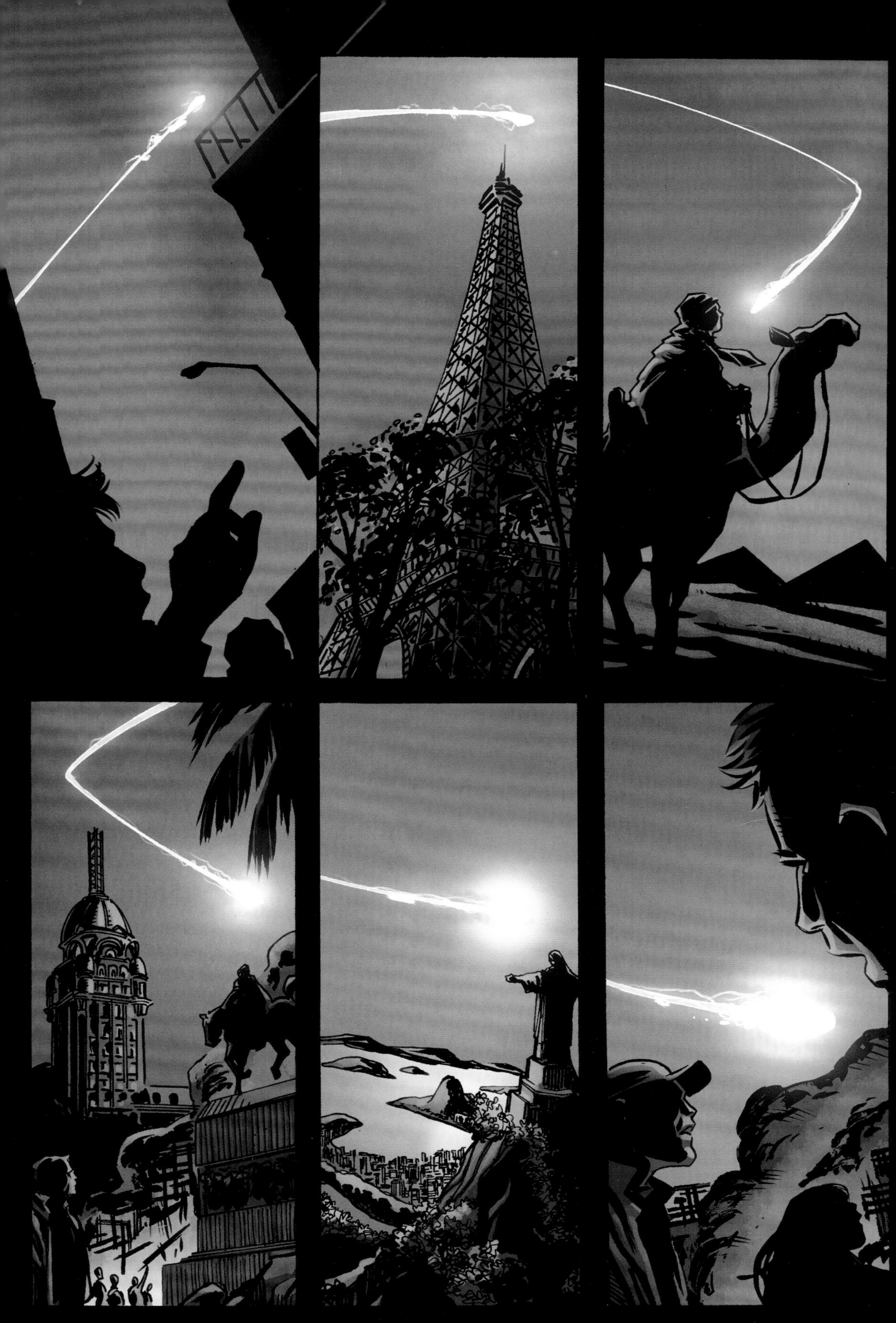

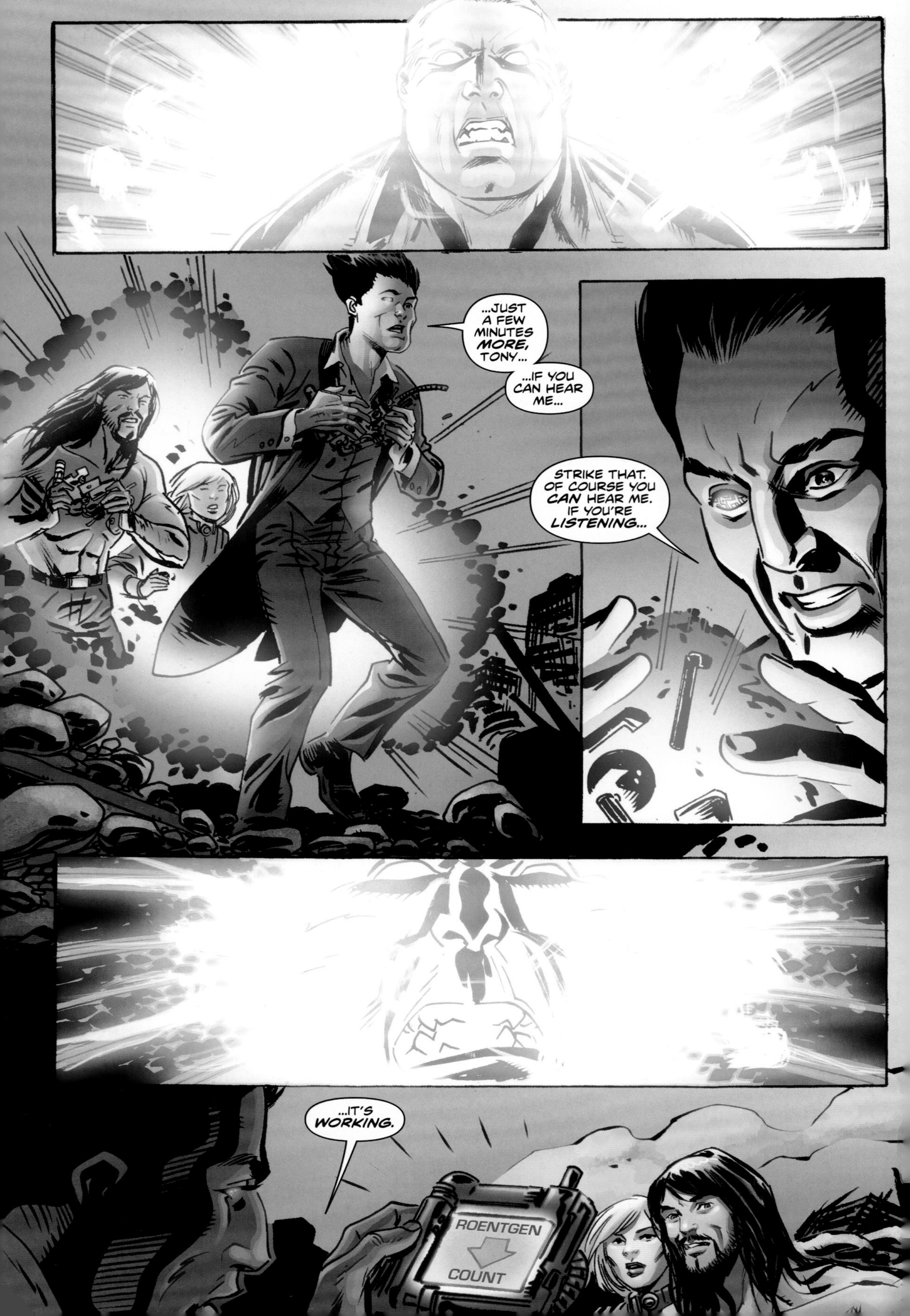
...JUST A FEW MINUTES MORE, TONY...
...IF YOU CAN HEAR ME...
STRIKE THAT. OF COURSE YOU CAN HEAR ME. IF YOU'RE LISTENING...
...IT'S WORKING.
ROENTGEN COUNT

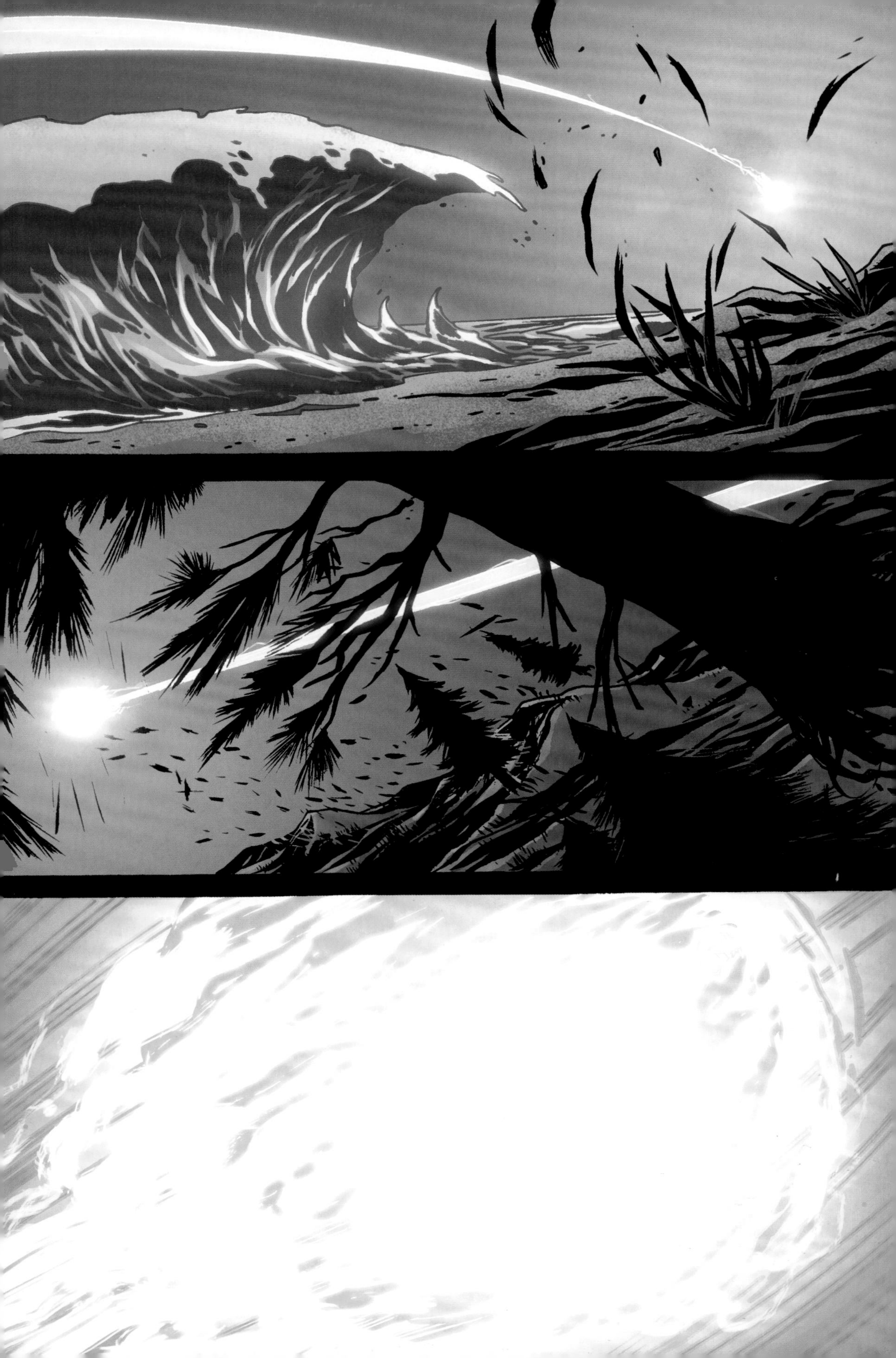

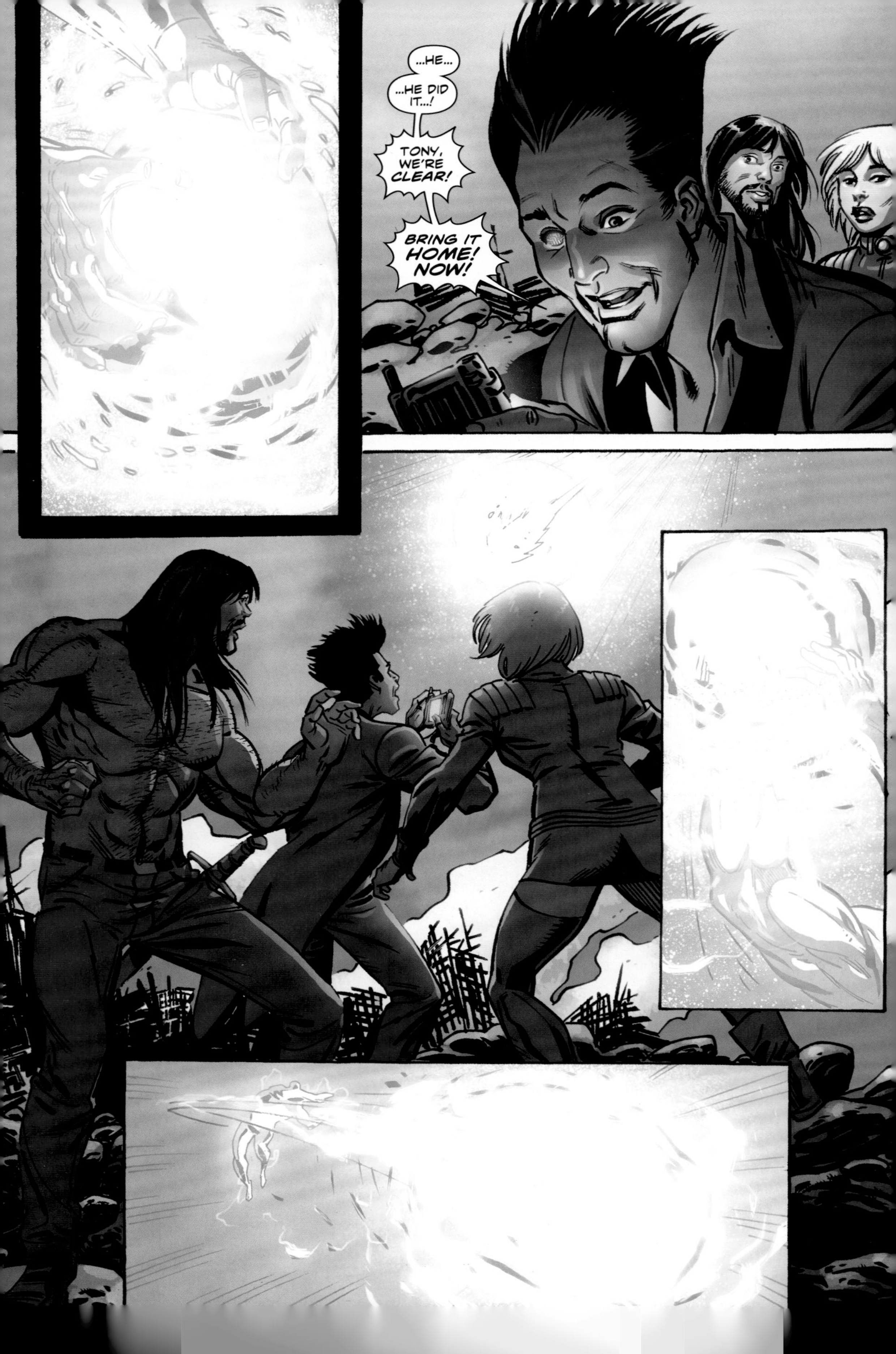
...HE...
...HE DID IT...!
TONY, WE'RE CLEAR!
BRING IT HOME! NOW!

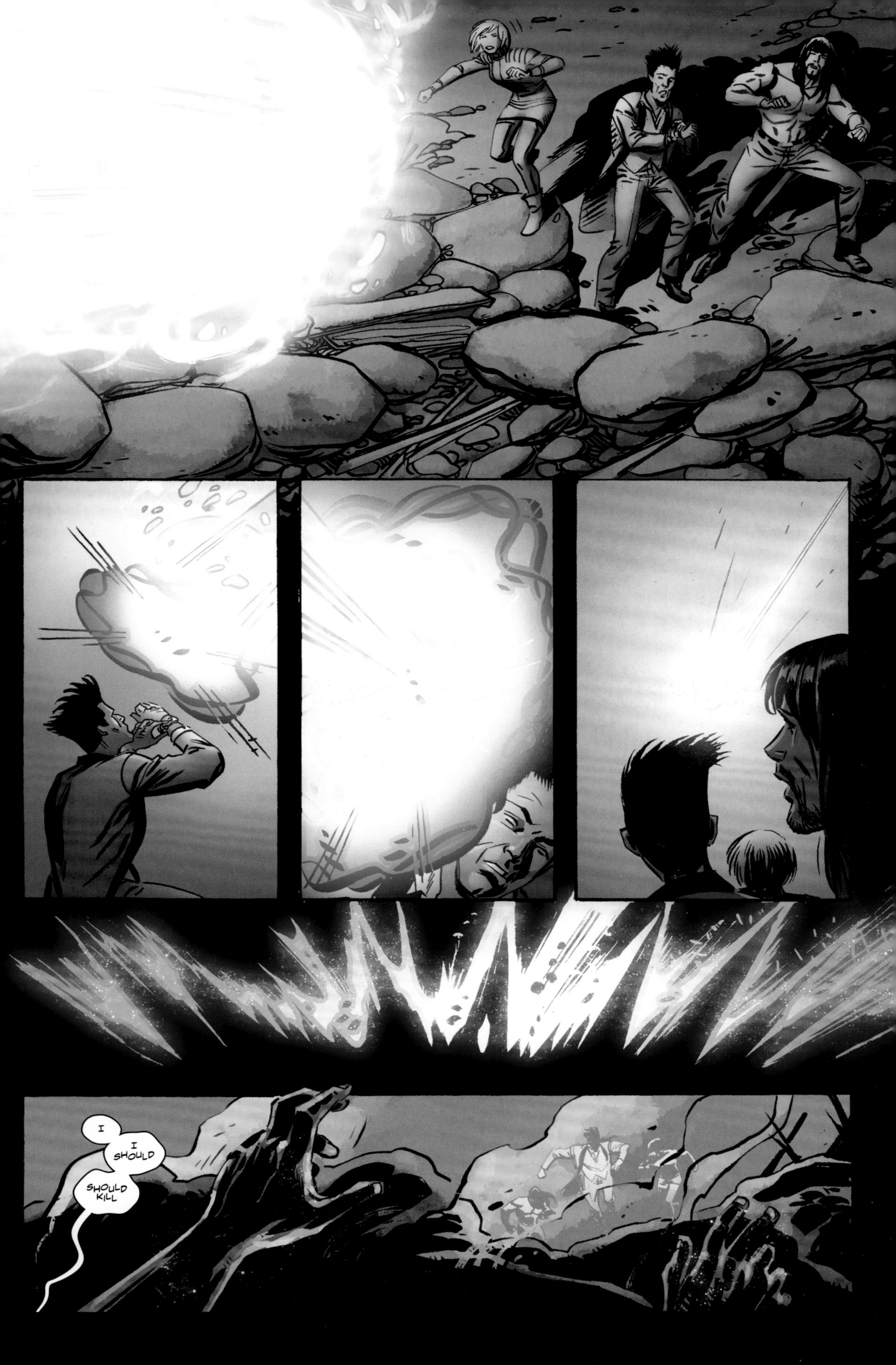
I
I SHOULD
SHOULD KILL

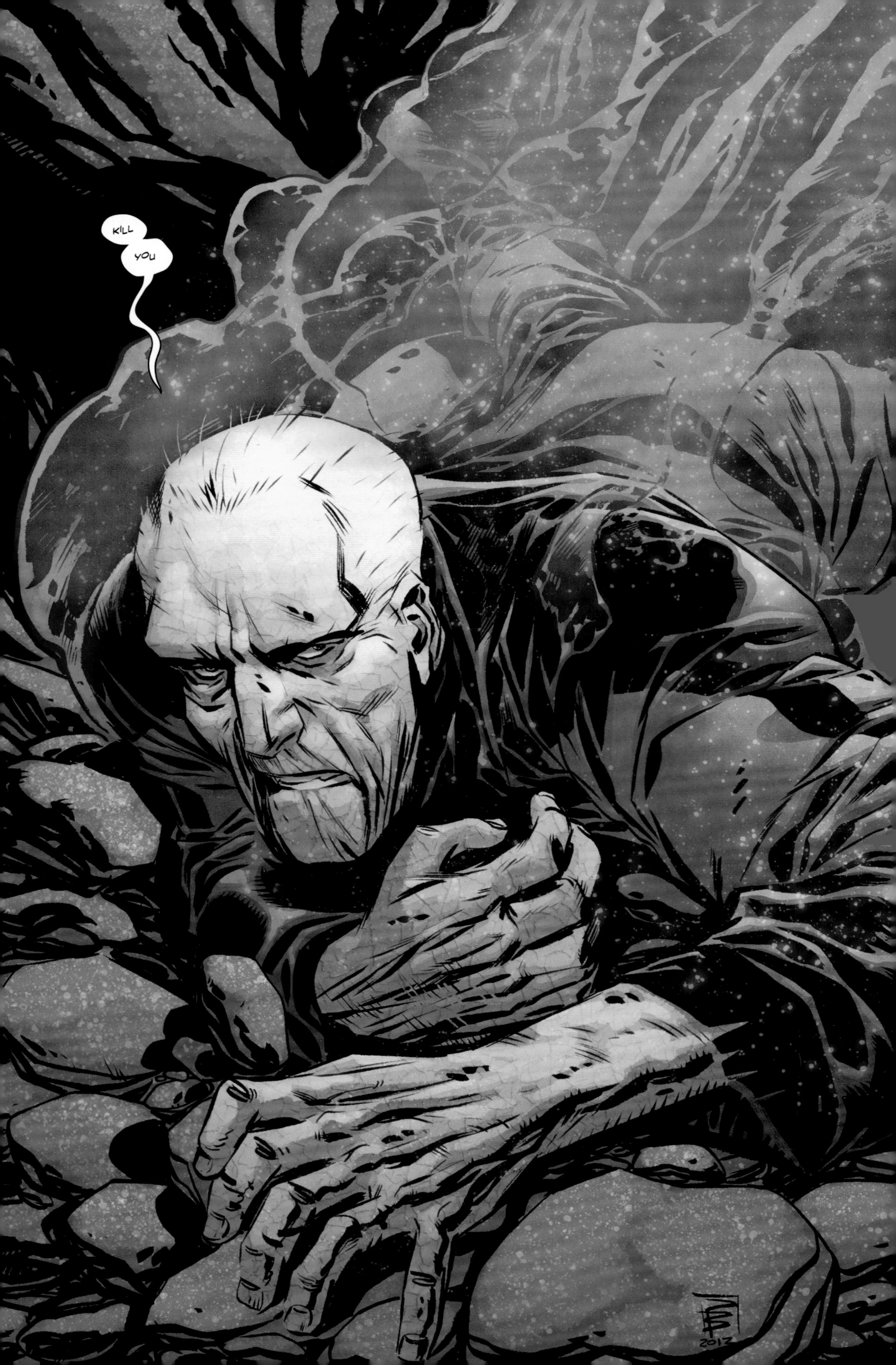
KILL
YOU

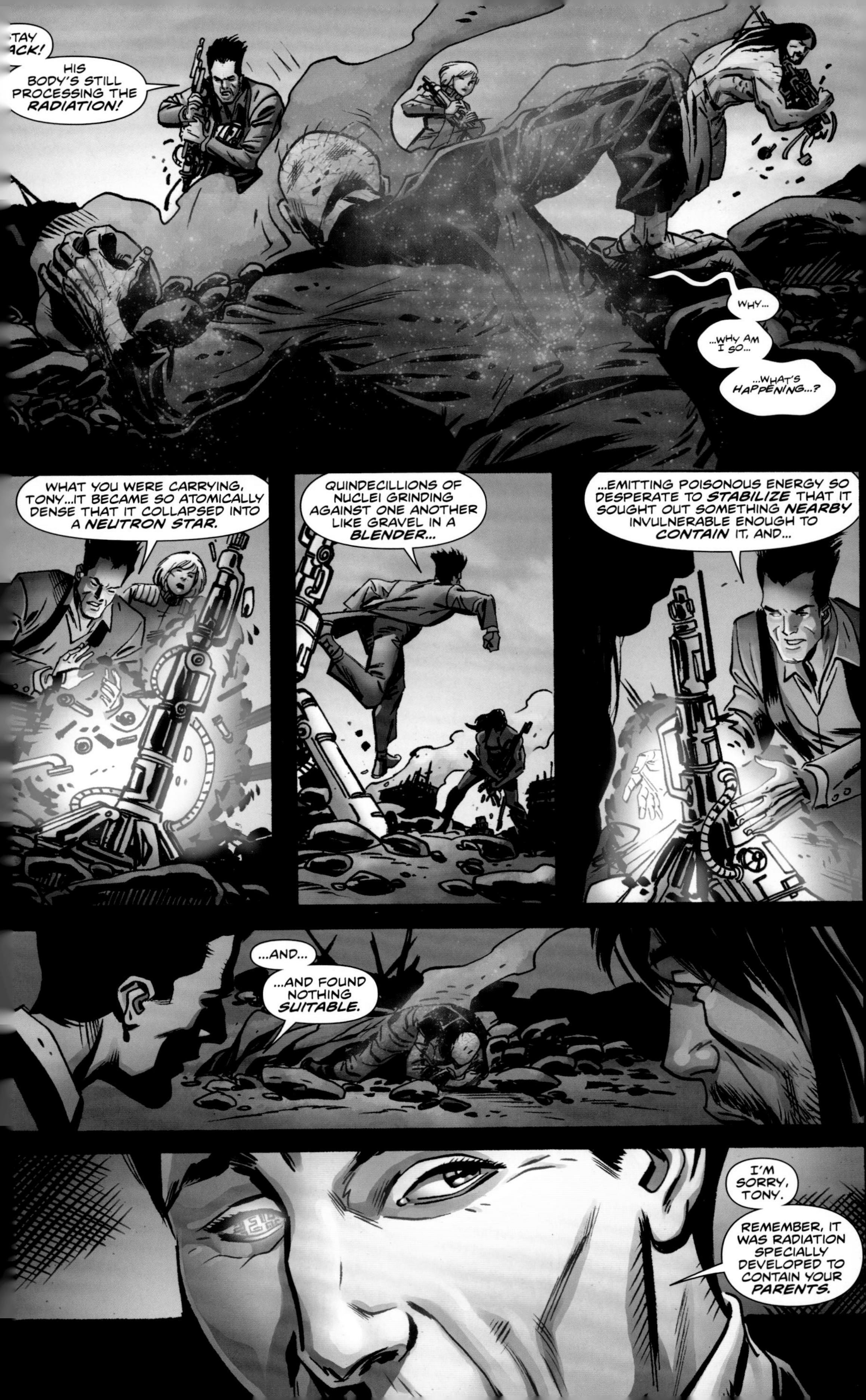

STAY BACK!
HIS BODY'S STILL PROCESSING THE RADIATION!
WHY...
...WHY AM I SO...
...WHAT'S HAPPENING...?
WHAT YOU WERE CARRYING, TONY...IT BECAME SO ATOMICALLY DENSE THAT IT COLLAPSED INTO A NEUTRON STAR.
QUINDECILLIONS OF NUCLEI GRINDING AGAINST ONE ANOTHER LIKE GRAVEL IN A BLENDER...
...EMITTING POISONOUS ENERGY SO DESPERATE TO STABILIZE THAT IT SOUGHT OUT SOMETHING NEARBY INVULNERABLE ENOUGH TO CONTAIN IT, AND...
...AND...
...AND FOUND NOTHING SUITABLE.
I'M SORRY, TONY.
REMEMBER, IT WAS RADIATION SPECIALLY DEVELOPED TO CONTAIN YOUR PARENTS.

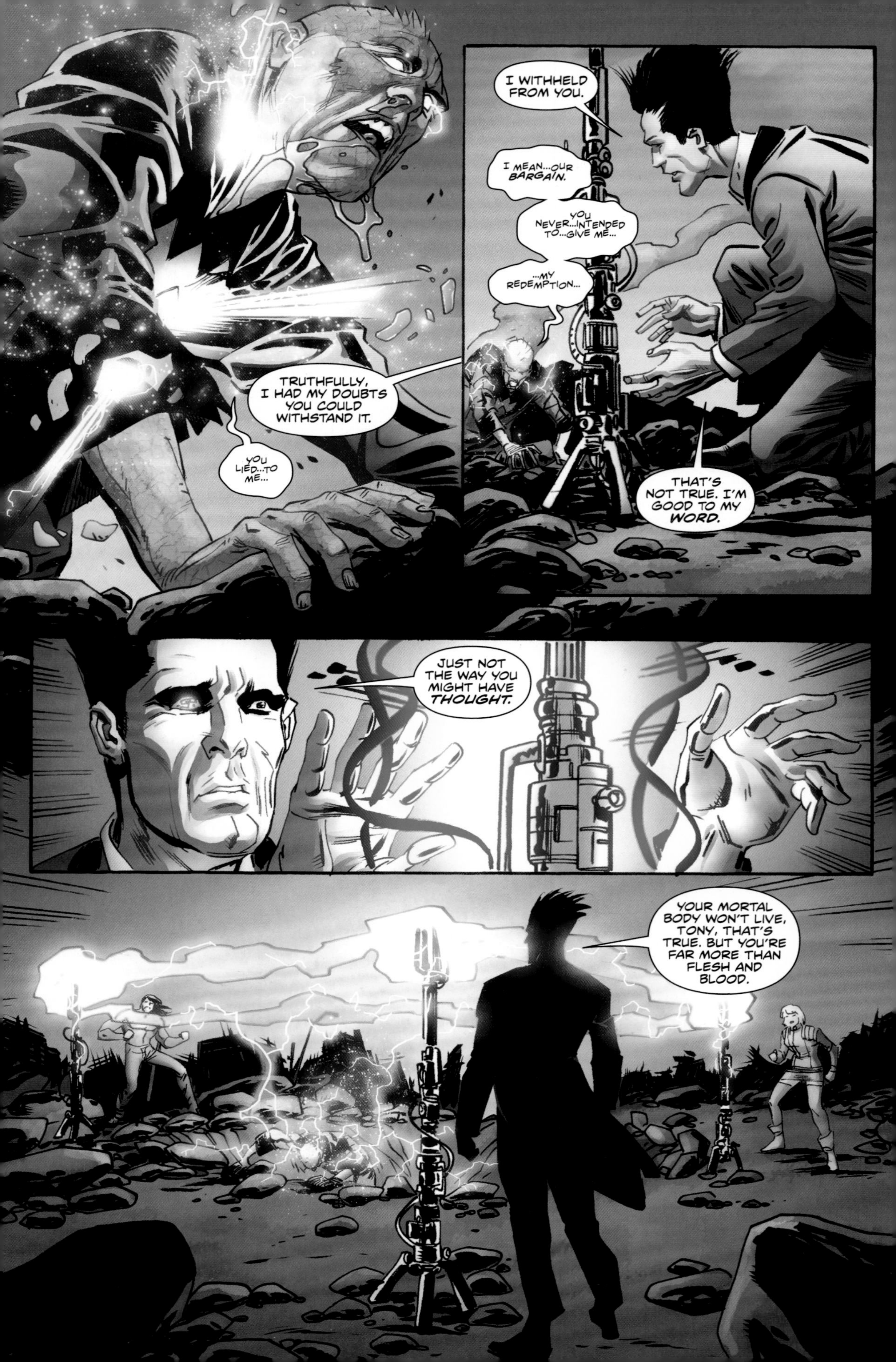
I WITHHELD FROM YOU.
I MEAN...OUR BARGAIN.
YOU NEVER...INTENDED TO...GIVE ME...
...MY REDEMPTION...
TRUTHFULLY, I HAD MY DOUBTS YOU COULD WITHSTAND IT.
YOU LIED...TO ME...
THAT'S NOT TRUE. I'M GOOD TO MY WORD.
JUST NOT THE WAY YOU MIGHT HAVE THOUGHT.
YOUR MORTAL BODY WON'T LIVE, TONY, THAT'S TRUE. BUT YOU'RE FAR MORE THAN FLESH AND BLOOD.

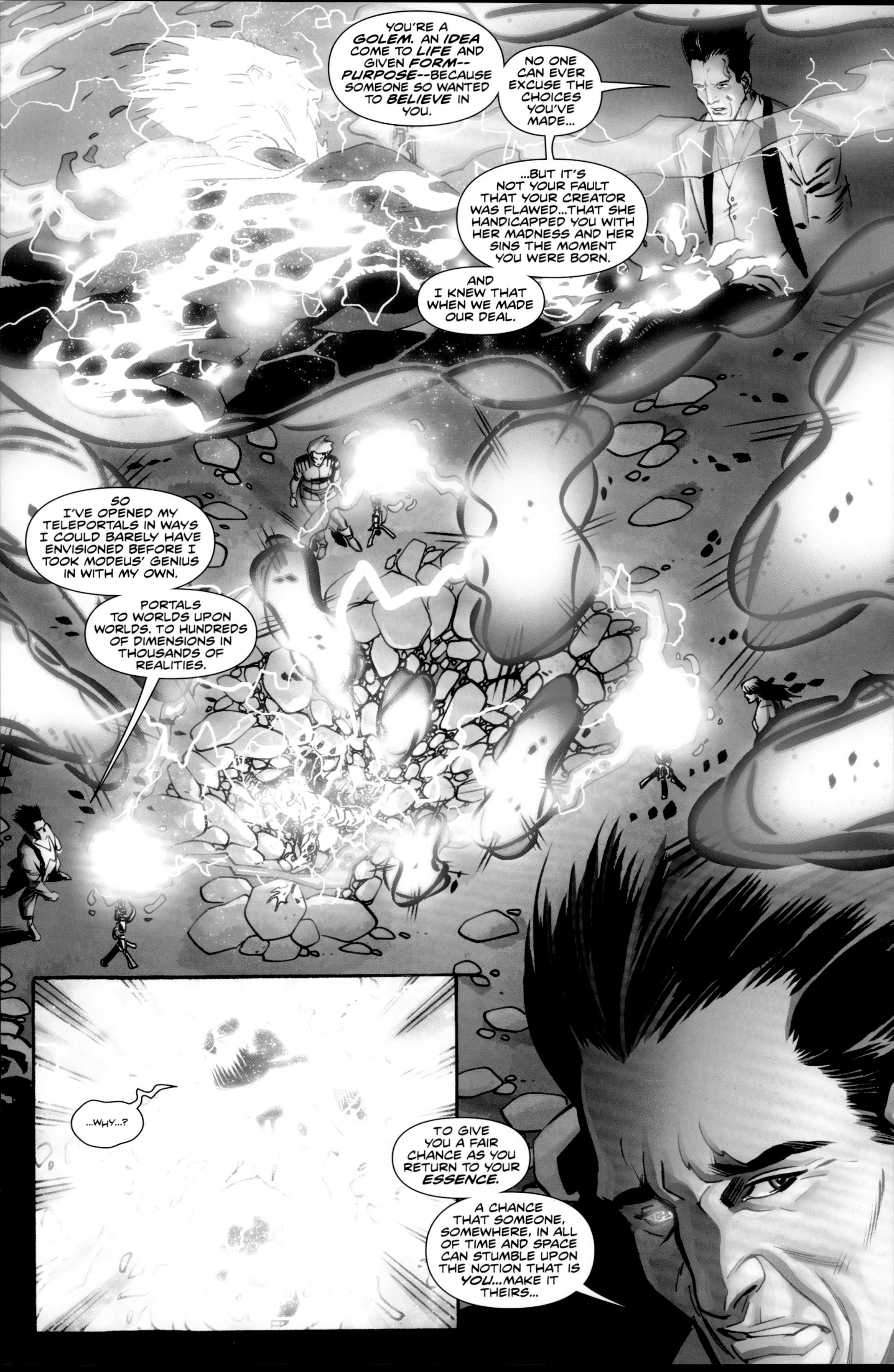
YOU'RE A GOLEM. AN IDEA COME TO LIFE AND GIVEN FORM--PURPOSE--BECAUSE SOMEONE SO WANTED TO BELIEVE IN YOU.
NO ONE CAN EVER EXCUSE THE CHOICES YOU'VE MADE...
...BUT IT'S NOT YOUR FAULT THAT YOUR CREATOR WAS FLAWED...THAT SHE HANDICAPPED YOU WITH HER MADNESS AND HER SINS THE MOMENT YOU WERE BORN.
AND I KNEW THAT WHEN WE MADE OUR DEAL.
SO I'VE OPENED MY TELEPORTALS IN WAYS I COULD BARELY HAVE ENVISIONED BEFORE I TOOK MODEUS' GENIUS IN WITH MY OWN.
PORTALS TO WORLDS UPON WORLDS. TO HUNDREDS OF DIMENSIONS IN THOUSANDS OF REALITIES.
...WHY...?
TO GIVE YOU A FAIR CHANCE AS YOU RETURN TO YOUR ESSENCE.
A CHANCE THAT SOMEONE, SOMEWHERE, IN ALL OF TIME AND SPACE CAN STUMBLE UPON THE NOTION THAT IS YOU...MAKE IT THEIRS...

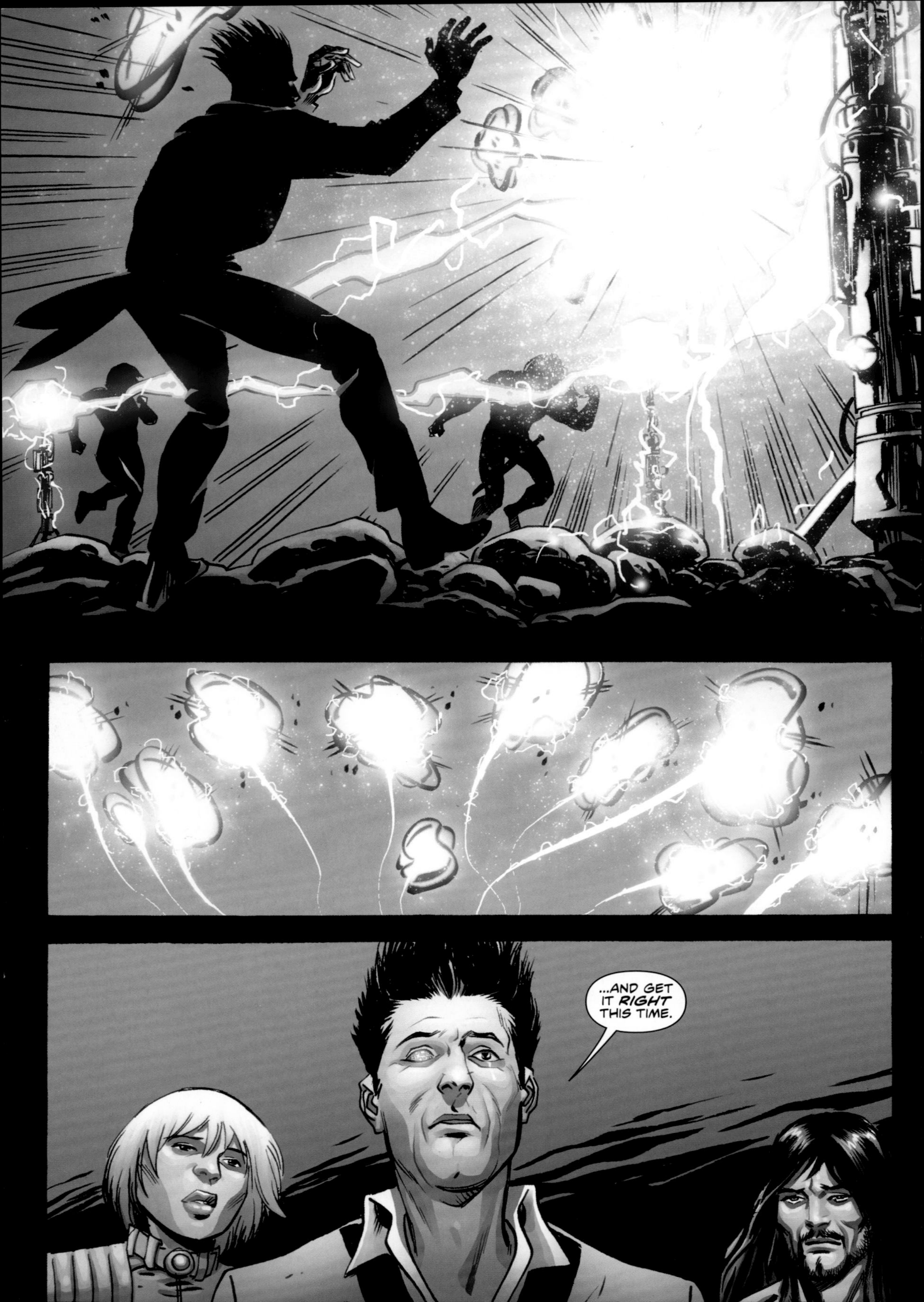
...AND GET IT RIGHT THIS TIME.

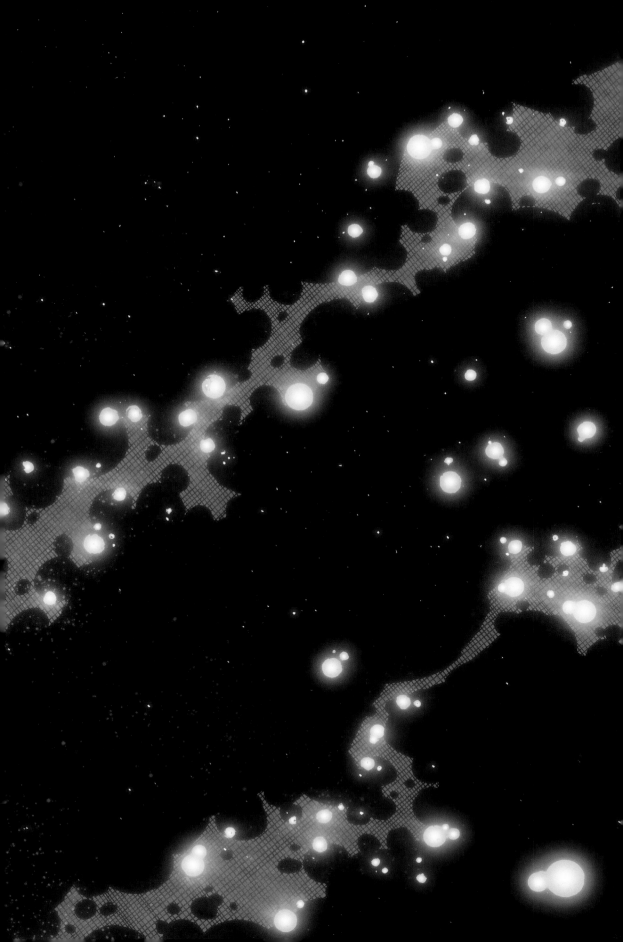

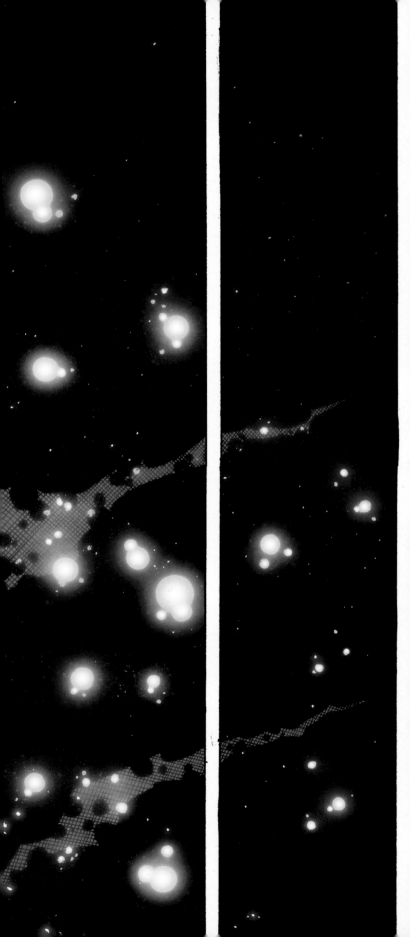

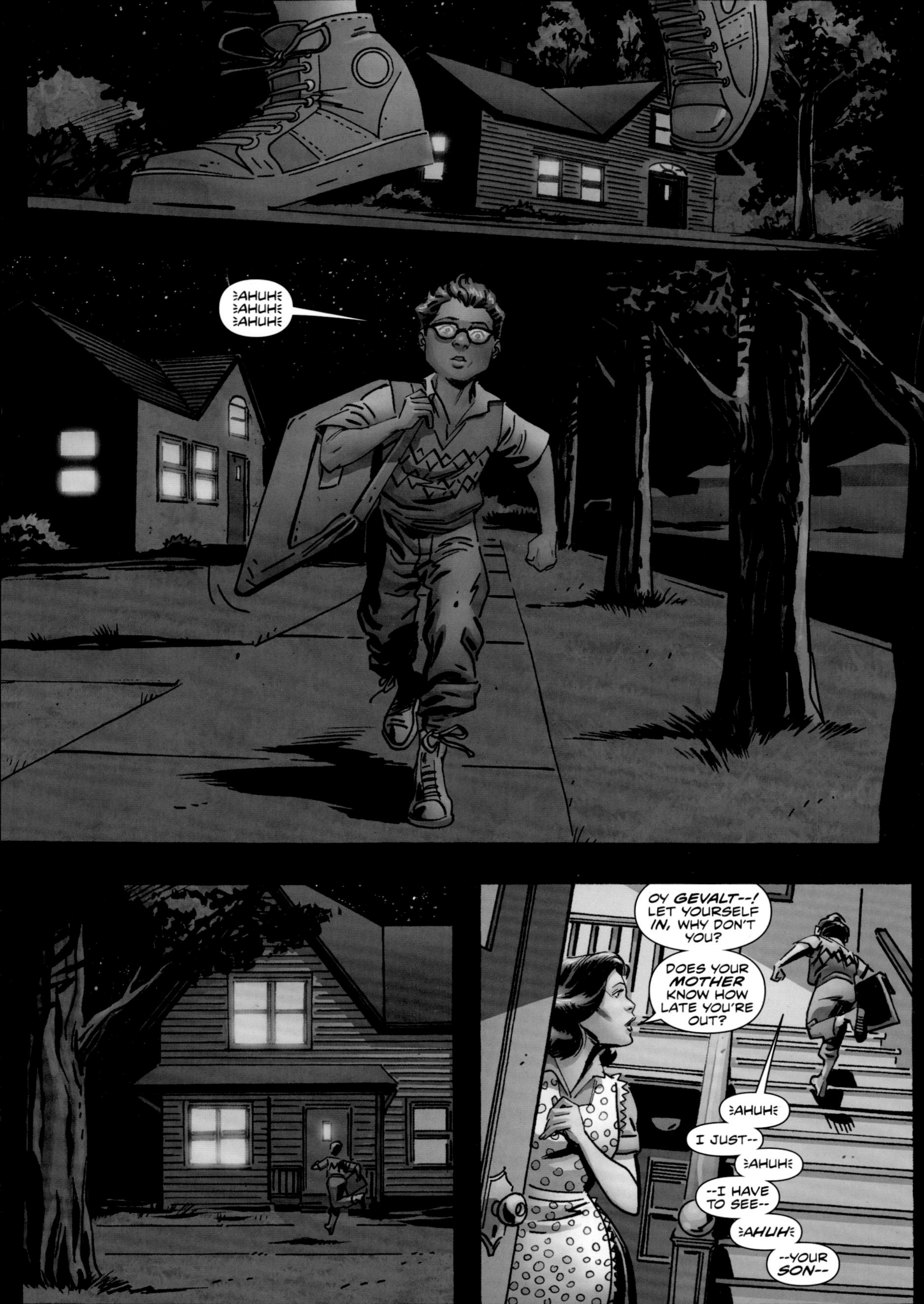
AHUH AHUH AHUH
OY GEVALT--! LET YOURSELF IN, WHY DON'T YOU?
DOES YOUR MOTHER KNOW HOW LATE YOU'RE OUT?
AHUH
I JUST--
AHUH
--I HAVE TO SEE--
AHUH
--YOUR SON--

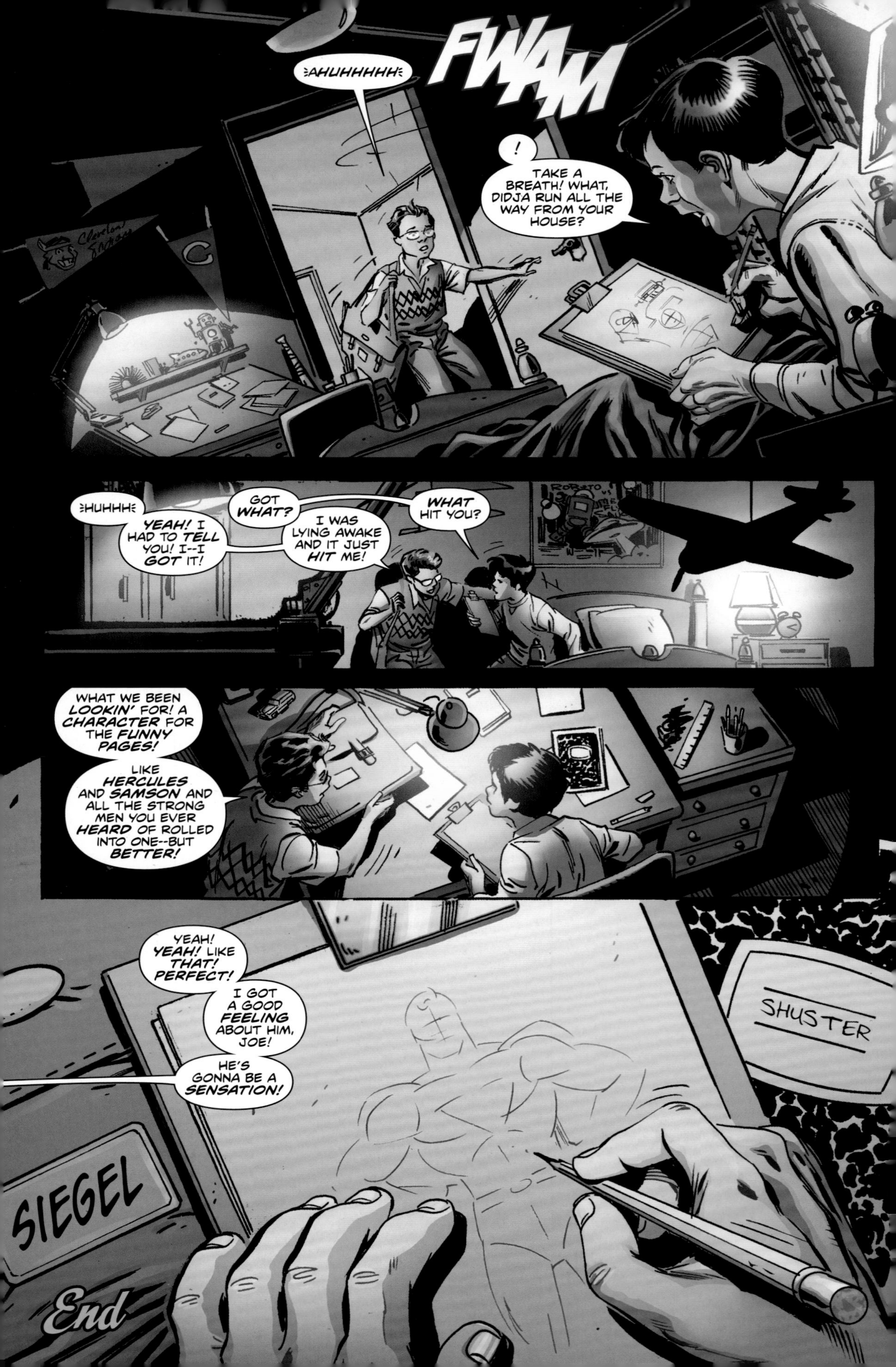
FWAM
AHUHHHHH
!
TAKE A BREATH! WHAT, DIDJA RUN ALL THE WAY FROM YOUR HOUSE?
HUHHH
YEAH! I HAD TO TELL YOU! I--I GOT IT!
GOT WHAT?
I WAS LYING AWAKE AND IT JUST HIT ME!
WHAT HIT YOU?
WHAT WE BEEN LOOKIN' FOR! A CHARACTER FOR THE FUNNY PAGES!
LIKE HERCULES AND SAMSON AND ALL THE STRONG MEN YOU EVER HEARD OF ROLLED INTO ONE--BUT BETTER!
YEAH! YEAH! LIKE THAT! PERFECT!
I GOT A GOOD FEELING ABOUT HIM, JOE!
HE'S GONNA BE A SENSATION!
SHUSTER
SIEGEL
End

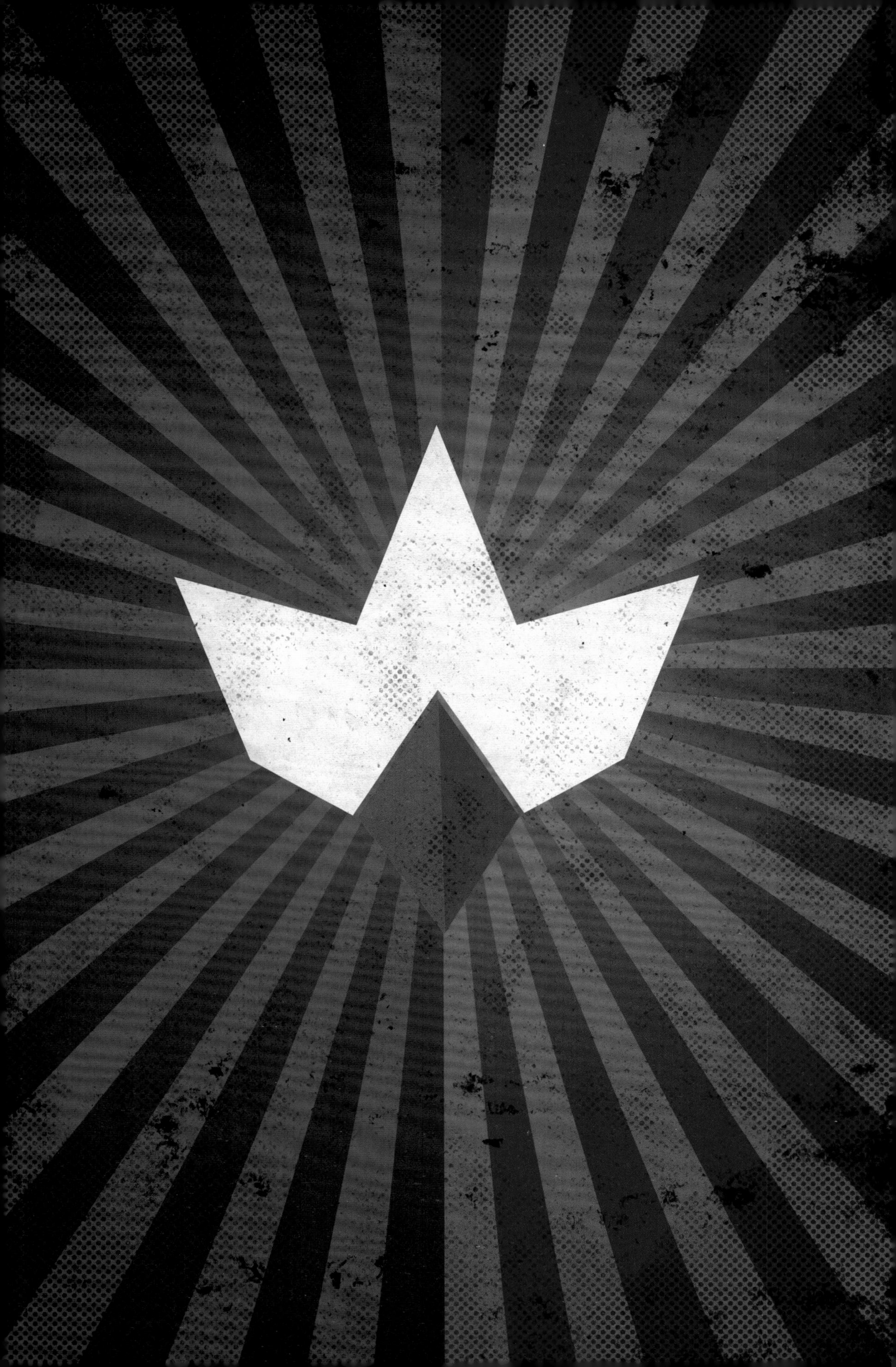

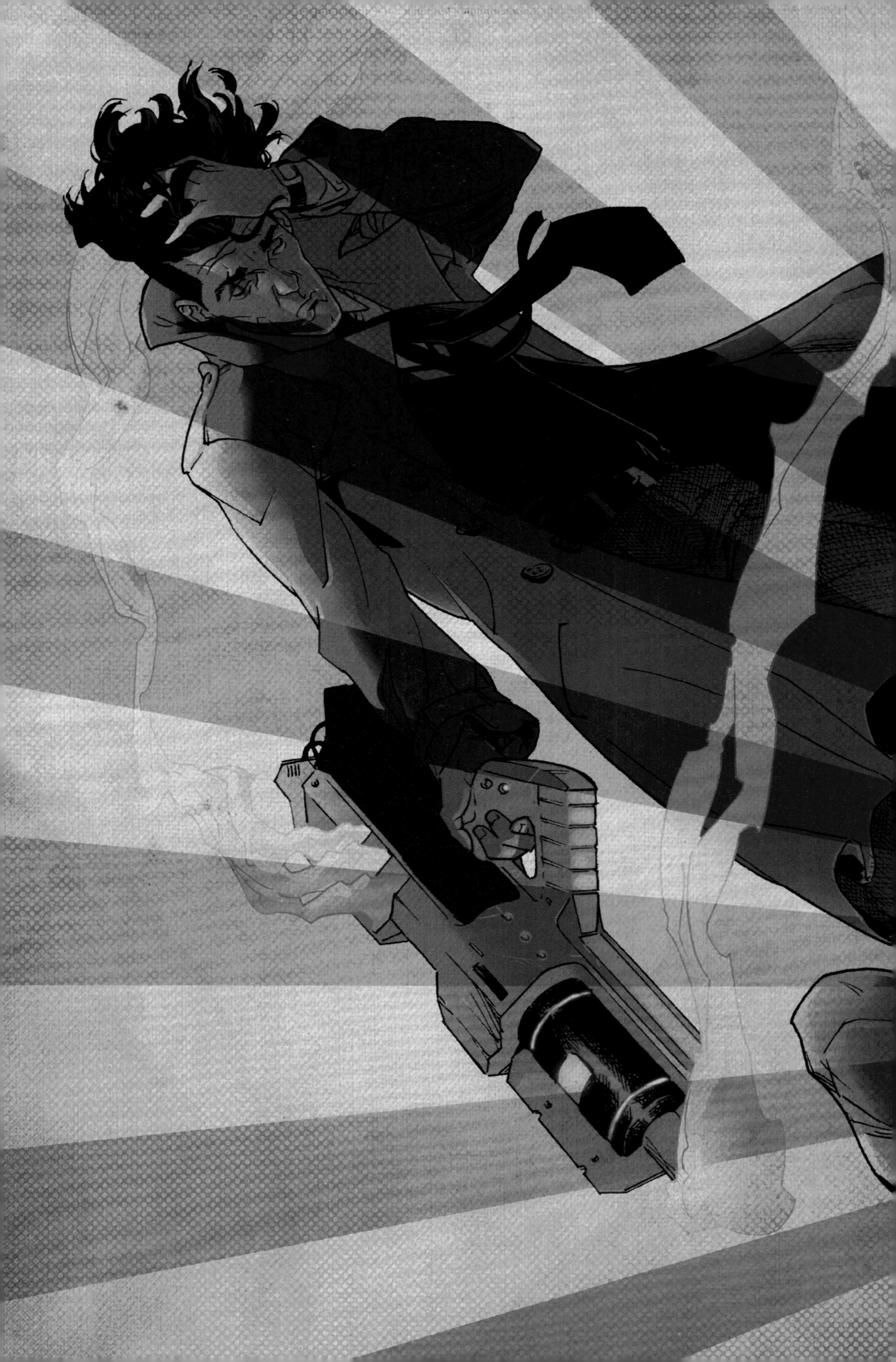

COVER GALLERY

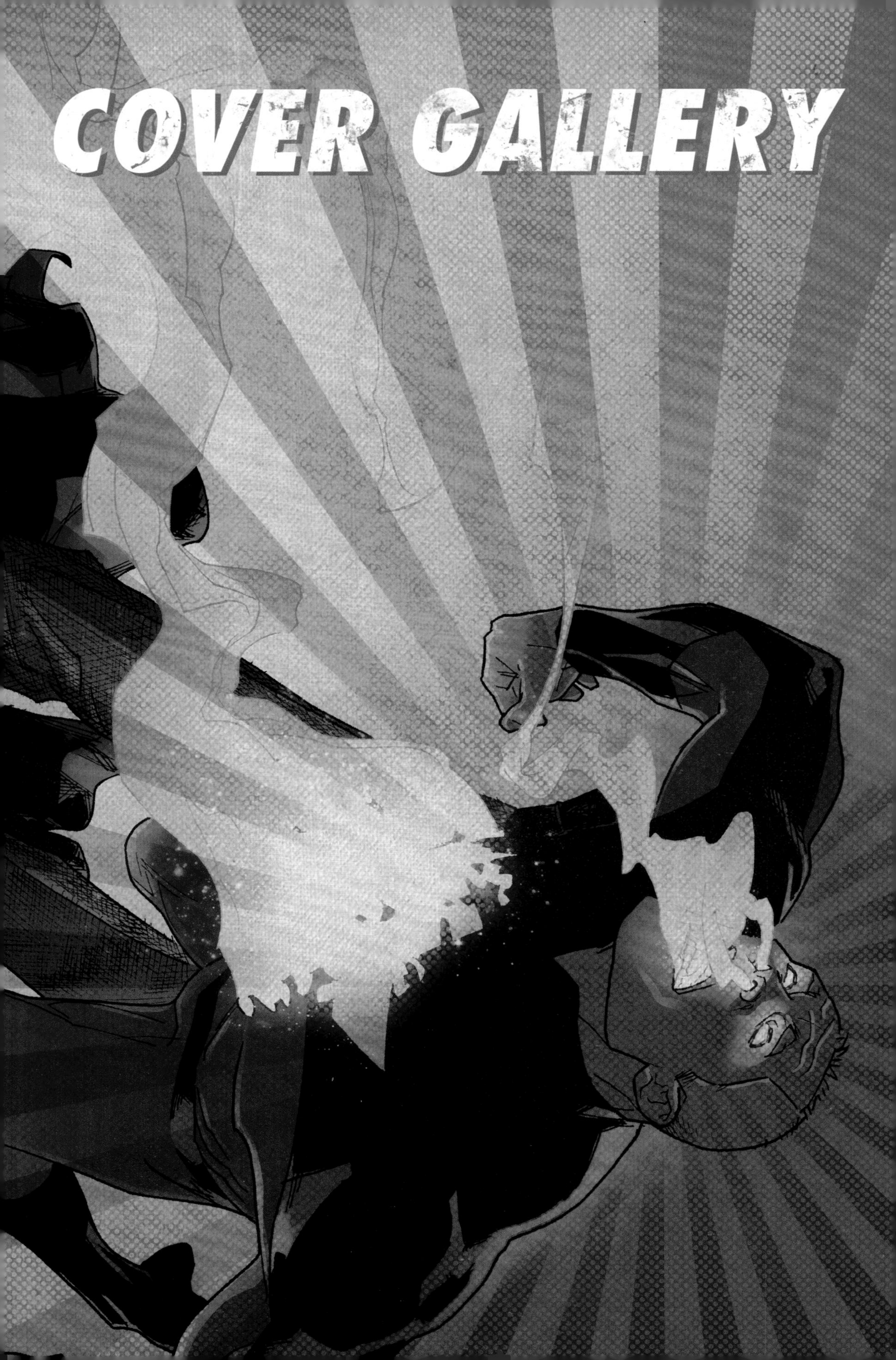

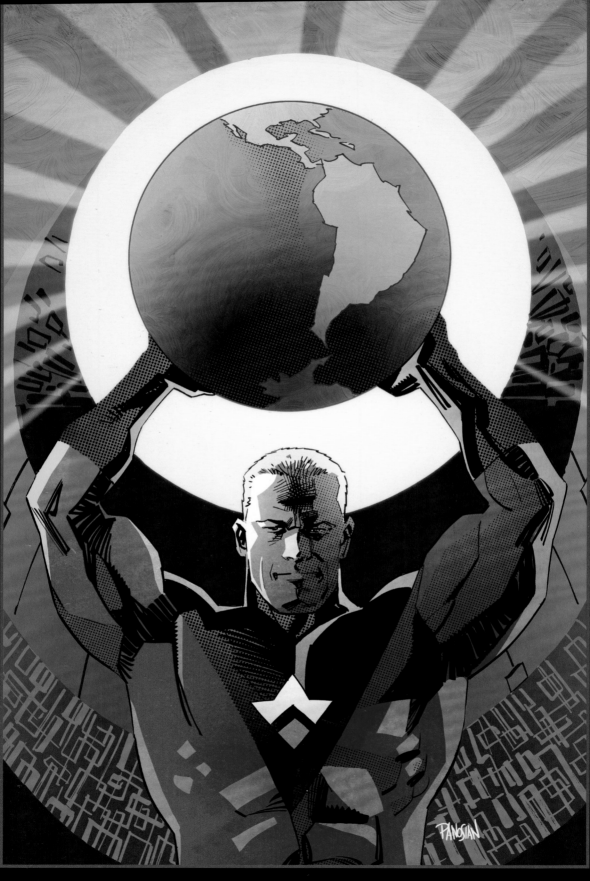

IRREDEEMABLE 34A: DAN PANOSIAN

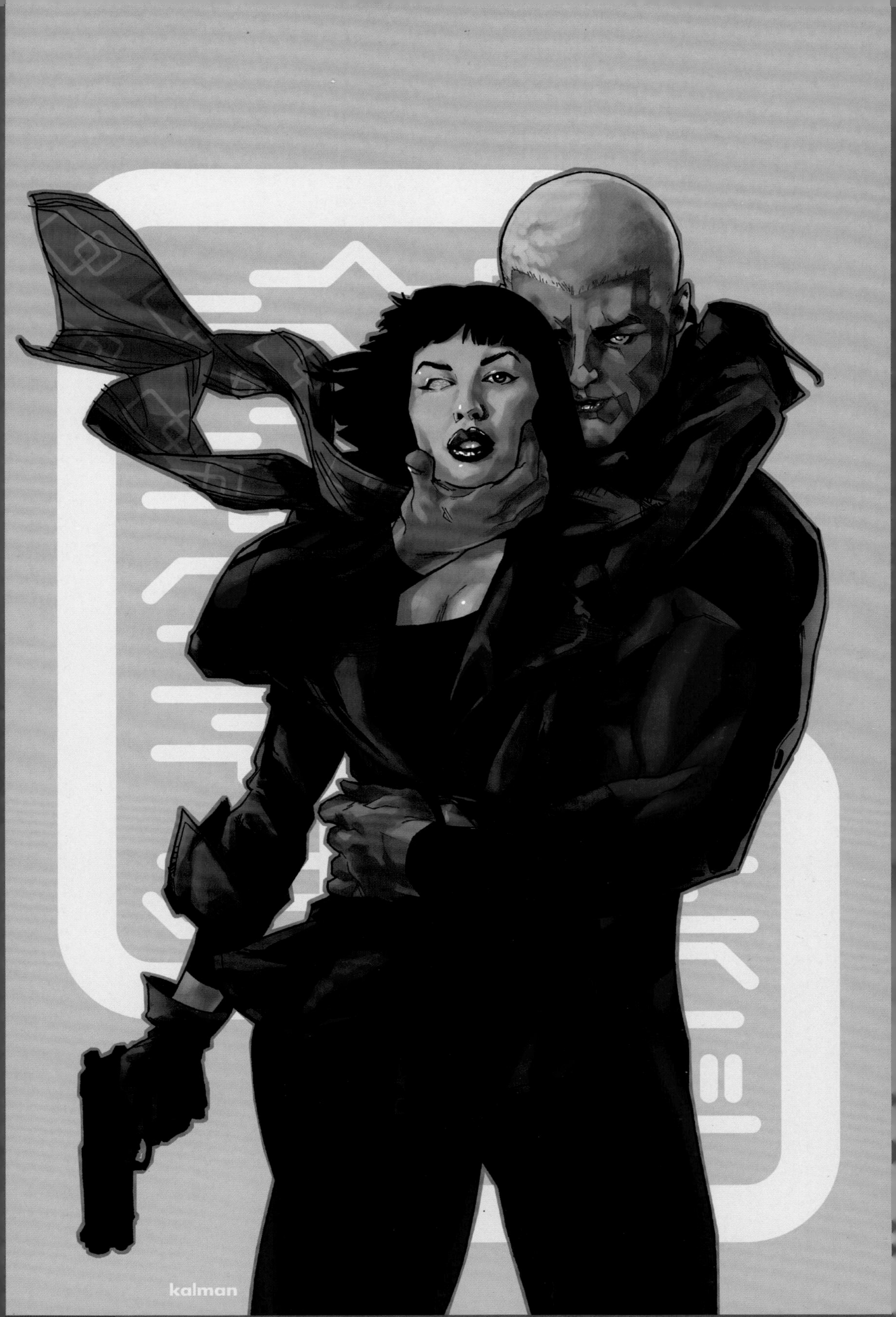
kalman

IAN ANDR

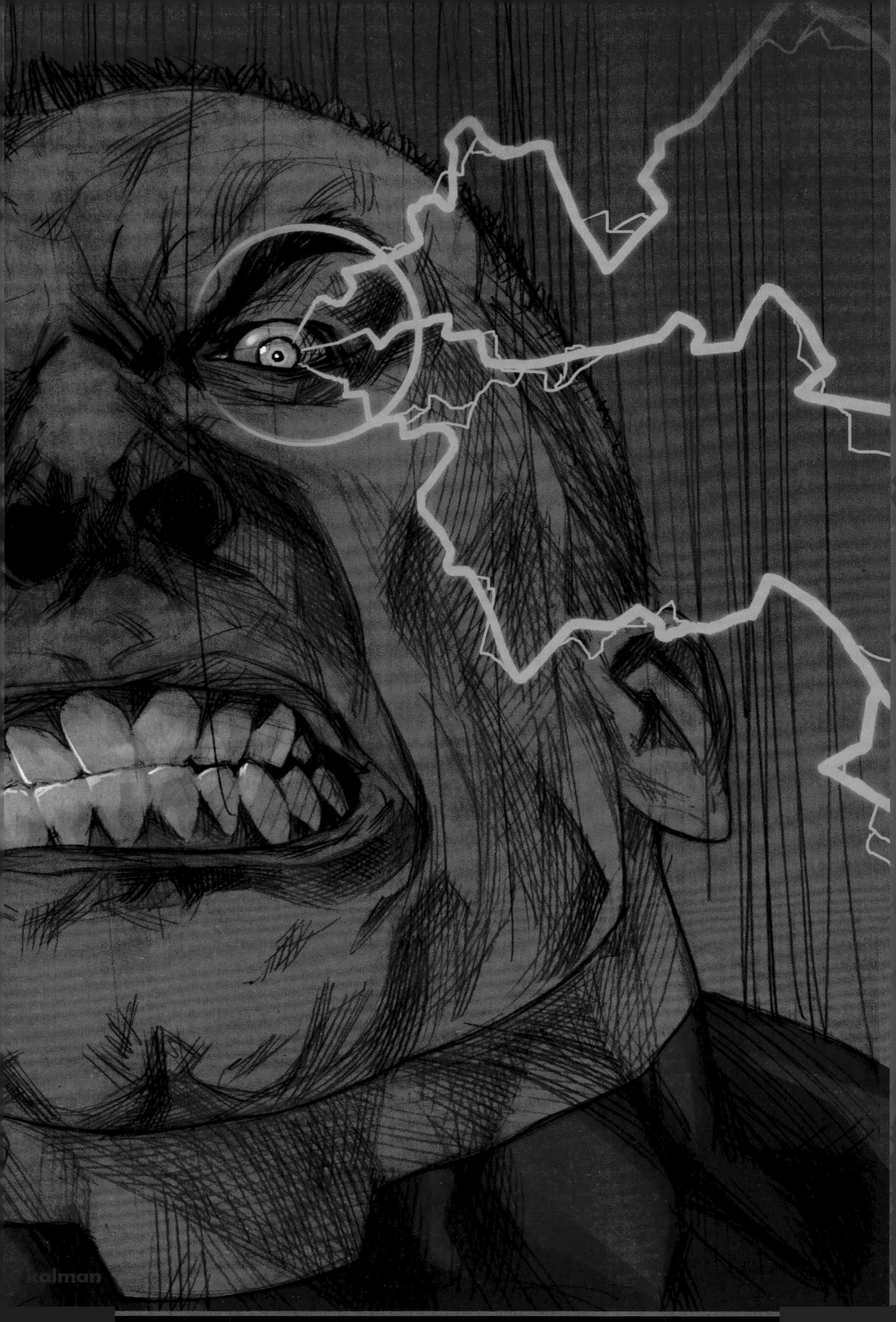
kalman

ABLE 35A:

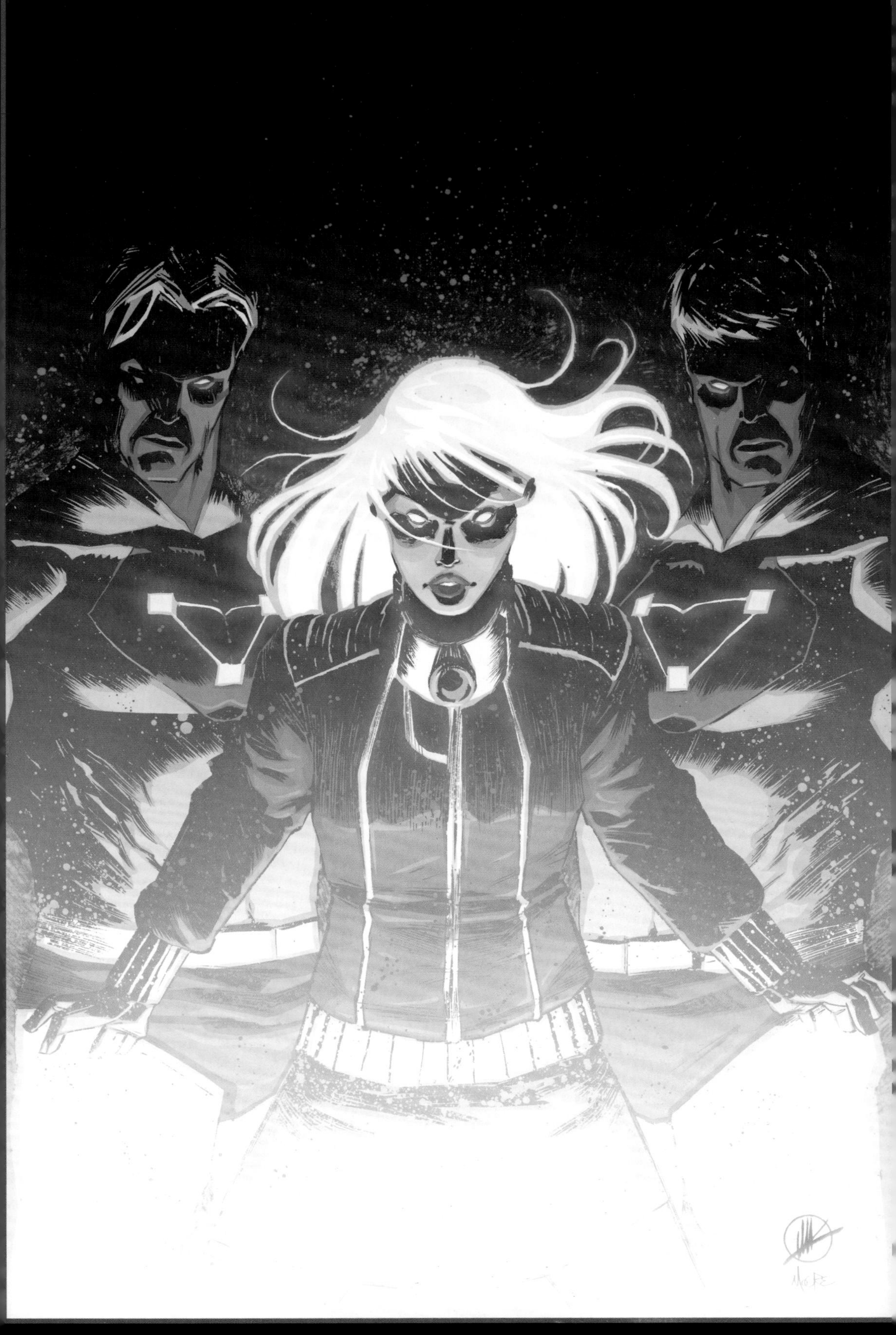

IRREDEEMABLE 35B: MATTEO SCALERA
COLORS: DARRIN MOOR

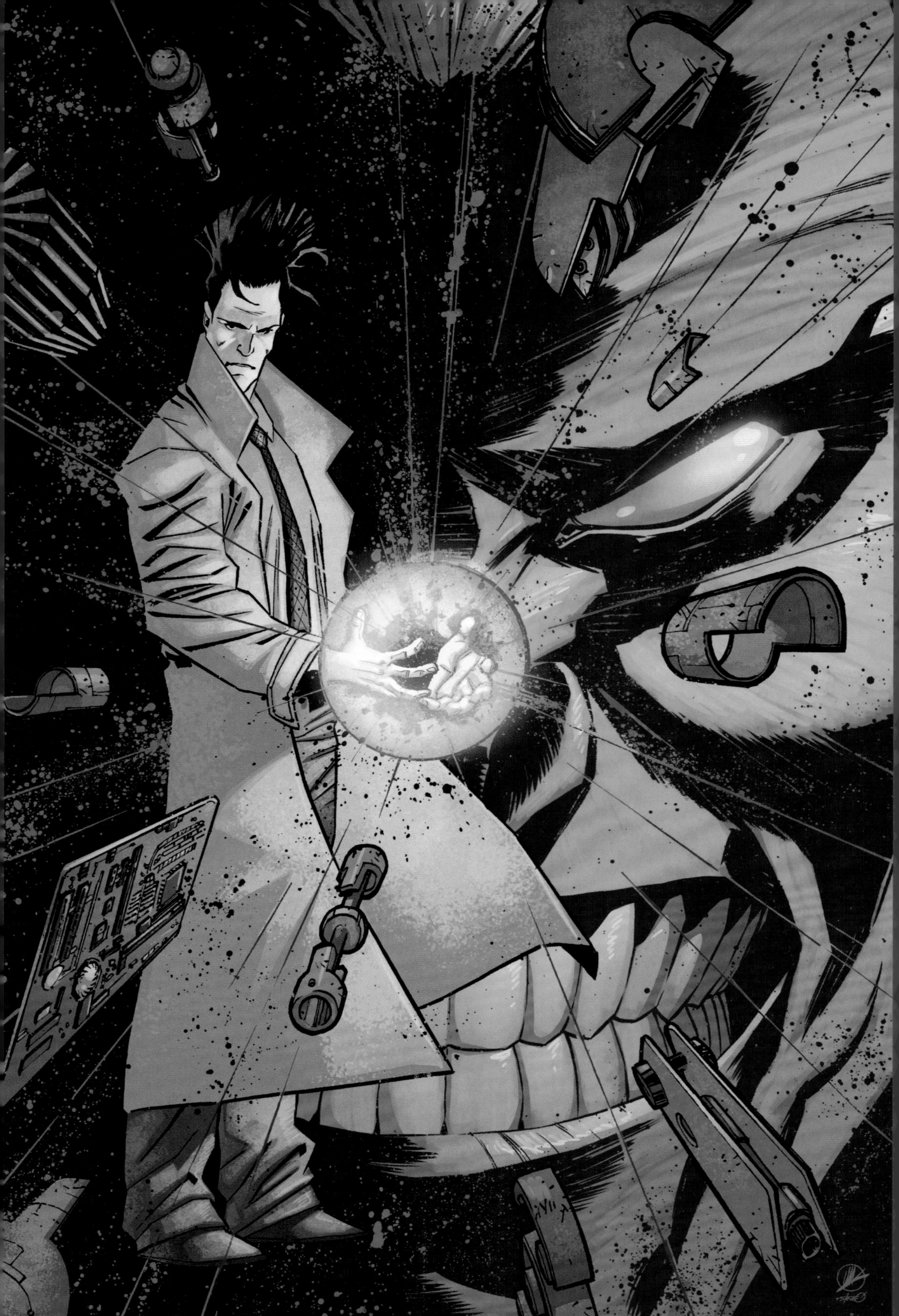

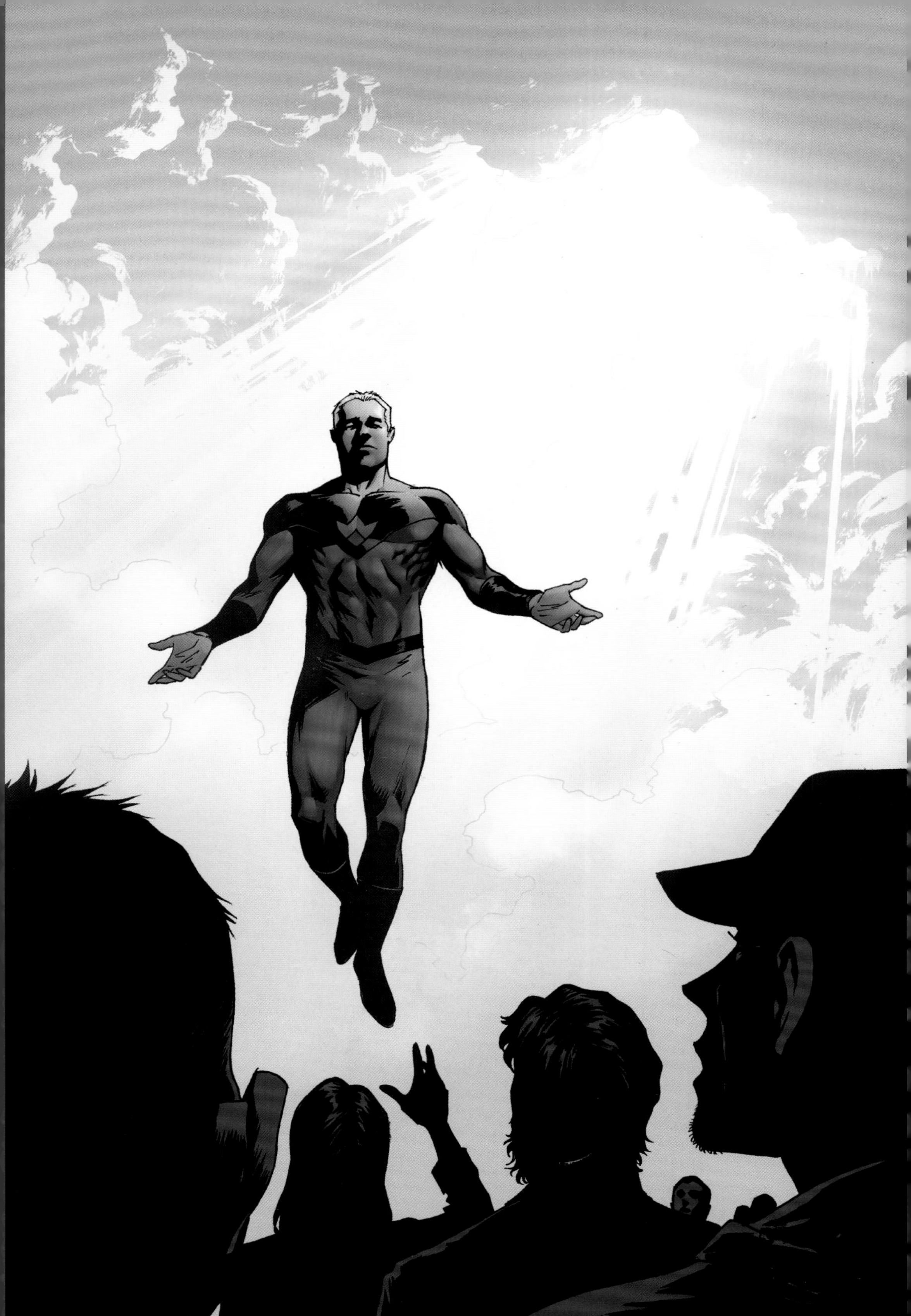

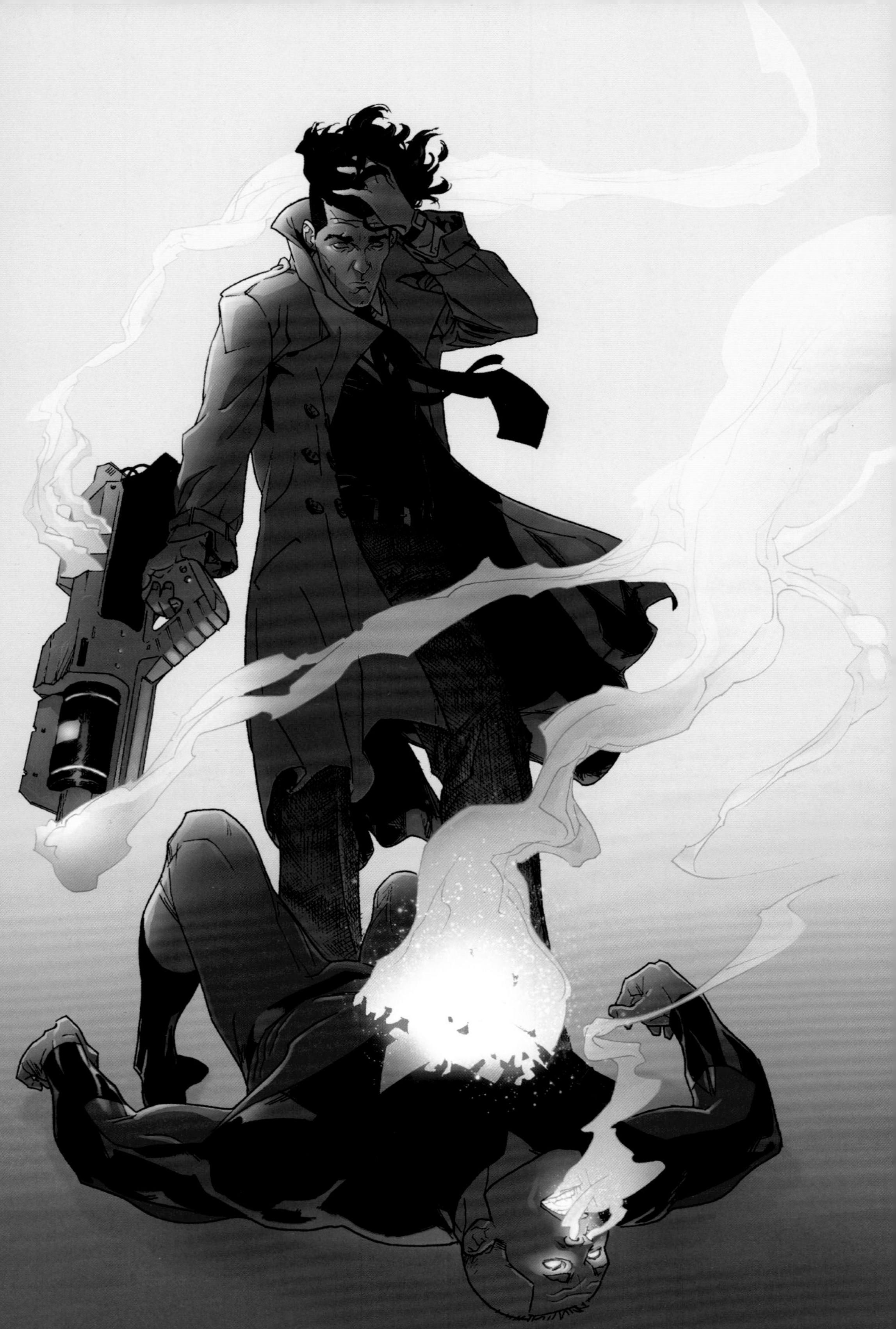

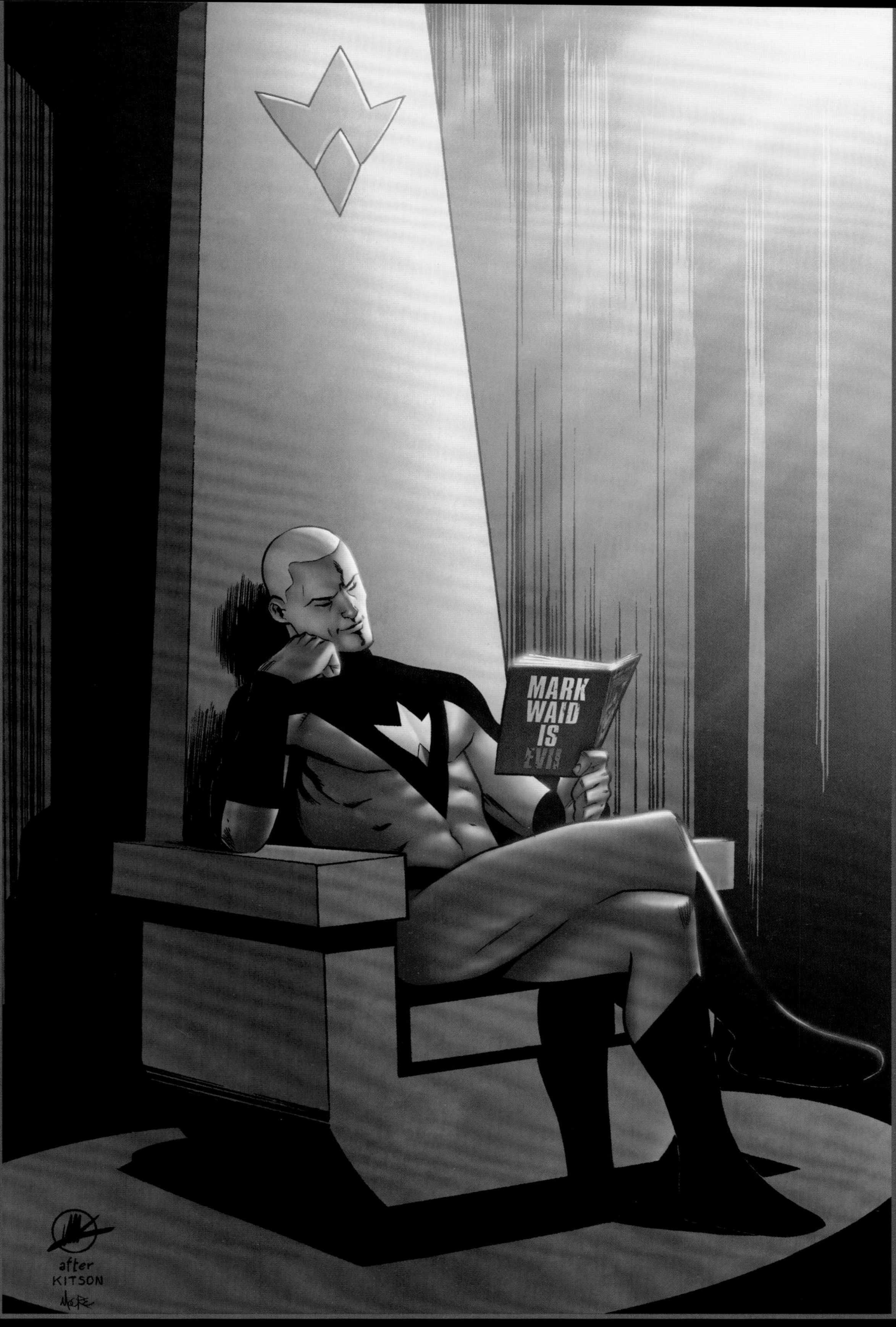
MARK
WAID
IS
EVIL
after
KITSON
MOORE

IRREDEEMABLE 37B: MATTEO SCALERA
COLORS: DARRIN MOORE

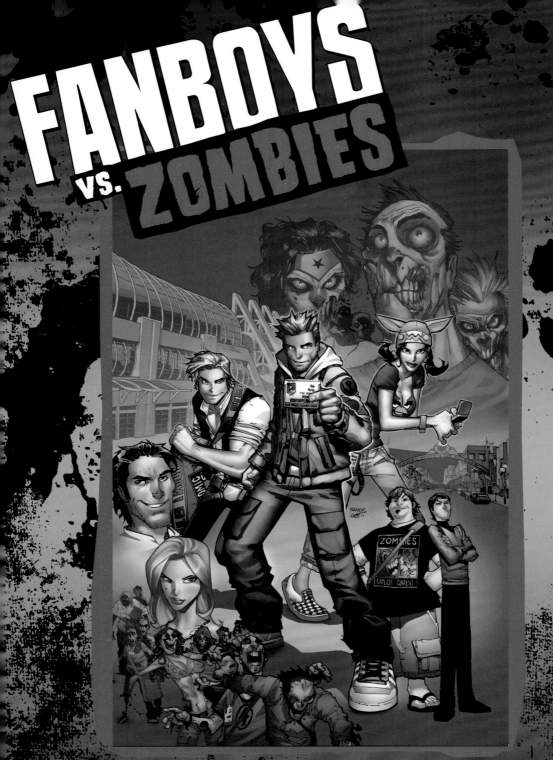

FANBOYS vs. ZOMBIES

SAM HUMPHRIES   JERRY GAYLORD

VOLUME 1
IN STORES JANUARY!

SPECIAL SIXTEEN
PAGE PREVIEW

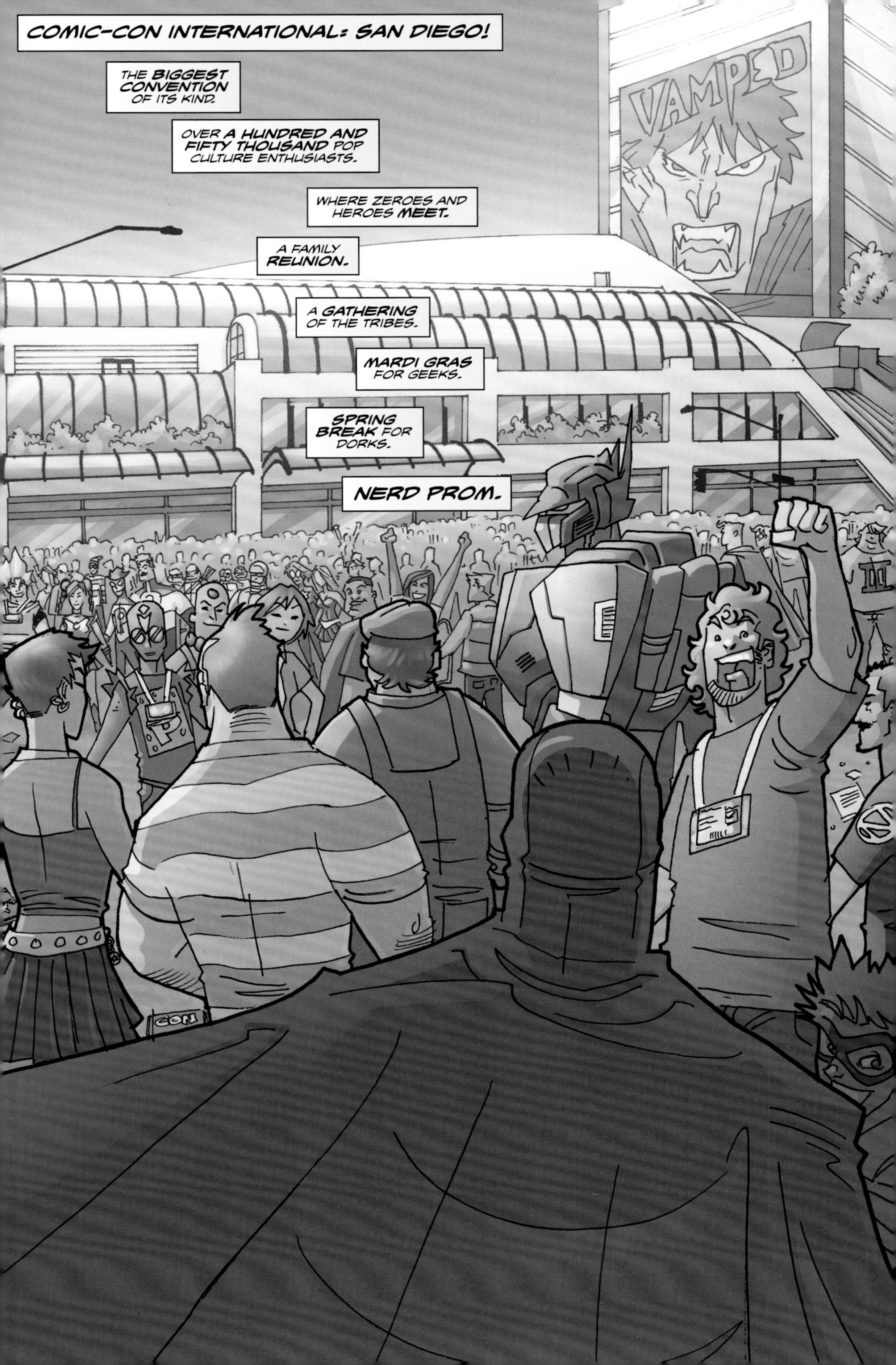
COMIC-CON INTERNATIONAL: SAN DIEGO!
THE BIGGEST CONVENTION OF ITS KIND.
OVER A HUNDRED AND FIFTY THOUSAND POP CULTURE ENTHUSIASTS.
WHERE ZEROES AND HEROES MEET.
A FAMILY REUNION.
A GATHERING OF THE TRIBES.
MARDI GRAS FOR GEEKS.
SPRING BREAK FOR DORKS.
NERD PROM.
VAMPED
CON

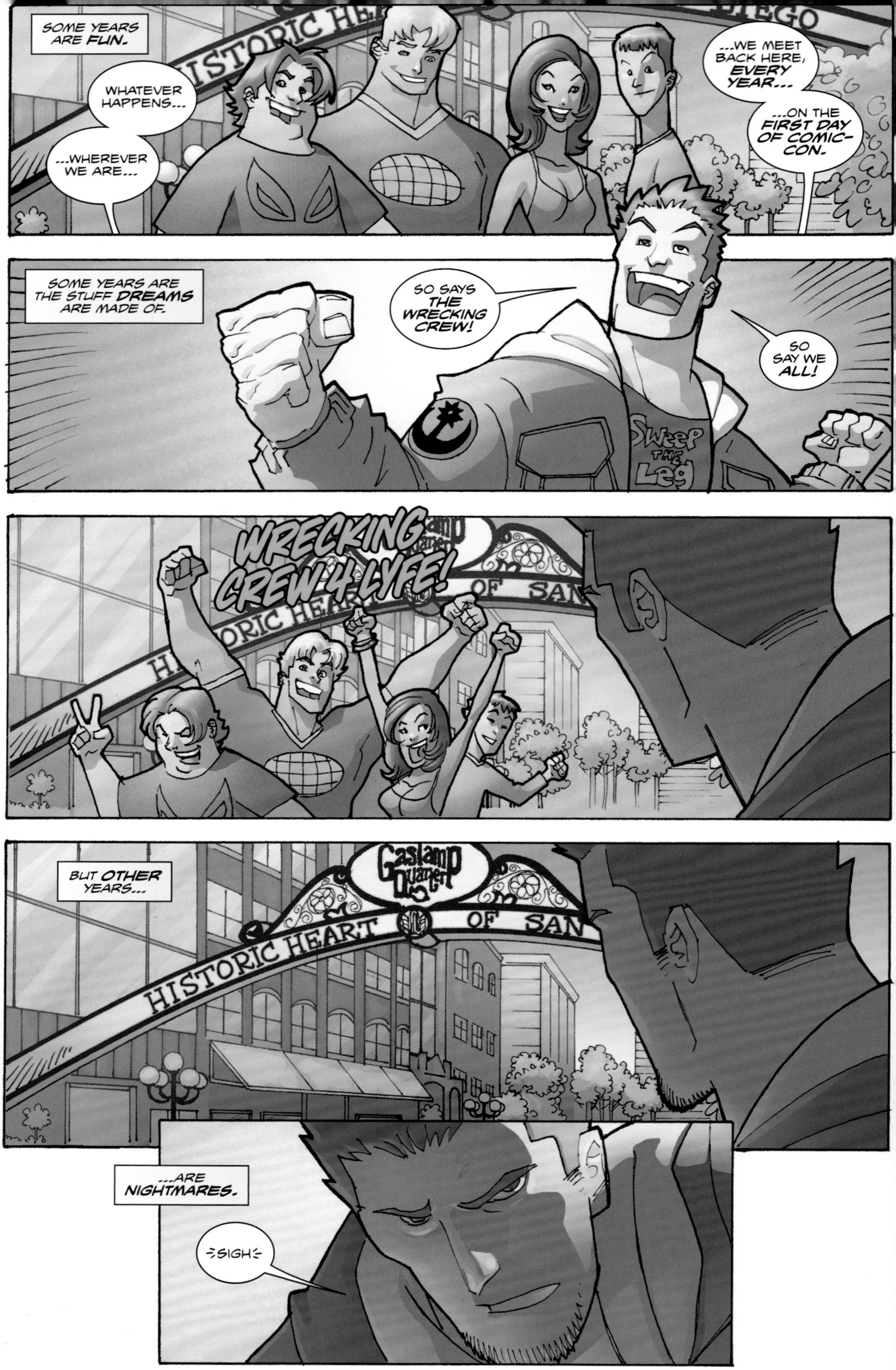
SOME YEARS ARE FUN.
WHATEVER HAPPENS...
...WHEREVER WE ARE...
...WE MEET BACK HERE, EVERY YEAR...
...ON THE FIRST DAY OF COMIC-CON.
SOME YEARS ARE THE STUFF DREAMS ARE MADE OF.
SO SAYS THE WRECKING CREW!
SO SAY WE ALL!
SWEEP THE LEG
WRECKING CREW 4 LYFE!
BUT OTHER YEARS...
HISTORIC HEART OF SAN
...ARE NIGHTMARES.
SIGH

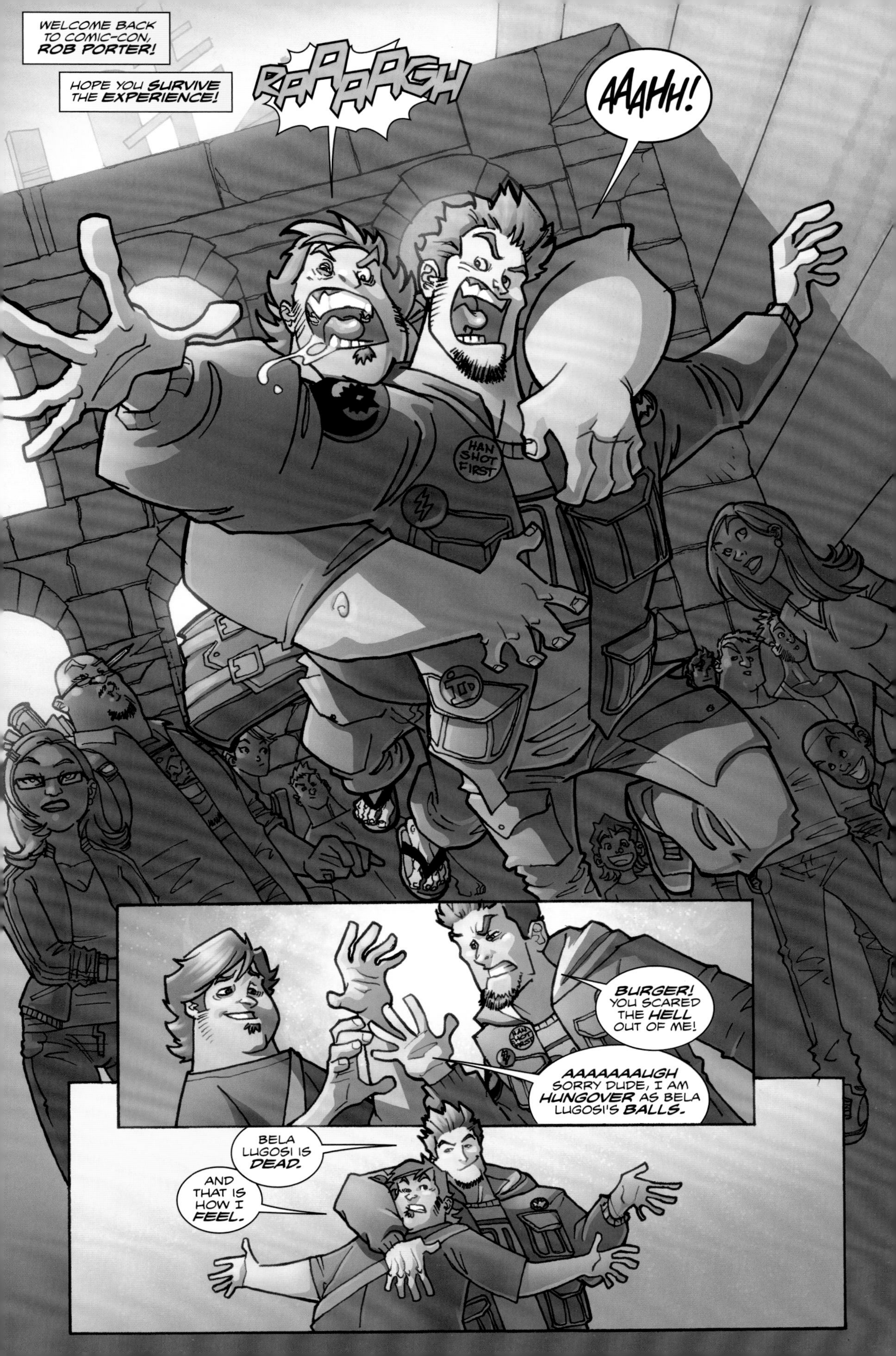
WELCOME BACK TO COMIC-CON, ROB PORTER!
HOPE YOU SURVIVE THE EXPERIENCE!
RAAAARGH
AAAHH!
HAN SHOT FIRST
BURGER! YOU SCARED THE HELL OUT OF ME!
AAAAAAAUGH SORRY DUDE, I AM HUNGOVER AS BELA LUGOSI'S BALLS.
BELA LUGOSI IS DEAD.
AND THAT IS HOW I FEEL.

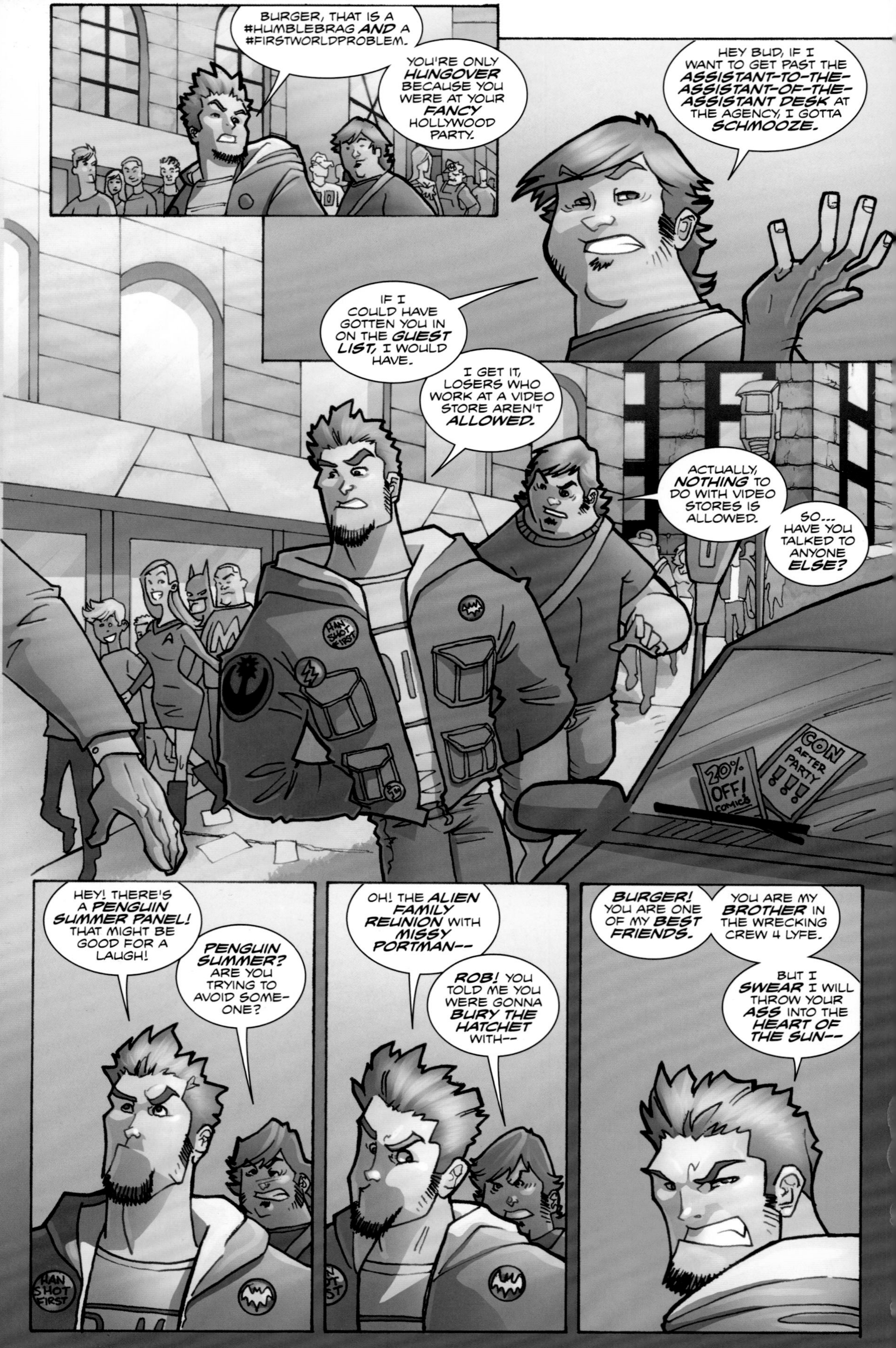
BURGER, THAT IS A #HUMBLEBRAG AND A #FIRSTWORLDPROBLEM.
YOU'RE ONLY HUNGOVER BECAUSE YOU WERE AT YOUR FANCY HOLLYWOOD PARTY.
HEY BUD, IF I WANT TO GET PAST THE ASSISTANT-TO-THE-ASSISTANT-OF-THE-ASSISTANT DESK AT THE AGENCY, I GOTTA SCHMOOZE.
IF I COULD HAVE GOTTEN YOU IN ON THE GUEST LIST, I WOULD HAVE.
I GET IT, LOSERS WHO WORK AT A VIDEO STORE AREN'T ALLOWED.
ACTUALLY, NOTHING TO DO WITH VIDEO STORES IS ALLOWED.
SO... HAVE YOU TALKED TO ANYONE ELSE?
HAN SHOT FIRST
20% OFF! COMICS
CON AFTER PARTY !!!
HEY! THERE'S A PENGUIN SUMMER PANEL! THAT MIGHT BE GOOD FOR A LAUGH!
PENGUIN SUMMER? ARE YOU TRYING TO AVOID SOME-ONE?
HAN SHOT FIRST
OH! THE ALIEN FAMILY REUNION WITH MISSY PORTMAN--
ROB! YOU TOLD ME YOU WERE GONNA BURY THE HATCHET WITH--
BURGER! YOU ARE ONE OF MY BEST FRIENDS.
YOU ARE MY BROTHER IN THE WRECKING CREW 4 LYFE.
BUT I SWEAR I WILL THROW YOUR ASS INTO THE HEART OF THE SUN--

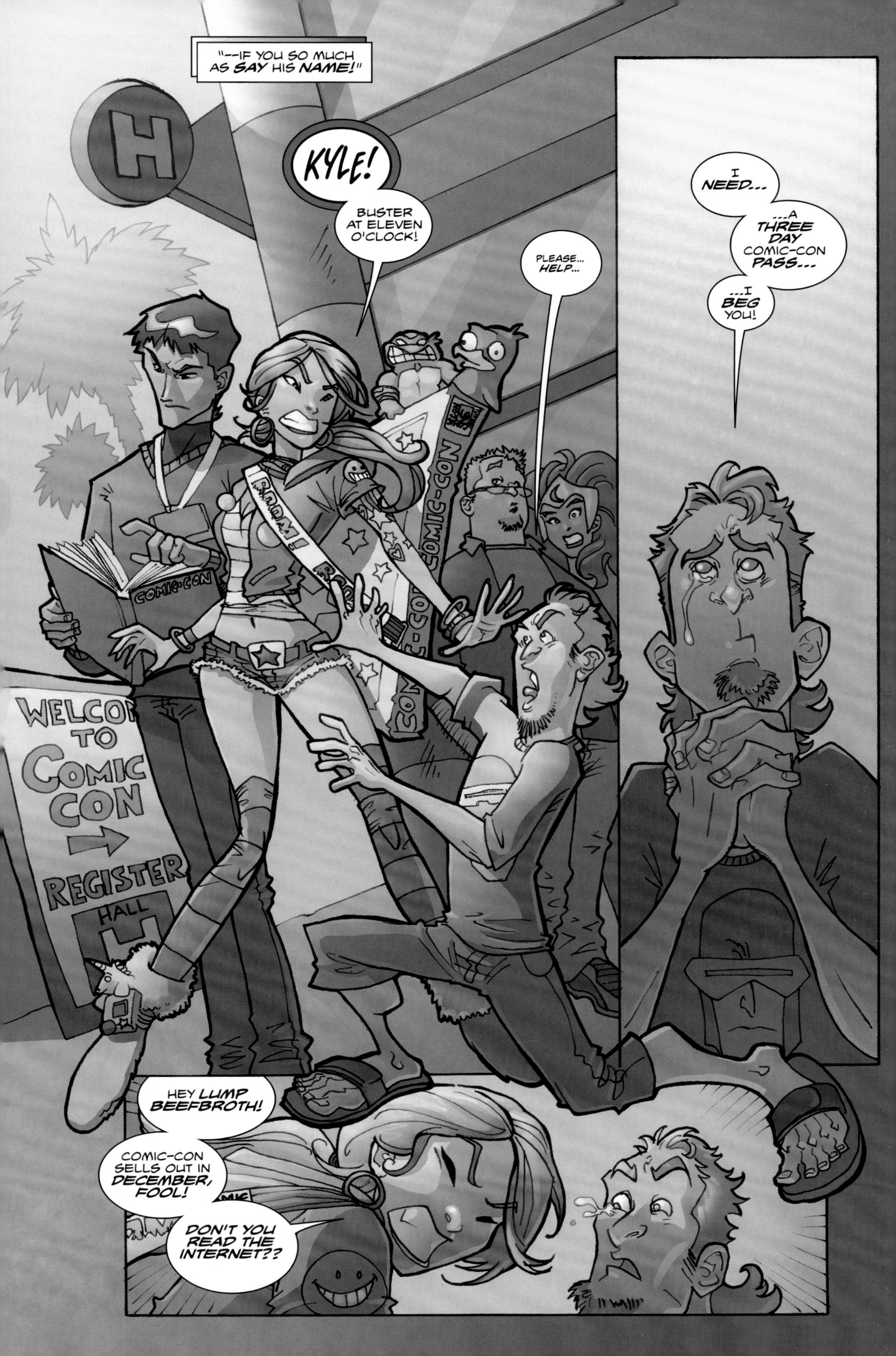
"--IF YOU SO MUCH AS SAY HIS NAME!"
H
KYLE!
BUSTER AT ELEVEN O'CLOCK!
PLEASE... HELP...
I NEED...
...A THREE DAY COMIC-CON PASS...
...I BEG YOU!
COMIC-CON
WELCO TO COMIC CON
REGISTER
HALL H
HEY LUMP BEEFBROTH!
COMIC-CON SELLS OUT IN DECEMBER, FOOL!
DON'T YOU READ THE INTERNET??

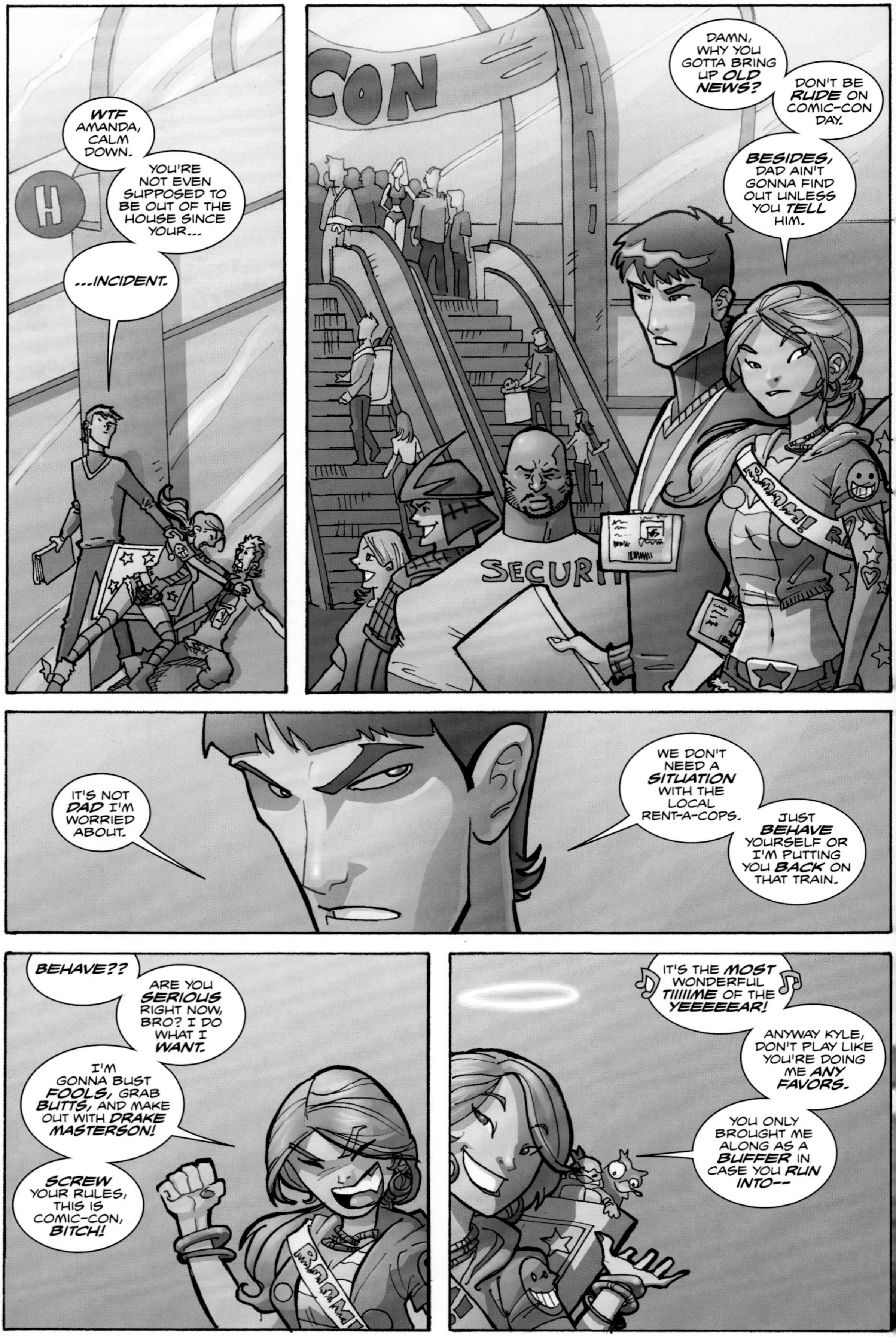
CON
WTF AMANDA, CALM DOWN.
YOU'RE NOT EVEN SUPPOSED TO BE OUT OF THE HOUSE SINCE YOUR...
...INCIDENT.
DAMN, WHY YOU GOTTA BRING UP OLD NEWS?
DON'T BE RUDE ON COMIC-CON DAY.
BESIDES, DAD AIN'T GONNA FIND OUT UNLESS YOU TELL HIM.
IT'S NOT DAD I'M WORRIED ABOUT.
WE DON'T NEED A SITUATION WITH THE LOCAL RENT-A-COPS.
JUST BEHAVE YOURSELF OR I'M PUTTING YOU BACK ON THAT TRAIN.
BEHAVE??
ARE YOU SERIOUS RIGHT NOW, BRO? I DO WHAT I WANT.
I'M GONNA BUST FOOLS, GRAB BUTTS, AND MAKE OUT WITH DRAKE MASTERSON!
SCREW YOUR RULES, THIS IS COMIC-CON, BITCH!
IT'S THE MOST WONDERFUL TIIIIIME OF THE YEEEEEAR!
ANYWAY KYLE, DON'T PLAY LIKE YOU'RE DOING ME ANY FAVORS.
YOU ONLY BROUGHT ME ALONG AS A BUFFER IN CASE YOU RUN INTO--

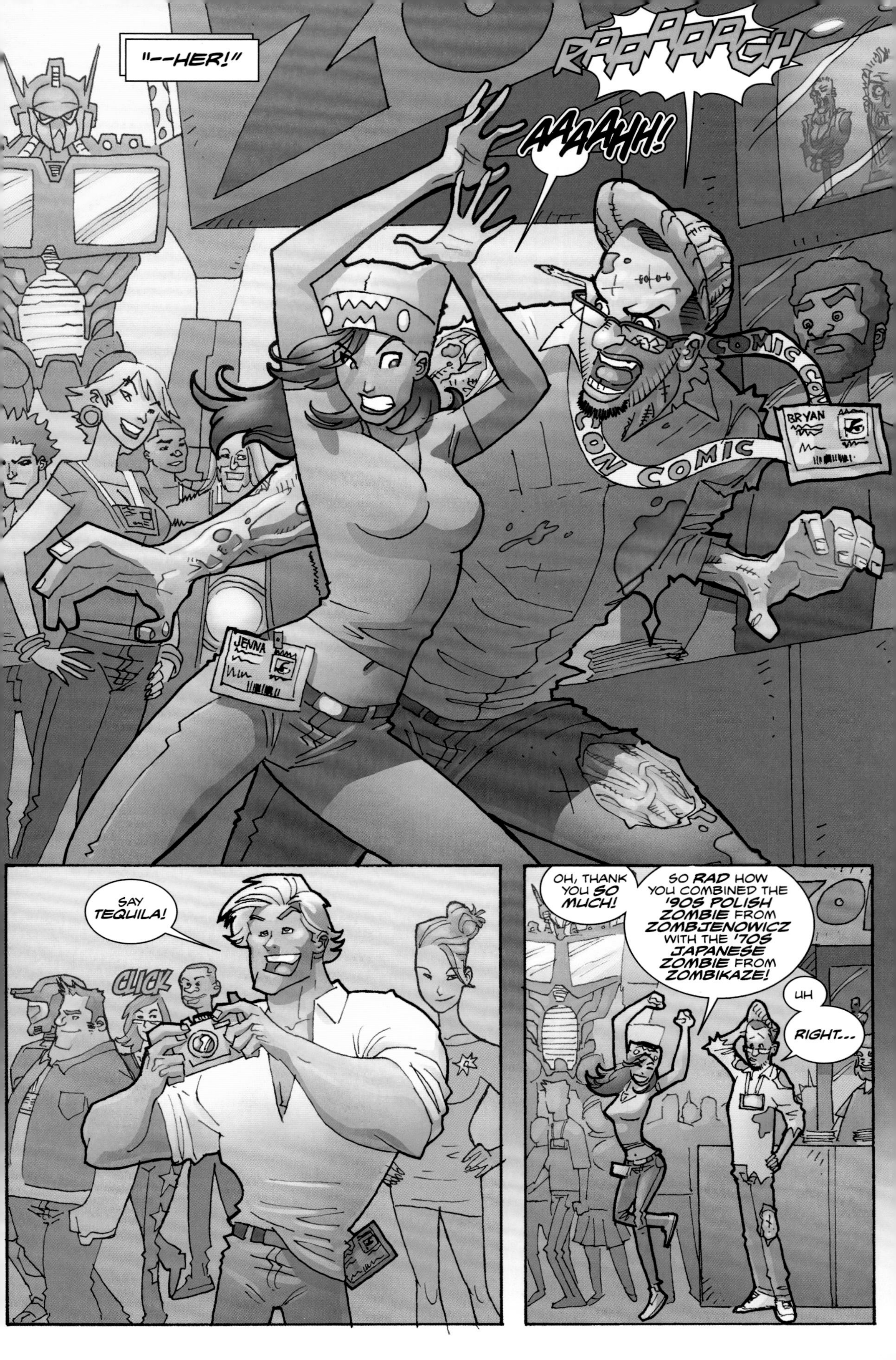
"--HER!"
RAAAAARGH
AAAAHH!
COMIC CON
BRYAN
JENNA
SAY TEQUILA!
CLICK
OH, THANK YOU SO MUCH!
SO RAD HOW YOU COMBINED THE '90S POLISH ZOMBIE FROM ZOMBJENOWICZ WITH THE '70S JAPANESE ZOMBIE FROM ZOMBIKAZE!
UH
RIGHT...

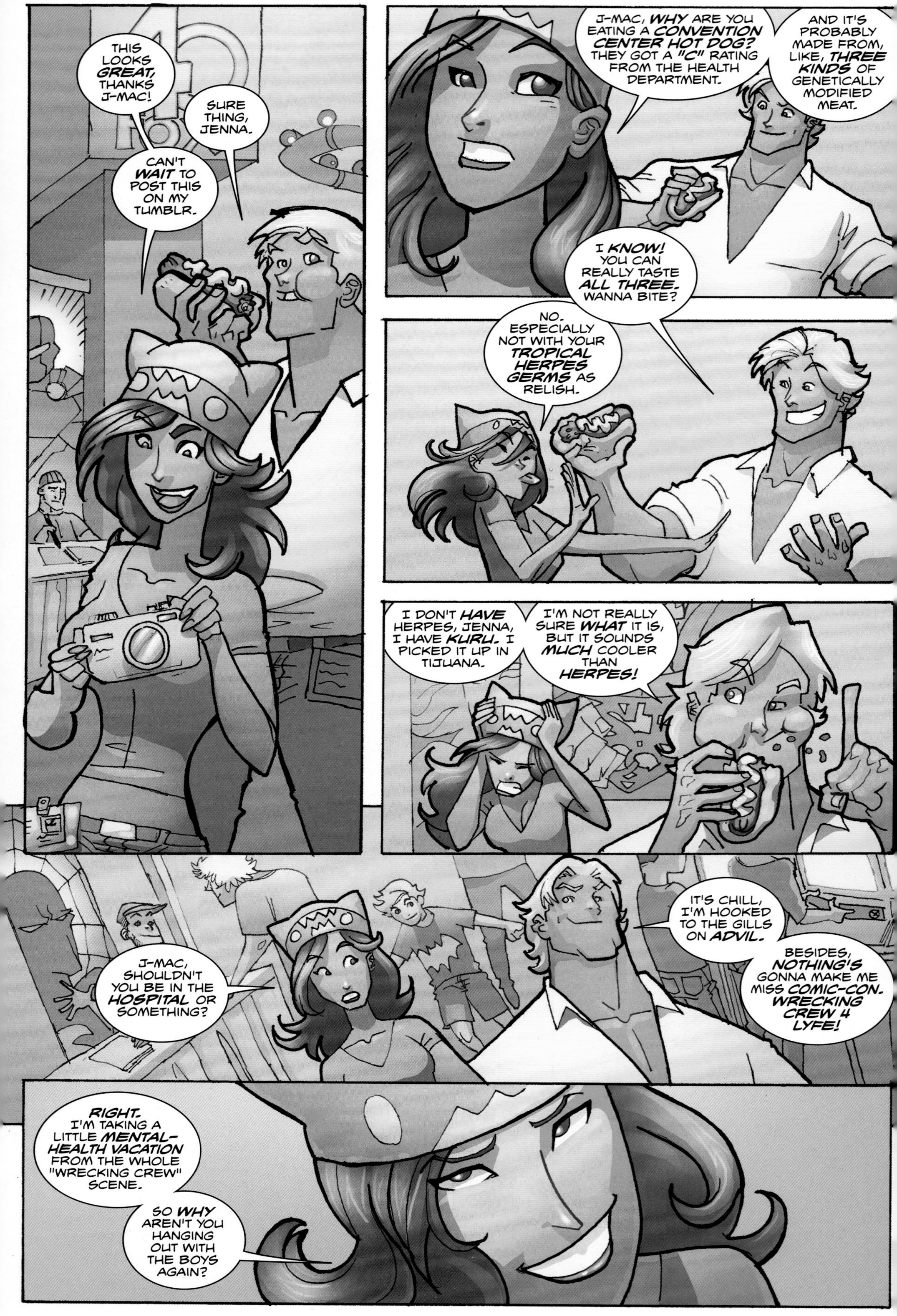
THIS LOOKS GREAT, THANKS J-MAC!
SURE THING, JENNA.
CAN'T WAIT TO POST THIS ON MY TUMBLR.
J-MAC, WHY ARE YOU EATING A CONVENTION CENTER HOT DOG? THEY GOT A "C" RATING FROM THE HEALTH DEPARTMENT.
AND IT'S PROBABLY MADE FROM, LIKE, THREE KINDS OF GENETICALLY MODIFIED MEAT.
I KNOW! YOU CAN REALLY TASTE ALL THREE. WANNA BITE?
NO. ESPECIALLY NOT WITH YOUR TROPICAL HERPES GERMS AS RELISH.
I DON'T HAVE HERPES, JENNA, I HAVE KURU. I PICKED IT UP IN TIJUANA.
I'M NOT REALLY SURE WHAT IT IS, BUT IT SOUNDS MUCH COOLER THAN HERPES!
J-MAC, SHOULDN'T YOU BE IN THE HOSPITAL OR SOMETHING?
IT'S CHILL, I'M HOOKED TO THE GILLS ON ADVIL.
BESIDES, NOTHING'S GONNA MAKE ME MISS COMIC-CON. WRECKING CREW 4 LYFE!
RIGHT. I'M TAKING A LITTLE MENTAL-HEALTH VACATION FROM THE WHOLE "WRECKING CREW" SCENE.
SO WHY AREN'T YOU HANGING OUT WITH THE BOYS AGAIN?

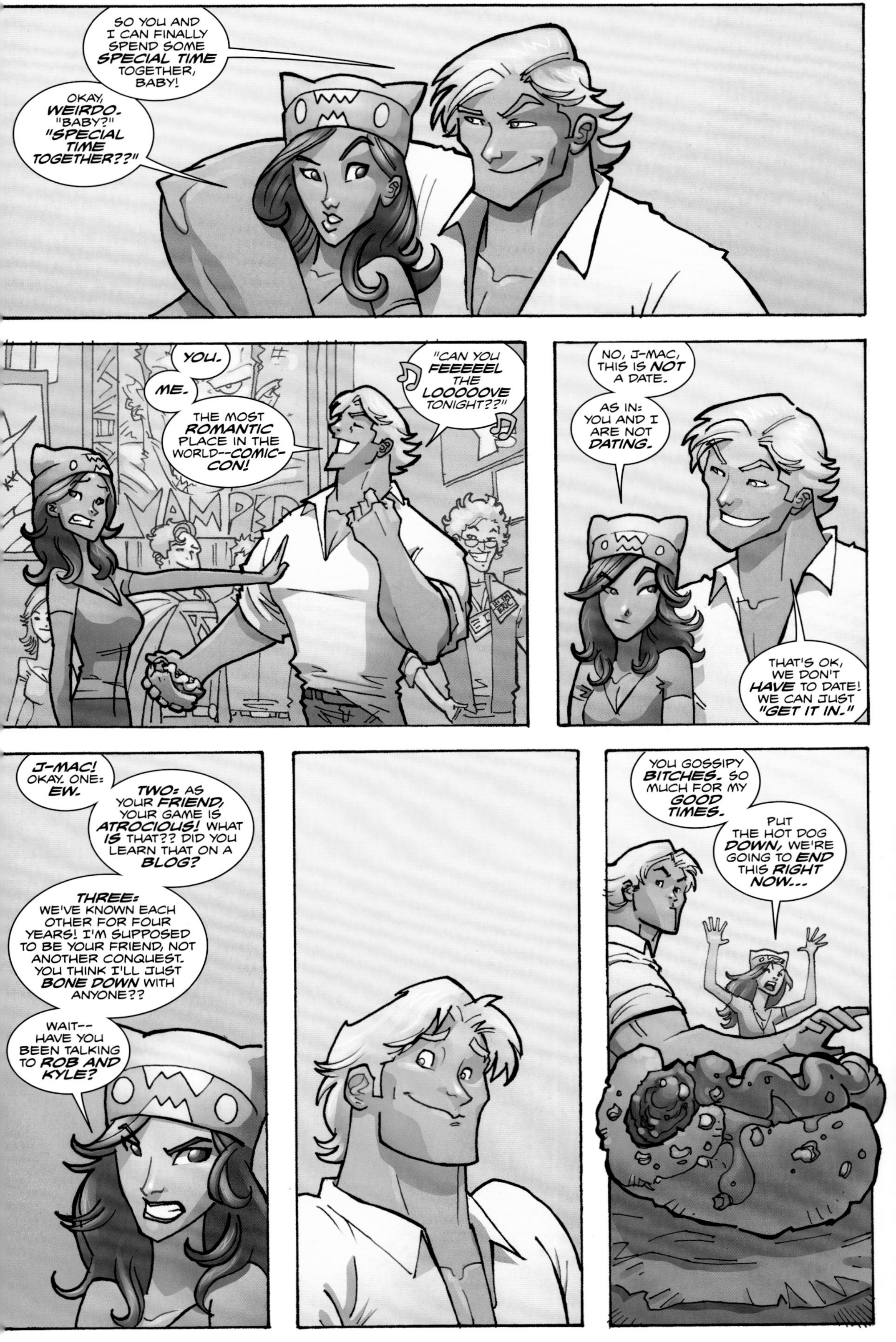
SO YOU AND I CAN FINALLY SPEND SOME SPECIAL TIME TOGETHER, BABY!
OKAY, WEIRDO. "BABY?" "SPECIAL TIME TOGETHER??"
YOU.
ME.
THE MOST ROMANTIC PLACE IN THE WORLD--COMIC-CON!
"CAN YOU FEEEEEL THE LOOOOOVE TONIGHT??"
NO, J-MAC, THIS IS NOT A DATE.
AS IN: YOU AND I ARE NOT DATING.
THAT'S OK, WE DON'T HAVE TO DATE! WE CAN JUST "GET IT IN."
J-MAC! OKAY. ONE: EW.
TWO: AS YOUR FRIEND, YOUR GAME IS ATROCIOUS! WHAT IS THAT?? DID YOU LEARN THAT ON A BLOG?
THREE: WE'VE KNOWN EACH OTHER FOR FOUR YEARS! I'M SUPPOSED TO BE YOUR FRIEND, NOT ANOTHER CONQUEST. YOU THINK I'LL JUST BONE DOWN WITH ANYONE??
WAIT-- HAVE YOU BEEN TALKING TO ROB AND KYLE?
YOU GOSSIPY BITCHES. SO MUCH FOR MY GOOD TIMES.
PUT THE HOT DOG DOWN, WE'RE GOING TO END THIS RIGHT NOW...

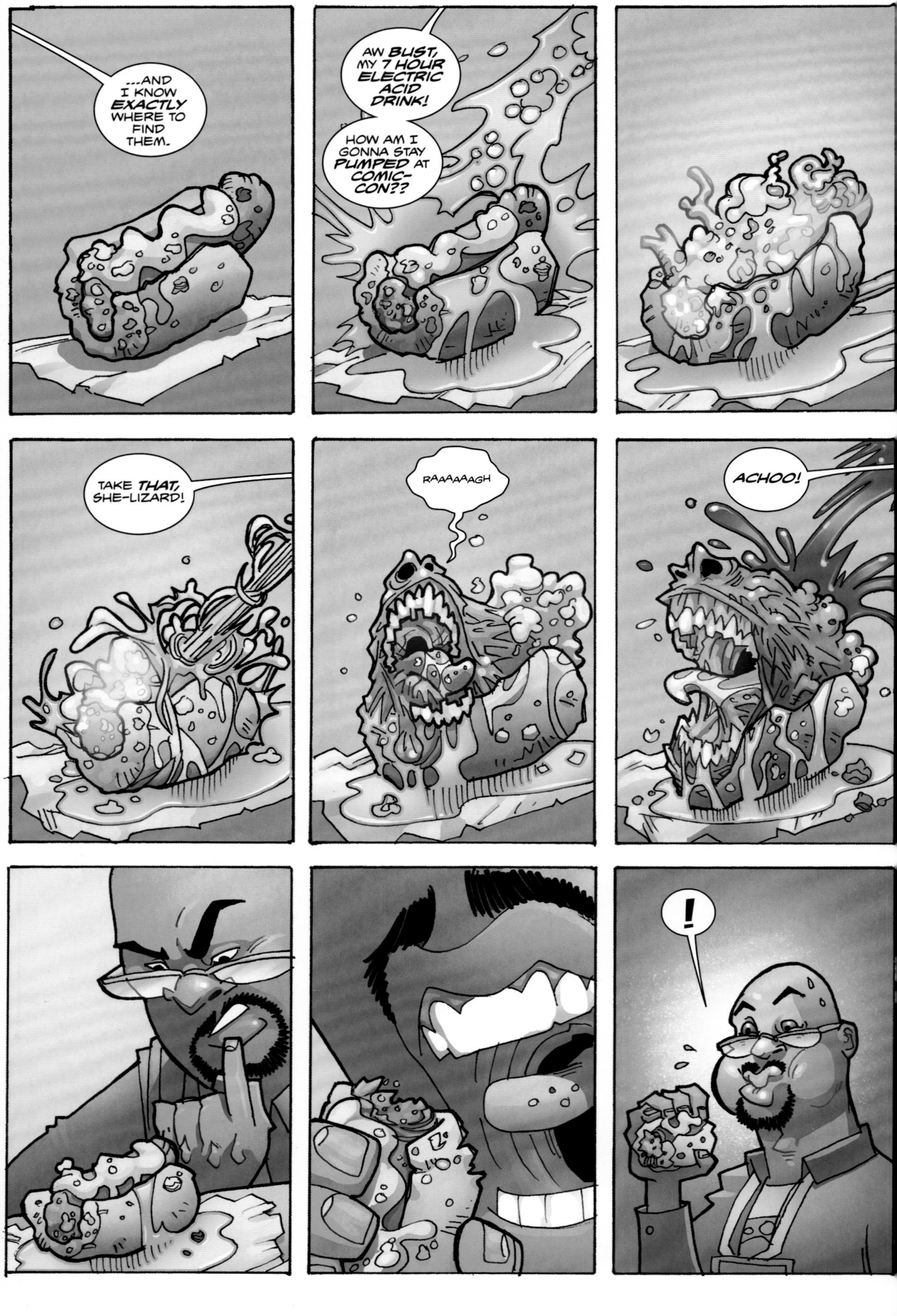
...AND I KNOW EXACTLY WHERE TO FIND THEM.
AW BUST, MY 7 HOUR ELECTRIC ACID DRINK!
HOW AM I GONNA STAY PUMPED AT COMIC-CON??
TAKE THAT, SHE-LIZARD!
RAAAAAAGH
ACHOO!
!

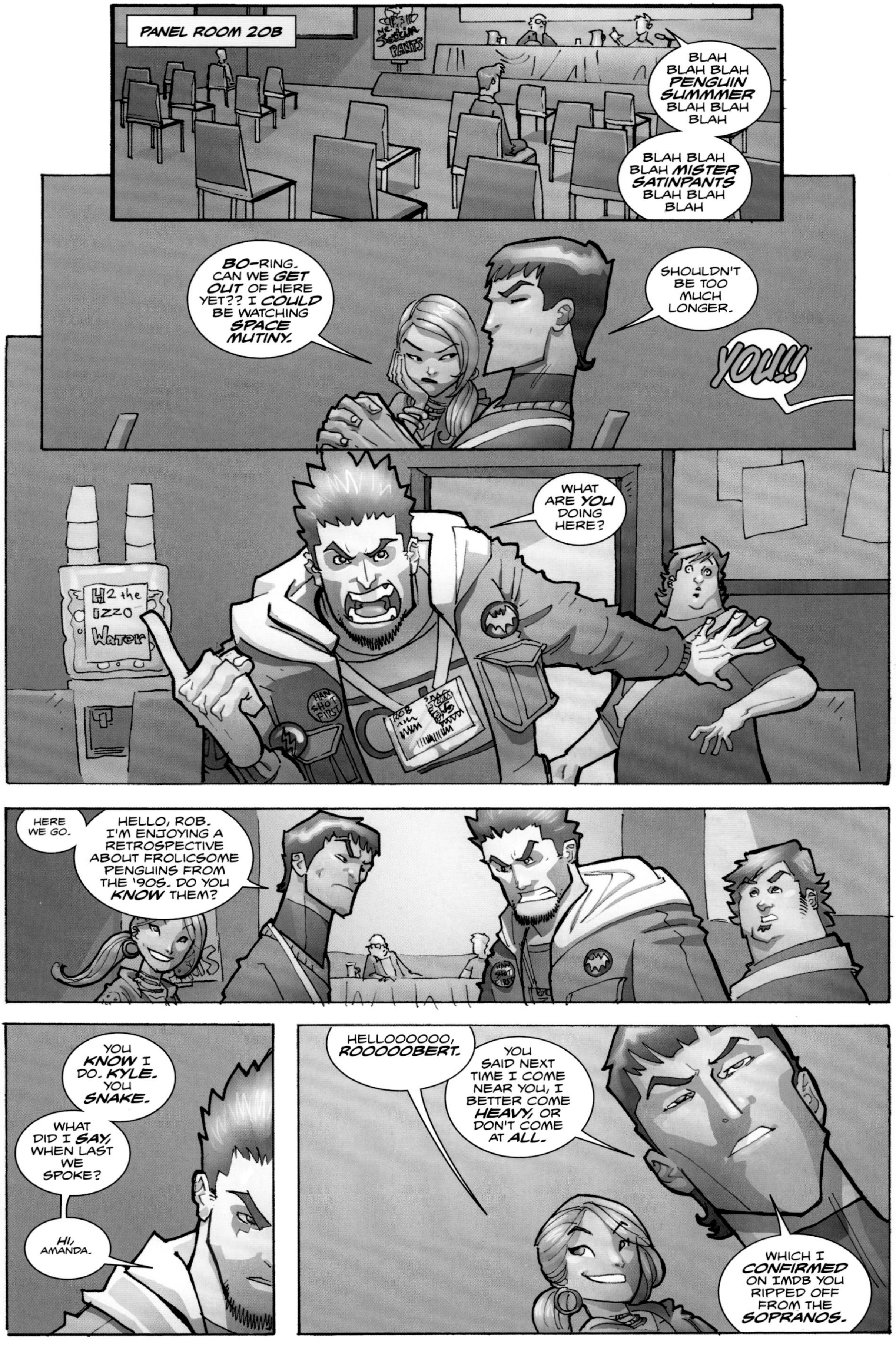
PANEL ROOM 20B
BLAH BLAH BLAH PENGUIN SUMMMER BLAH BLAH BLAH
BLAH BLAH BLAH MISTER SATINPANTS BLAH BLAH BLAH
BO-RING. CAN WE GET OUT OF HERE YET?? I COULD BE WATCHING SPACE MUTINY.
SHOULDN'T BE TOO MUCH LONGER.
YOU!!
WHAT ARE YOU DOING HERE?
H2 the IZZO Water
HAN SHOT FIRST
HERE WE GO.
HELLO, ROB. I'M ENJOYING A RETROSPECTIVE ABOUT FROLICSOME PENGUINS FROM THE '90S. DO YOU KNOW THEM?
YOU KNOW I DO. KYLE. YOU SNAKE.
WHAT DID I SAY, WHEN LAST WE SPOKE?
HI, AMANDA.
HELLOOOOOO, ROOOOOBERT.
YOU SAID NEXT TIME I COME NEAR YOU, I BETTER COME HEAVY, OR DON'T COME AT ALL.
WHICH I CONFIRMED ON IMDB YOU RIPPED OFF FROM THE SOPRANOS.

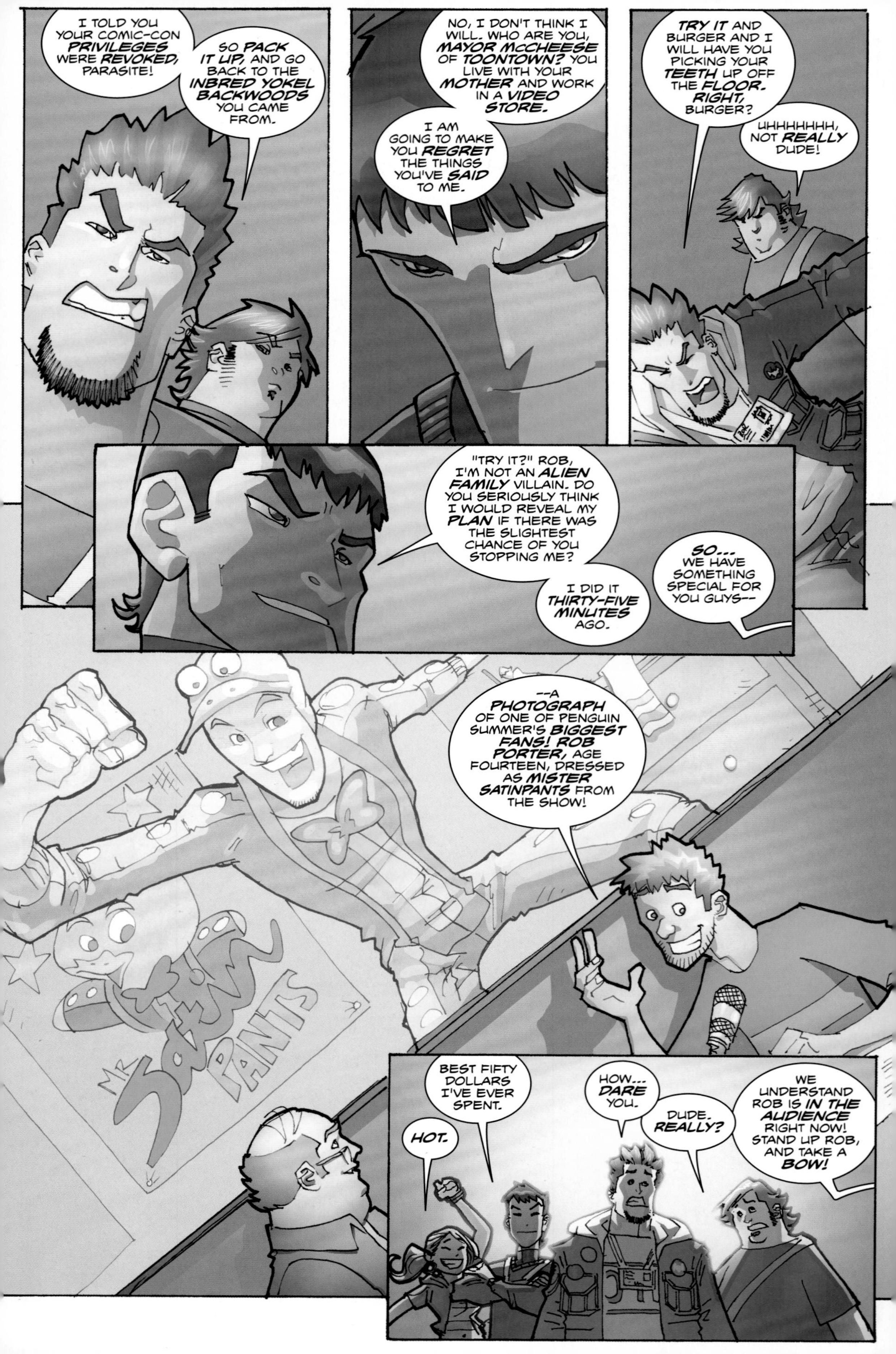
I TOLD YOU YOUR COMIC-CON PRIVILEGES WERE REVOKED, PARASITE!
SO PACK IT UP, AND GO BACK TO THE INBRED YOKEL BACKWOODS YOU CAME FROM.
NO, I DON'T THINK I WILL. WHO ARE YOU, MAYOR McCHEESE OF TOONTOWN? YOU LIVE WITH YOUR MOTHER AND WORK IN A VIDEO STORE.
I AM GOING TO MAKE YOU REGRET THE THINGS YOU'VE SAID TO ME.
TRY IT AND BURGER AND I WILL HAVE YOU PICKING YOUR TEETH UP OFF THE FLOOR. RIGHT, BURGER?
UHHHHHHH, NOT REALLY DUDE!
"TRY IT?" ROB, I'M NOT AN ALIEN FAMILY VILLAIN. DO YOU SERIOUSLY THINK I WOULD REVEAL MY PLAN IF THERE WAS THE SLIGHTEST CHANCE OF YOU STOPPING ME?
I DID IT THIRTY-FIVE MINUTES AGO.
SO... WE HAVE SOMETHING SPECIAL FOR YOU GUYS--
--A PHOTOGRAPH OF ONE OF PENGUIN SUMMER'S BIGGEST FANS! ROB PORTER, AGE FOURTEEN, DRESSED AS MISTER SATINPANTS FROM THE SHOW!
MR. SATIN PANTS
HOT.
BEST FIFTY DOLLARS I'VE EVER SPENT.
HOW... DARE YOU.
DUDE. REALLY?
WE UNDERSTAND ROB IS IN THE AUDIENCE RIGHT NOW! STAND UP ROB, AND TAKE A BOW!

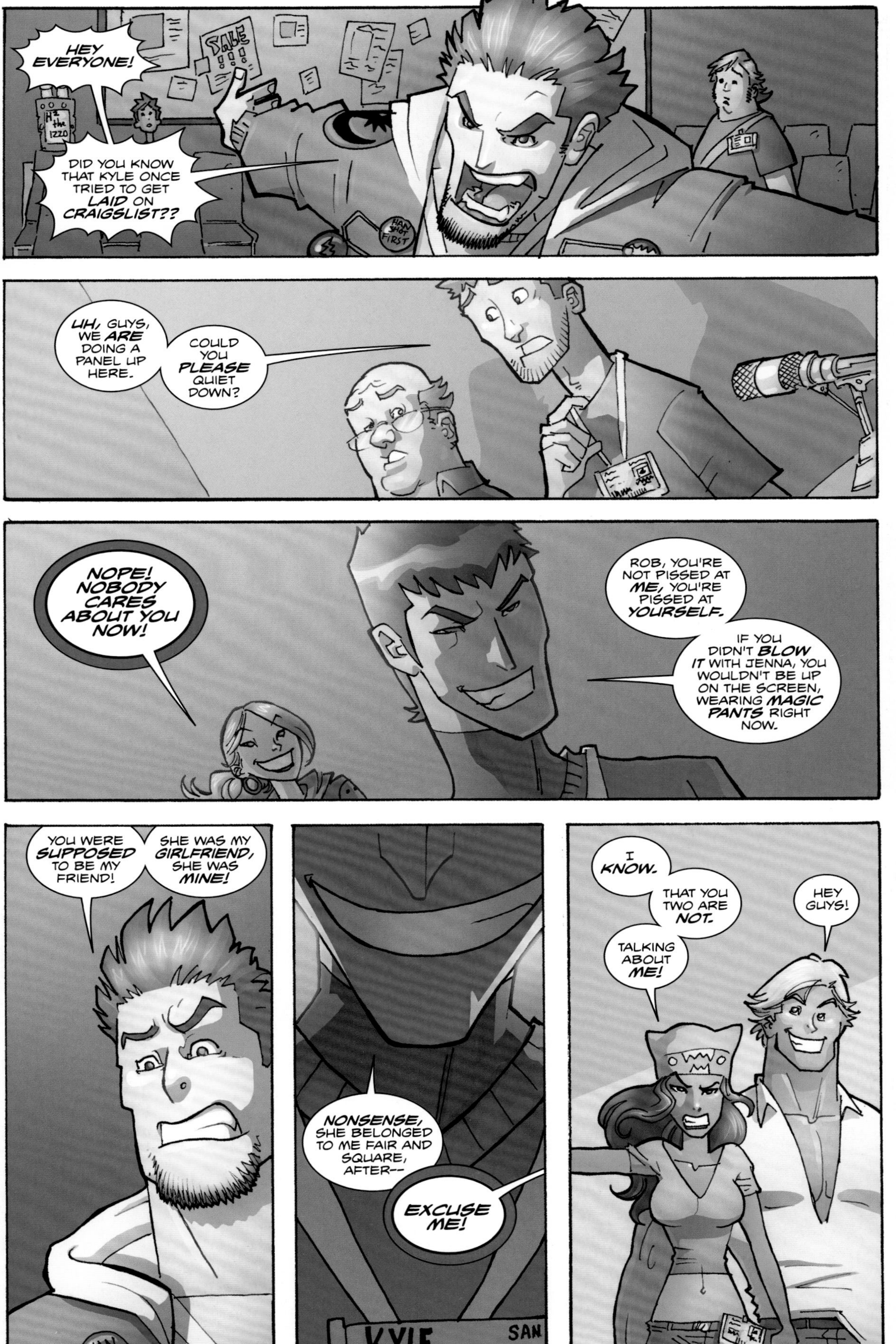
HEY EVERYONE!
DID YOU KNOW THAT KYLE ONCE TRIED TO GET LAID ON CRAIGSLIST??
SALE
HAN SHOT FIRST
UH, GUYS, WE ARE DOING A PANEL UP HERE.
COULD YOU PLEASE QUIET DOWN?
NOPE! NOBODY CARES ABOUT YOU NOW!
ROB, YOU'RE NOT PISSED AT ME, YOU'RE PISSED AT YOURSELF.
IF YOU DIDN'T BLOW IT WITH JENNA, YOU WOULDN'T BE UP ON THE SCREEN, WEARING MAGIC PANTS RIGHT NOW.
YOU WERE SUPPOSED TO BE MY FRIEND!
SHE WAS MY GIRLFRIEND, SHE WAS MINE!
HAN
NONSENSE, SHE BELONGED TO ME FAIR AND SQUARE, AFTER--
EXCUSE ME!
KYLE
SAN
I KNOW.
THAT YOU TWO ARE NOT.
TALKING ABOUT ME!
HEY GUYS!

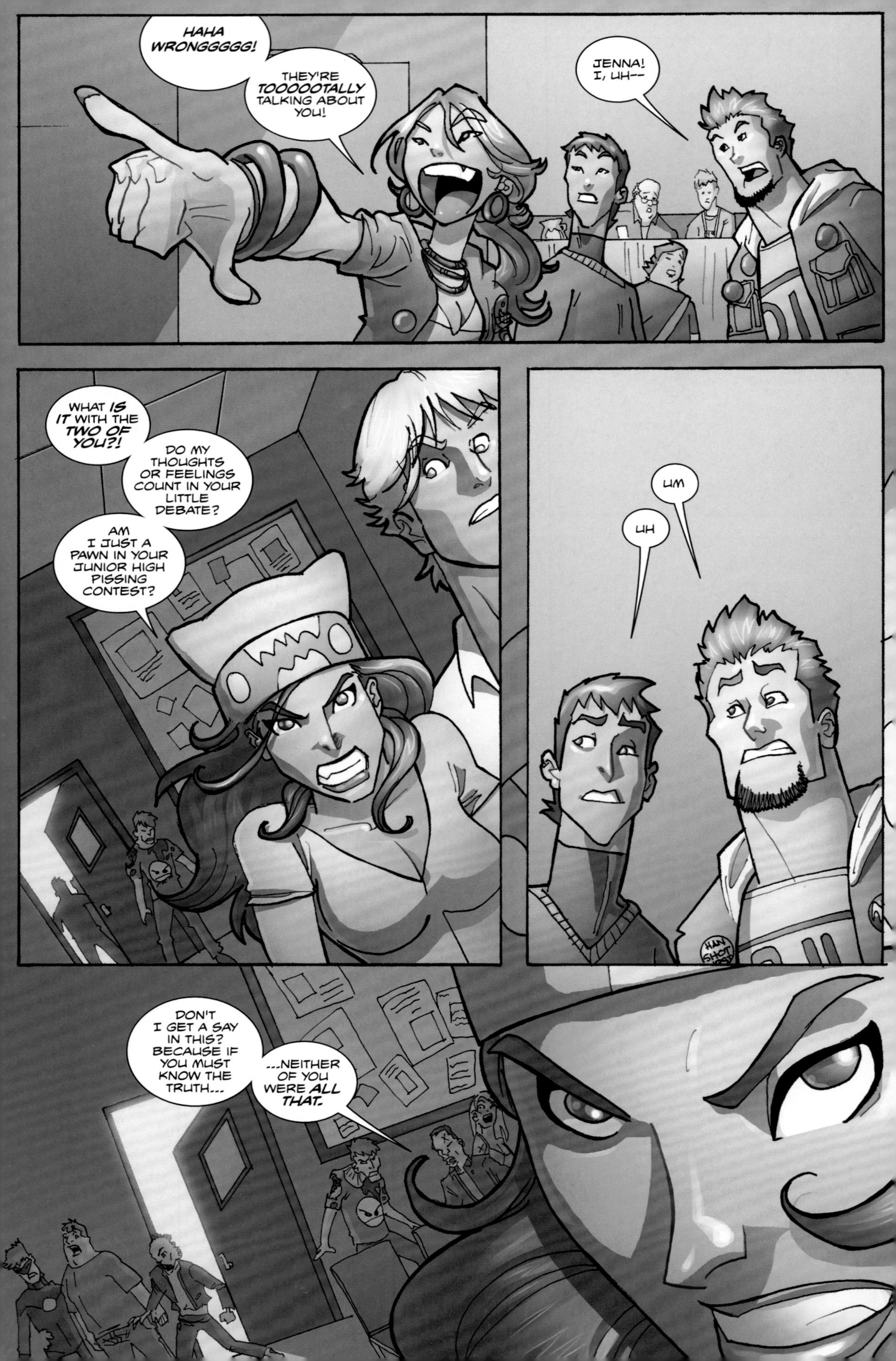

HAHA WRONGGGGG!
THEY'RE TOOOOOTALLY TALKING ABOUT YOU!
JENNA! I, UH--
WHAT IS IT WITH THE TWO OF YOU?!
DO MY THOUGHTS OR FEELINGS COUNT IN YOUR LITTLE DEBATE?
AM I JUST A PAWN IN YOUR JUNIOR HIGH PISSING CONTEST?
UH
UM
DON'T I GET A SAY IN THIS? BECAUSE IF YOU MUST KNOW THE TRUTH...
...NEITHER OF YOU WERE ALL THAT.

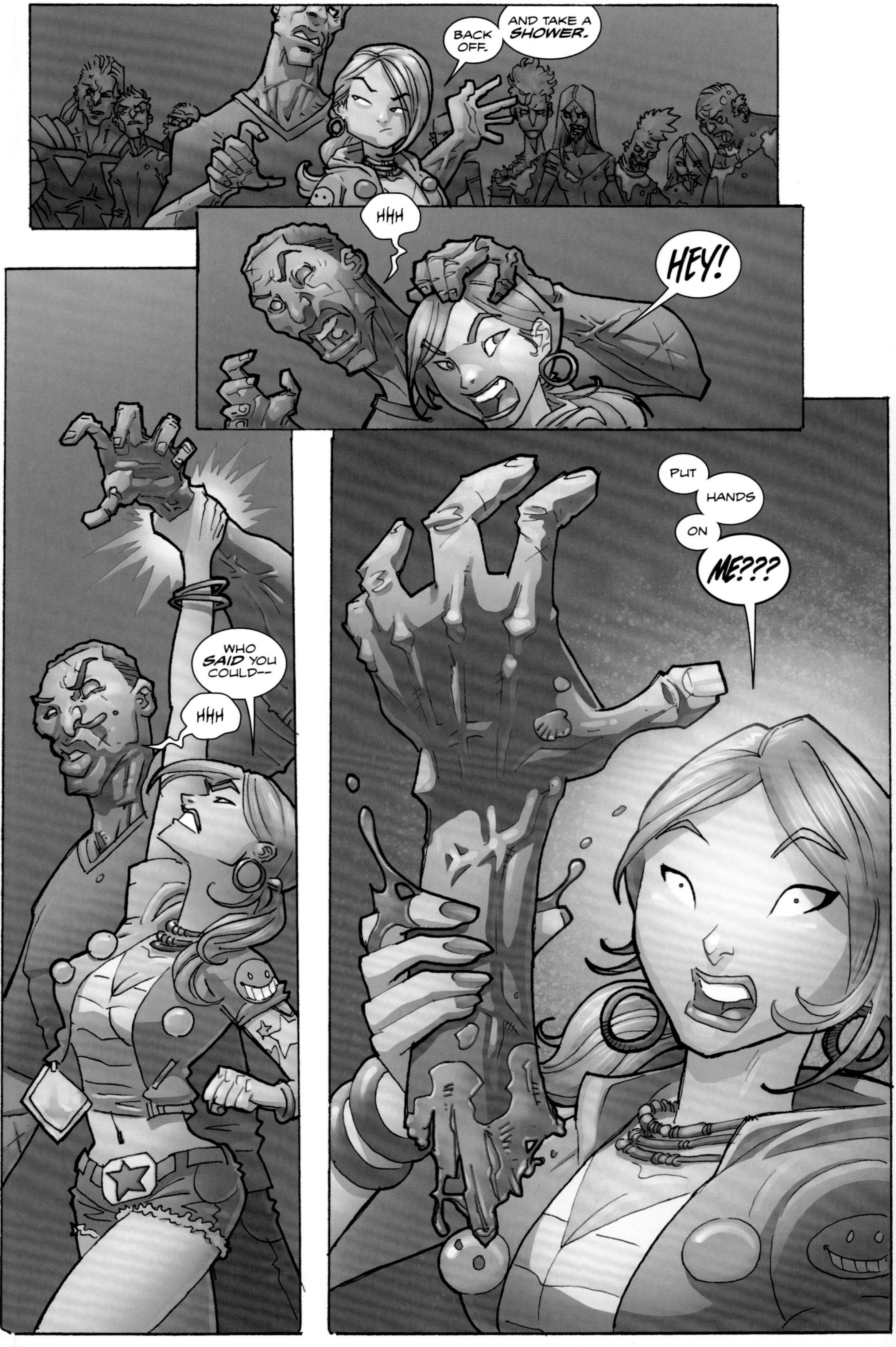
BACK OFF.
AND TAKE A SHOWER.
HHH
HEY!
WHO SAID YOU COULD--
HHH
PUT
HANDS
ON
ME???

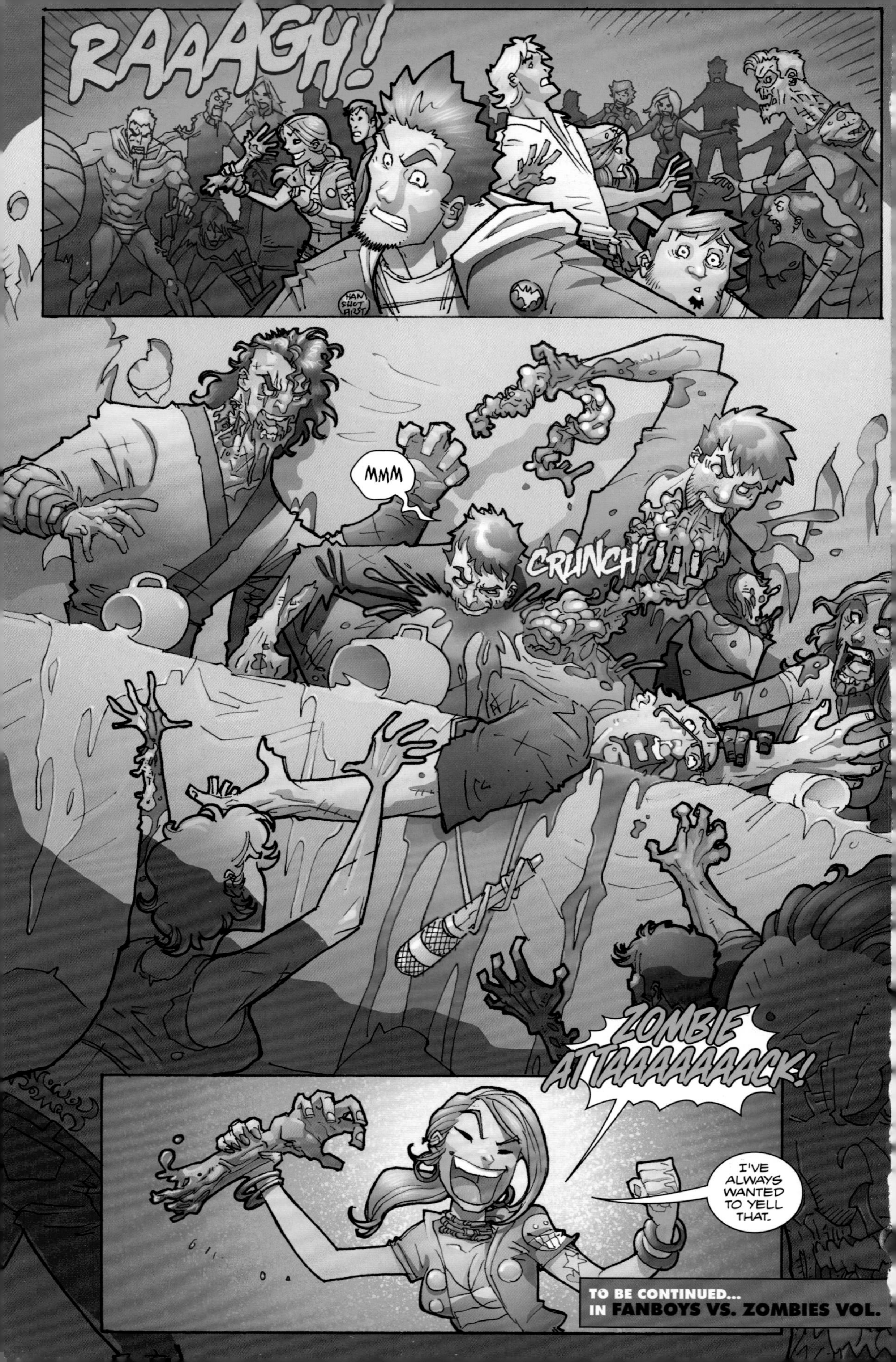
RAAAGH!
HAN SHOT FIRST
MMM
CRUNCH
ZOMBIE ATTAAAAAAAACK!
I'VE ALWAYS WANTED TO YELL THAT.
TO BE CONTINUED...
IN FANBOYS VS. ZOMBIES VOL.